REFRAMING CULTURE

REFRAMING CULTURE

The
Case of the
VITAGRAPH
QUALITY FILMS

William Uricchio and
Roberta E. Pearson

PRINCETON UNIVERSITY PRESS

PRINCETON, NEW JERSEY

Library of Congress Cataloging-in-Publication Data

Uricchio, William.
Reframing culture : the case of the Vitagraph quality films /
William Uricchio and Roberta E. Pearson.
p.   cm.
Includes bibliographical references and index.
ISBN 0-691-04774-X (cl. : alk. paper) —
ISBN 0-691-02117-1 (pb. : alk. paper)
1. Motion pictures—Social aspects—United States.   2. Vitagraph
Company of America.   I. Pearson, Roberta E.   II. Title.
PN1995.9.S6U75   1993
302.23'43'0973—dc20   93-16641   CIP

If the Movies Had Moved in the Days of the Past

I wonder what the screens would show,
If in the golden past,
The movie-man had filmed the scenes
And held the captives fast:

And would the Red Sea's waters part
And let the hordes pass through,
Or would the ferry ply its trade
And free the poor Hebrew?
If Caesar's slaying had been filmed,
To Brutus would he shout,
"You cheap ward-heeler, have a care,
Look out what you're about!"
Would Cleopatra nurse the asp
And tease it, to be slain?
Or shout, "Come Antony, old sport,
With more of that champagne!"
And Bonaparte at Waterloo,
Where lay the sunken road,
Would he stand pat and take the gaff,
or try to shift the load?
And would we behold upon the screen
At Valley Forge, the sigh
Of Washington, or read these words,
"Oh, say, but coal is high!"

—Lloyd Kenyon Jones
(*The Photoplay Magazine*, November 1914)

Contents

Illustrations

Acknowledgments

WE WOULD LIKE to begin where the book began, that is, by thanking the organizers of the Giornate del Cinema Muto in Pordenone, Italy for the 1987 Vitagraph retrospective that inspired this volume. Joanna Hitchcock, then of Princeton University Press, acted as the guiding spirit of the project, providing the advance contract and encouragement that enabled us to turn a visit to Italy into a book. We are indebted to our copy editor, Pamela MacFarland Holway, for cleaning up both our prose and our notes. Brian Winston, then dean of the School of Communications at Penn State, supported some of the travel neces- sary for our extensive archival research and also arranged course reductions. And the knowledge and assistance of the following librarians and archivists all greatly facilitated this research: Charles Mann, Rare Books Room, and Ruth Senior and the staff, interlibrary loan, Pattee Library, Penn State; Elaine Bur- rows, Jackie Morris, Roger Holman, Markku Salmi, and Luke McKernan, the National Film Archive, the British Film Institute; Steven Higgins, Bobst Li- brary, New York University; Elias Savada, researcher, The American Film In- stitute Catalogue; Bernard McTeague and the staff, New York Public Library Rare Books and Manuscripts Division; David Ment, special collections, the Milbank Memorial Library, Teachers' College, Columbia University; Dale Neighbors, Prints and Photos, The New York Historical Society; Sam Gill, Academy of Motion Picture Arts and Sciences; Ned Comstock, special collec- tions, University of Southern California Library; Anne Caiger, special collec- tions, University of California at Los Angeles Library; Eileen Bowser, Jon Gar- tenberg, and Charles Silver, Museum of Modern Art; Ula Volk, Cooper Union Library; the staff of the Motion Picture Division of the Library of Congress; the staff of the Prints and Photos Room of the Metropolitan Museum of Art; Ann Harris, Amberg Center, New York University, and the staff of the Folger Shakespeare Library. Our research assistants, Tom Schumacher and Dan Paige, photocopied many pages and scanned many microfilm reels.

Several of our colleagues have at various stages of the project given us very helpful readings: Karen Backstein, Tony Bennett, Michael Denning, Tom Gun- ning, Charlie Keil, Barbara Klinger, Richard Maltby, Charles Musser, David Nasaw, and Pierre Sorlin. The obligatory caveat about responsibility for errors of course applies. Earlier versions of portions of the manuscript have appeared in R. Cosandey, A. Gaudreault, and T. Gunning, eds., *An Invention of the Devil?*

Religion and Early Cinema (Lausanne: Presses de l'Université Laval, 1992), and *Cinémas, RSSI* (Recherches Semiotiques/Semiotic Inquiry), *Persistence of Vision, Screen,* the *Journal of Communication Inquiry,* and the *Journal of Film and Video.* We thank all the editors.

Finally, the authors wish to acknowledge their debt to each other for a thoroughly equal collaboration. The realities of publication force one name to precede another on the cover of this volume, but academic Realpolitik forces us to state that the name sequence does not indicate "seniority." We have collaborated to such an extent throughout the writing of this volume that we could not ourselves distinguish our "individual" contributions.

REFRAMING CULTURE

"IT WAS, to put it mildly, literary sabotage to boil Shakespeare down to thirty minutes."[1] So said Albert E. Smith, who together with James Stuart Blackton cofounded the Vitagraph Company of America, the largest film studio of the pre-Hollywood era and the most prolific producer of "high-art" subjects, that is, films based on literary, biblical, and historical texts. Smith, writing his memoirs in the early 1950s, recalled his partner's productions of numerous Shakespearean films between 1908 and 1912. Literary sabotage or no, Smith humorously speculated that these films may have bolstered the Bard's popularity.

> Shakespeare can and perhaps by now has thanked Jim Blackton for introducing his comedies and tragedies to films: *Romeo and Juliet*, *King Lear*, *Richard the Third*, *Macbeth*, *A Midsummer Nights Dream* [sic], *Twelfth Night*.
>
> Some pundit no doubt will hold that Shakespeare has suffered enormous torment over the treatment of his plays by picture people. To this one might capriciously say that millions of film patrons have suffered as much, but this would not be the full truth. I contend that "Old Will" has the movies to thank for an appreciable segment of new Shakespearean followers. Even the Bard himself would at least concede that among his new fans are many who, irritated by film versions, decided to look into the original Shakespeare to see if his plays are really as bad as the movies made out, and then found themselves implacably drawn into a new world.[2]

The reader may well ask what perverse motivation has led us to devote an entire book to films that were dismissed by their own producer, that accounted for only a small fraction of Vitagraph's overall output, and, worst of all, that to the modern eye seem primitive even relative to other American films of the period. Smith's evaluation of Vitagraph's Shakespearean productions, predicated upon forty-year-old memories and recast by decades of exposure to the classical Hollywood cinema, accords with our own period's assumptions about the absurdity of thirty-minute Shakespeare. Yet interrogating Smith's statement by placing the Shakespeare films within their own cultural context quickly exposes the inadequacy of latter-day recollections and assumptions, revealing these films as fascinating markers of cultural formation and contestation at a critical moment for the film industry and the nation.

Contemporary cultural hierarchies, in which theatrical Shakespeare ranks far above the "movies," would lead us to accept Smith's rather negative assessment of the Vitagraph productions. Common sense would lead us to conclude that a silent, black-and-white vehicle could not possibly provide a faithful adaptation of a complex verbal text. Textual analysis would compound our doubts, showing that Vitagraph had boiled the Swan of Avon down not to thirty minutes but to fifteen (one reel) and that the cinematic signifying practices—editing, camera scale, performance—seem somewhat archaic compared to those of other contemporary films. But textual analysis tells us nothing about reception, leading us to ponder whether the original audiences may, as Smith suggests, have considered these films "bad." Broadening the scope of inquiry to the trade press reveals that critics and exhibitors had doubts about the suitability of Shakespearean films for nickelodeon audiences, wondering whether any viewer not already familiar with the Bard's work would understand or appreciate these adaptations.

But common sense, textual analysis, and the trade press can neither confirm nor repudiate Smith's assertion that Shakespeare acquired some new fans through cinematic adaptations. As we will discuss in chapter 3, many viewers might already have encountered Shakespeare in various forms, since Shakespearean texts, ranging from free performances to school books to advertising trade cards and relating to both the plays and the poet, pervaded turn-of-the-century America to such an extent that an individual would have been hard-pressed to avoid contact with the author whom some considered the greatest writer in the English language. Perhaps even more surprisingly, those thought to be outside the cultural mainstream, such as the Jewish and Italian immigrants reputed to compose a large portion of New York City's nickelodeon audiences, may have seen more Shakespeare, both in terms of number of productions and textual completeness, than their uptown counterparts.

Evidence from textual analysis or trade press discourse cannot correct Smith's very inaccurate picture of the conditions of reception for the Vitagraph Shakespeares. The same holds true for Smith's implications about the conditions of production, since Vitagraph's adaptations are not particularly anomalous compared with many noncinematic period Shakespearean texts. As chapter 3 will show, turn-of-the-century America valorized Shakespeare but not the textual integrity of his works. Broadway productions, children's books, and meat advertisements all committed "literary sabotage," shortening, rearranging, and reducing Shakespeare's plays to familiar quotations and misquotations. And the "sabotage" that ensured a widespread circulation of Shakespeareana constituted part of an ongoing effort to forge a cultural consensus at a time of contested national identity, as ruling elites administered the poet to the masses as an effective tonic. Rather than dismissing the Vitagraph

Shakespeares, along with the rest of the "high-art" films, as retrograde and uninteresting, this book uses these texts as an entry point to a fuller illumination of conditions of cinematic production and reception at a time of crisis for the film industry and the larger society, as film producers sought respectability and the country's elites sought cultural cohesion.

The book uses eleven reels produced by the Vitagraph Company between 1907 and 1910 as a means of relating a crucial moment in the history of the early American cinema to the larger cultural dynamics of the period: Dante's *Francesca di Rimini* (made 1907, released 1908); Shakespeare's *Julius Caesar* (1908); *The Life Drama of Napoleon Bonaparte and the Empress Josephine of France* and *Napoleon, The Man of Destiny* (1909); *Washington under the British Flag* and *Washington under the American Flag* (1909); and *The Life of Moses* (five reels, 1909–10).[3] Between 1880 and 1920 urbanization, labor unrest, and massive immigration all challenged the social/cultural status quo, a crisis that encouraged repressive responses from dominant social formations.[4] The strategies ranged from state-endorsed violence to more subtle attempts to control popular culture, particularly the so-called cheap amusements, as well as attempts to maintain national unity through the dissemination of shared cultural values. In a period roughly coincident with the third decade of this crisis, the American film industry sought to distance itself from forces perceived as disruptive, differentiating its product from expressive forms that continued to be associated with marginalized social formations while seeking to ally with the emerging mainstream mass culture. In the few short years between 1907 and 1913, changes in signifying practices, economic organization, exhibition venues, and audience composition gained the new medium the approval of many who had formerly castigated moving pictures for fomenting disorder among the "lower orders."

This study is neither exclusively about the positioning of cultural figures such as Shakespeare nor exclusively about the Vitagraph high-art films. Rather, we use intertextual evidence about these cultural figures to explore the interface between film and culture. Although the high-art films, also known as "quality films" and even "films deluxe," constituted a relatively small (though highly publicized) component of the industry's overall output, they represented one of the most visible markers of the film industry's desire to improve its cultural status, explicitly invoking "high" culture referents but offering them in a "low" culture venue, the moving picture shows. We have chosen three discursive realms—literature, history, and religion—that members of all social formations participated in to some extent, and specific characters within those realms—Shakespeare, Dante, Washington, Napoleon, and Moses— that particularize the conjunction of high and low the film industry sought to exploit.

In the absence of further evidence, the disjunction between "high" cultural references and "low" cultural venues might lead to conceiving of the production and reception of these texts in overly simplistic terms. The production of these films could be understood as evidence of the industry's drive for respectability: its desire to attract new audiences and to placate its most powerful critics. It could also be seen as attesting to the film industry's desire to ally itself with dominant social formations in creating consensual values. The reception of these films might be interpreted in terms of appeals to the assimilationist and upwardly mobile tendencies of the workers and immigrants alleged to have constituted the bulk of the nickelodeon audience.

These initial perceptions are to some extent correct but are predicated largely on the traditional sources of evidence in film history. Scholars of the early cinema regularly have to contend with gaps in evidence, since the disappearance of the great majority of studio records makes the trade press the primary, but problematic, source of production information. The Vitagraph studio records are, unfortunately, numbered among the missing, leaving us to extrapolate much from the few remaining documents. Almost no traditional documentation of the conditions of reception exists. The few shreds of evidence that do remain derive mostly from elites such as reviewers, reformers, censors, and the occasional memorialist, all of whom obviously reflected the tastes of a relatively restricted social formation, while the preponderance of nickelodeon audiences have left behind virtually no contemporary reports of their viewing experiences. Such class-inflected patterns of evidence inevitably lead to the perception of a disjunction between "high" culture subjects and "low" culture venues, since we literally have no idea how "real" nickelodeon audiences in fact responded to particular quality films.

Refining our understanding of the conditions of production and reception for the quality films requires going beyond traditional sources and adducing intertextual evidence. Indeed, intertextuality forms the linchpin of this project. The term *intertextuality* encompasses both a narrow construction of directly related textual references and a broader construction that includes less directly related cultural expressions. By directly related references, we mean, in the context of film, sources readily identifiable from either the producers' discourse or easily discernible textual homologies. For example, Vitagraph's *Julius Caesar* stages Jean Léon Gérôme's famous depiction of the assassination of Caesar. By less directly related cultural expressions, we mean any text pertaining to our cultural figures that might have inflected conditions of production or reception. For example, the "reduced" Shakespeare that circulated in the form of key scenes and key phrases authorized Vitagraph's boiling down of the Bard and informed the producers' representations of the plays. Intertextuality embraces everything from plays and paintings to advertising, stereographs, and current events. It thus presents a daunting array of potential evidence.

In the next five chapters we use intertextual evidence to address questions that traditional evidence leaves largely unanswered. In terms of conditions of production, why might Vitagraph have chosen the particular subjects it did and the particular means of representing them? What sources did the Vitagraph producers reference, what constituencies did they specifically attempt to engage, and what approaches did they exclude? In terms of conditions of reception, what preexisting intertextual frames—based on their cultural exposures, through education, public libraries, free public lectures, and so on—could viewers have used to make sense of these texts? And were the meanings that viewers produced from the quality films always in the interests of the dominant social formations?

Despite its central position in the book, an intertextual approach does not imply a monocausal understanding of conditions of production and reception. Instead, we see these conditions as the dialectical interplay of producers, viewers, texts, intertexts, and contexts. We look at the choices that the producers made from the rich intertextual frames available to them and the way their publicity sought to position these choices in order to shape the reception of their films. We also look at the rich intertextual frames available to potential audiences, considering how differently situated viewers may have deployed different intertextual frames to make different sense(s) of the texts. But using this intertextual evidence to illuminate production and, most particularly, reception requires a speculative leap. By roughly estimating the probable intertextual exposures of specific populations, we can hypothesize a range of possible conditions of reception and thereby open a route for conjecture about the meanings made by viewers in their interactions with the quality films.[5] Although this procedure may lack the positivist certainty beloved by the more hardheaded of social scientists and historians, without such evidentially grounded speculation the experiences of socially and culturally marginalized populations remain forever beyond our grasp.

At this juncture, we wish to offer a provisional sketch of our understanding of the construction and operation of culture during this period, specifically with regard to the discursive realms of literature, history, and religion. The work of Antonio Gramsci and Pierre Bourdieu, together with recent developments in reception studies, informs our understanding, although our analytic perspective arises dialectically from the interplay between our empirical evidence and theoretical and methodological constructs. Gramsci's notion of hegemony conceives of culture as a means of social control. Bourdieu provides a detailed analysis of the operation of a particular hegemonic order, mid-twentieth-century France, explicating more fully than Gramsci the social control hypothesis and addressing the class-based conditions of production and reception for cultural commodities. Recent developments in reception studies help us to understand how social subjects contest and negotiate cultural commodities, and by so doing challenge the notion of elite cultural control.

As we argue in the first chapter, many members of the period's dominant social formations sought to defuse perceived threats to the social order through the construction of consensual cultural values—through the construction and maintenance of a hegemonic order rather than through political domination, to use Gramsci's bifurcated model of social control. Gramsci's work offers one of the most suggestive elaborations of the scattered references to culture found in Marx. Whereas Marx had rejected an idealist notion of "taste" or "art," many of his epigones saw culture simply as a totally determined epiphenomenon of society's economic base. Gramsci reformulated Marx's concepts of base and superstructure, developing the latter in order to provide a provocative yet often sketchy consideration of the role of culture in the construction of a complex and interactive notion of political consensus.

According to Gramsci, those in power maintain control over both the state and civic, or private, society through two means: hegemony and direct domination. In a much-quoted passage, Gramsci defines hegemony as "the 'spontaneous' consent given by the great masses of the population to the general direction imposed on social life by the dominant fundamental group [class]; this consent is 'historically' caused by the prestige (and consequent confidence) which the dominant group enjoys because of its position and function in the world of production."[6] This "general direction" is charted by intellectuals and by such institutions as the church, trade unions, and schools. Gramsci contrasts hegemony with direct domination, which he defines as "the apparatus of state coercive power which 'legally' enforces discipline on those groups who do not 'consent' either actively or passively. This apparatus is, however, constituted for the whole of society in anticipation of moments of crisis of command and direction when spontaneous consent has failed."[7] State coercive power is exercised by agents of political domination, such as the police and the militia, and its active deployment usually suggests a lapse in the hegemonic order.

The concept of hegemony has been taken up by cultural studies because it permits a nuanced and complex approach to the production and consumption of culture that remains sensitive to the constant negotiations and contestations within any social order. This approach offers an alternative to the model of totalizing and monolithic top-down control advanced by such Marxists as the members of the Frankfurt school.[8] As Raymond Williams said,

> A lived hegemony is always a process. It is not, except analytically, a system or a structure. It is a realized complex of experiences, relationships, and activities, with specific and changing pressures and limits. In practice, that is, hegemony can never be singular. Its internal structures are highly complex, as can readily be seen in any concrete analysis. Moreover . . . it does not just passively exist as a form of dominance. It has continually to be renewed, recreated, defended, and modified. It is also continually resisted, limited, altered, challenged by pressures not at all its own.[9]

The quality films, as we have suggested above, can be seen as part of the defense of a particular hegemonic order at a moment of intense renewal and resistance. As T. J. Jackson Lears remarks, "The period from 1877 to 1919 . . . offers abundant evidence that subordinate groups did not consent to the hegemony of industrial capitalism."[10] The clearest evidence of this lack of consent comes from the state's attempt to use agents of political domination to quell dissent. Yet, as chapter 1 will demonstrate, the period's dominant social formations also attempted to renew, recreate, defend, and even modify the existing hegemony, in a desperate bid to reestablish "order."

While Gramsci made it clear that hegemony did not operate in a unilateral, top-down fashion, he did not fully theorize the manner in which the hegemonic order served the interests of "the dominant fundamental group" nor did he elaborate upon the formation of hegemonic culture. Although Pierre Bourdieu does not explicitly acknowledge the influence of Gramsci or the notion of hegemony, *Distinction*, his massive, empirically based analysis of taste and cultural reproduction in mid-twentieth-century France can be seen as a thorough explication of the workings of cultural hegemony.[11]

Consistent with Gramsci's formulation, Bourdieu suggests that members of all social formations in a particular society have a shared perception of the natural workings of the world that leads them to accept the existing social order and their place within it. But he goes further than Gramsci in explicating the workings of a hegemonic order by acknowledging its broadly cohesive function while positing a series of binary oppositions in the production and consumption of culture that define classes and class fractions. "One only has to bear in mind that goods are converted into distinctive signs, which may be signs of distinction but also of vulgarity, as soon as they are perceived relationally, to see that the representation which individuals and groups inevitably project through their practices and properties is an integral part of social reality."[12]

Bourdieu's empirical survey data offer a grounded look at the formation and operation of taste hierarchies, in which certain kinds of engagements—predicated on the possession of what Bourdieu terms "cultural capital"—with certain cultural commodities and/or figures distinguish the participating subject from members of other social formations. Those capable of these engagements possess a symbolic power, stemming from this cultural capital often reinforced by economic capital. This symbolic power in turn helps to maintain distinctions among groups, to which members of all groups willingly assent. Distinction ultimately serves the project of consensus by articulating hierarchies of "taste" that essentially serve to naturalize and sustain the unequal distribution of economic and political power within a social system. On the one hand, engagement with certain cultural products marks some individuals as superior to others, and, on the other, it provides a delineated sequence of levels through which the upwardly (or downwardly) mobile can chart their movement, serving as a stimulus for ever deeper commitment to the goals and rewards of a given social order.[13]

Bourdieu's fuller articulation of hegemonic processes helps to elucidate the particular strategies employed by the film industry in its attempt to align itself with its perceptions of high culture, a strategy most evident in the quality films, and thus gives us a position from which to interrogate Vitagraph's choice of film subjects. With regard to the first point, a reading of Bourdieu provides more than the rather obvious insight that the film industry sought to change its cultural status. Bourdieu not only discusses the production of culture in terms of its relation to those whose interests it most directly serves (the dominant fraction of the dominant class, who possess economic and political power) but looks in detail at its actual producers (the dominated fraction of the dominant class, who possess cultural power). "The field of cultural production is the area par excellence of clashes between the dominant fractions of the dominant class, who sometimes fight there in person but more often through producers oriented towards defending their 'ideas' and satisfying their 'tastes,' and the dominated fractions who are totally involved in this struggle."[14] Bourdieu's empirical examination of the mechanics of cultural production delineates the struggles among various producers as they compete for economic and political support, as opposed to theories that simply view cultural production as a direct expression of the dominant classes. Our evidence concerning the conditions of production for the quality films will detail Vitagraph's attempts to position itself among and elicit the support of other cultural producers within the dominated fraction.

With regard to the second point, that is, the subject matter of the Vitagraph quality films, we borrow more freely from Bourdieu. In *Distinction*, Bourdieu examines a functioning and relatively unchallenged hegemonic order and therefore seeks evidence related to the creation and maintenance of cultural hierarchies. By contrast, we examine a potentially dysfunctional hegemonic order, the defense and rebuilding of which required attempts, not necessary in a functional hegemonic order, to instill shared cultural values. Hence, we have deliberately selected quality films that represent cultural figures who functioned to construct consensus (such as Shakespeare) to compare with those that represent cultural figures who functioned to maintain distinctions (such as Dante). By so doing, we can explore the reciprocal processes of a hegemonic order.

Since it is our intertextual evidence that enables us to locate the film industry within a wider cultural matrix and to detail the precise nature of the industry's relationship to other producers and cultural products, we must now discuss the agents involved in the contemporary production and circulation of our intertexts. From the plurality of groups whose members shared common standards for creating meaning—interpretive communities—some, which we term authorized interpretive communities, were granted greater influence by virtue of such factors as tradition, state empowerment, or even self-appointment.[15] These authorized interpretive communities selected, valorized, and circulated certain expressive forms rather than others and attempted to delimit the meanings derived therefrom.[16] Some authorized interpretive communities operated exclusively within the realm of the literary or the historical or the biblical while others were more interdisciplinary in nature. So, for example, literature was valorized and interpreted by academics, critics, and librarians, among others; history by academics, archivists, museum curators, and historical preservation societies, among others; religion by academics and clerics, among others. Obviously there were bids for power both among and between these authorized interpretive communities, and hints of such complexities will emerge in the following chapters. Although Bourdieu does not use this language, all these interpretive communities would be, in his terms, part of that dominated fraction of the dominant classes responsible for cultural production.

Authorized interpretive communities circulated their vision of culture through institutions of cultural reproduction, created and funded by those with economic and political power.[17] In a fully dialectical manner, these institutions of cultural reproduction further bolstered the authority of the interpretive communities and perpetuated the ongoing interpretive process. Yet, while all institutions of cultural reproduction disseminated the cultural meanings created by interpretive communities, authorized and unauthorized, not all interpretive communities had attendant institutions of cultural reproduction. Moreover, not all institutions of cultural reproduction were equivalent in their impact, in their economic base, or in their clienteles. Some state-supported and almost inescapable institutions of cultural reproduction, such as schools and public festivities, circulated canonized texts and delimited the meanings thereof across all social formations. Some more "voluntary" institutions, such as libraries and churches, which could potentially reach all social formations although in practice probably did not, circulated both canonized and noncanonized texts and had fewer mechanisms for constraining interpretation. Commercial institutions of cultural reproduction, such as publishing, the theatre, and advertising, tended to define and serve particular social formations, reflecting the views of a more idiosyncratic array of interpretive communities than state-supported or mandated institutions and resulting in the most diverse mix of canonized and noncanonized texts. We have tried to gather our evidence from a representative range of institutions of cultural reproduction and will, where possible, speak to the implications of institutional origin.

Rather than simply asserting that cultural elites strove to forge a common culture, we have sought an empirical manifestation of this project in the congruences among canonized texts that circulated across many institutions of cultural reproduction. By contrast, the restricted circulation of other canonized texts and meanings points to the creation and maintenance of social/cultural hierarchies within an overarching consensus. We have also sought textual evidence of counterhegemonic voices that strove to advance alternative interpretations.

Our quality films, representing the cultural figures of Shakespeare, Dante, Washington, Napoleon, and Moses, permit us to explore the role of the film industry within the contested hegemonic order. The cultural figures featured in the quality films all shared a prominent (and sometimes surprisingly contentious) position in late-nineteenth- and early-twentieth-century culture that facilitates the exploration of (1) the range of their portrayals—their interpretations and modes of representation—produced by interpretive communities; (2) the patterns of their circulation generated by institutions of cultural reproduction; (3) the uses that both interpretive communities and institutions of cultural reproduction wished to make of these figures; and (4) the exposures and possible responses of audiences.

Our discussion of Gramsci and Bourdieu, together with the concepts of interpretive communities and institutions of cultural reproduction, relate primarily to points one, two, and three. We must now more fully consider point four. No matter how the film industry sought to conform its texts to the texts and meanings circulated by dominant social formations through institutions of cultural reproduction, the possibilities for viewer negotiation were myriad. Even if a social control hypothesis could adequately account for the conditions of production, it could not do the same for the conditions of reception. The tensions among the infinite interpretive possibilities of the individual subject, the salient properties of the text, the structuring frameworks of intertexts, and the effects of social factors must be addressed.

The study of audiences and their receptions is a growth industry within mass communications, cultural studies, and film studies. Since others have provided overviews of the developments within these fields, we simply wish briefly to position our approach to historical reception vis-à-vis the work of other scholars.[18] Reception research within mass communications and cultural studies has focused almost exclusively on relatively presentist concerns, much of this research examining the processes by which real viewers produce meaning in their interactions with specific texts. Most exemplary in this latter regard are the oft-cited works of Janice Radway, David Morley, and Ien Ang, which spurred a shift away from the quantitative positivism that had dominated mass communications for decades toward the consideration of more qualitative issues. Given the rich range of evidence available for these presentist studies, these researchers have of necessity had to construct a priori formulations to delimit the relevant data. Radway used a combination of survey techniques and focus groups; Morley observed television watching in the home; and Ang relied upon letters reporting the receptions of a group of respondents to *Dallas*.[19]

In constructing their formulations, these and other scholars drew heavily upon the theorizing of audiences, texts, and cultural institutions associated with the University of Birmingham Centre for Contemporary Cultural Studies, which in turn drew upon the pioneering works of Raymond Williams, Richard

Hoggart, and E. P. Thompson. We, too, are heavily indebted to the perspectives on cultural production and viewer negotiation deriving from British cultural studies, yet we differ from Radway, Morley, and Ang in our focus upon historical reception.[20]

Within film studies, the impetus for the consideration of spectatorship came from those, such as Christian Metz, who applied a psychoanalytic paradigm to the study of cinema.[21] This impetus was most fully taken up and developed by the feminist film theorists, who postulated a textually extrapolated reader predicated on psychoanalytic principles.[22] Feminist film theory has traversed the terrain from Laura Mulvey's denial of any position for a female spectator in the classical Hollywood cinema to the full-blown consideration of the "spectatrix" taken up in an issue of *Camera Obscura*.[23]

Some scholars, among them Patrice Petro and Miriam Hansen, both influenced by the Frankfurt school, have sought to reconfigure feminist film theory by enhancing the psychoanalytic paradigm with historical evidence.[24] In fact, film scholars of many theoretical persuasions have increasingly focused on issues of historical reception. Janet Staiger has explored the theoretical and methodological problems inherent in historical reception studies and has identified the evidential constraints that have forced the majority of scholars working in this area to investigate conditions of reception rather than reception per se.[25] Thus, although film historians have investigated how such factors as theatre architecture, publicity and promotional campaigns, regional attitudes, and exhibition conditions have structured viewers' filmgoing experiences generally, they have not considered how these factors may inflect the reception of specific texts.[26] Other historians have employed intertextual evidence to investigate the mediation of historical viewers' receptions, showing how intertextual determinants reinforced particular meanings of film texts.[27]

Film scholars' research on the conditions of reception has not usually attempted to connect these conditions with the multiple meanings viewers may have constructed from particular texts in the process of negotiation between text and reader taking place within the context of particular social determinants. While we do not claim to have access to the multiple meanings actually constructed by historical viewers, we have attempted to evolve an intertextually based approach for extrapolating historically grounded possible readings. Our central assumption is that any individual's meanings are conditioned by his or her socially determined experiences in the world and that the shaping of those meanings with regard to materially embodied expressive forms is most proximately evident in the socially circulated interpretations of interpretive communities. This is neither to assert a causal and unilateral relationship between the utterances of interpretive communities and the meanings individuals make from texts nor to preclude the consideration of such vital social determinants as gender and ethnicity. As Tony Bennett points out, both texts and readers exist at the juncture of historically determined conditions and are "socially and politically mobilised in different ways within different class practices, differentially inscribed within the practices of educational, cultural and linguistic institutions and so on."[28] Readings, then, are produced by a dialectically inflected process with intertextuality as a crucial activating component. As Bennett and Woollacott say,

> The process of reading is not one in which the reader and the text meet as abstractions but one in which the inter-textually organised reader meets the inter-textually organised text. The exchange is never a pure one between two unsullied entities, existing separately from one another, but is rather "muddied" by the cultural debris which attach to both texts and readers in the determinate conditions which regulate the specific forms of their encounter.[29]

Hence, the reader does not precede or create the text any more than the text precedes or creates the reader. Rather, both result from the dialectical interaction of intertextual and social determinants.[30] The multiple meanings potentially arising from this dialectical interaction point to the contestation and negotiation of texts that might otherwise be seen as part of a top-down social control strategy.

Before proceeding further, however, we should offer some key provisos.

1. This book will not, indeed, cannot, given its historical orientation and the nature of its evidence, concern itself with the readings of actual historical viewers.[31] Thus, we cannot discuss the meanings that individual viewers may have constructed from film images and narratives or the pleasures that they may have derived from them. Instead, we employ the term *readings* to refer to the historically grounded possible meanings produced by historical readers. We arrive at these probable readings through examining the circulations of particular intertexts and how the probable intertextual exposures of readers and groups of readers may have colored their production of meanings in specific textual encounters. This examination of the interpretations in circulation at any given historical moment constitutes at least as significant a component in the conditions of reception as the others thus far examined by scholars. In fact, given the specifically foregrounded intertextual derivations of the quality films discussed in this book, this approach seems particularly suited for investigating their conditions of reception.

2. We try to avoid traditional formal analysis of the quality films. Our materially based interrogation of the conditions of production and reception for these films does not entail treating them as aesthetic objects to be "interpreted" in accord with the presentist schemata of the analyst, and we avowedly reject the imposition of our own "interpretations" that would arise solely from practicing textual hermeneutics. Rather, these texts provide the best possible entry point for the consideration of the role of the film industry at a moment of cultural reconfiguration and for a broader analysis of that reconfiguration.

We cannot, of course, avoid all presentist interpretation. The meanings we ascribe to our intertexts are as subject to negotiation as are the quality films that we take as our central texts. But, in order to preclude an infinite regress of interpretation, we have been forced to impose our own readings on our intertextual evidence. As partial compensation for this problem of infinite regress, we rely where possible on period discourse that is self-consciously "interpretive"—lectures, reviews and commentaries, for example.

3. Texts originating from the dominant social formations are more likely to survive the vicissitudes of historical filtration than those originating from marginalized social formations, since they are produced, circulated, and preserved by institutions of cultural reproduction. We have searched for the traces left by marginalized voices, attempting to remain sensitive to the possible receptions of members of various social formations by considering factors such as class, ethnicity, and gender. Historical filtration inevitably biases our evidence, however, making it easier to adduce conditions of reception for dominant social formations than for marginalized social formations.

4. Our intertextual evidence is drawn from a relatively broad period, usually ranging from the 1880s to the period when the quality films were produced, given that this was the key moment in the contestation and renegotiation of cultural hegemony. This evidentiary time frame is also necessitated by the fact that the circulation half-life of books, statuary, lithographs, and so forth, was significantly longer in this period than in our own and that our discussions of possible reception include audiences whose cultural experiences encompassed the closing decades of the nineteenth century.

And now a few words about the book's organization. Chapters 1 and 2 deal primarily with conditions of production, taking a social control perspective on the quality films. Chapter 1 adumbrates the broad social context, focusing on the contestation of the hegemonic order. The chapter discusses the perceived threat of workers and immigrants to the status quo at the turn of the century, particularly the most "dangerous" cultural embodiment of that threat: the cheap amusements with which the film industry was initially linked. Chapter 2 provides a brief overview of the film industry's own perceptions of its cultural status and its attempts to upgrade both film content and exhibition sites. The quality films, which were part of this overall strategy, help to illustrate the industry's dual strategy of forging a rhetorical alliance with the dominant fraction of the dominant class while jockeying for economic and political power within the dominated fraction of cultural producers.

Chapters 3, 4, and 5 deal with the conditions of production and reception for the five films or eleven reels enumerated above. Drawing on intertextual evidence, these chapters detail conditions of production and reception. They look at the film industry's attempts to reposition itself within the culture through selective alliances with particular interpretive communities and the ways in which members of various social formations may have negotiated the quality films. The intertextual delineation of production and reception helps to illuminate both the broad cultural reconfiguration of the period and the film industry's position within it. Chapter 3 deals with literary films, defined as those adapting canonized literary texts, and contrasts the consensual function of Shakespeare with the distinction function of Dante. Chapter 4 focuses on historical films, defined as those depicting particular historical personages, and contrasts the consensual function of Washington with the distinction function of Napoleon. Chapter 5 examines biblical films, defined as those illustrating characters and incidents from the Bible, and assesses the consensual function of the Moses films, in which Vitagraph struggled to avoid contentious distinctions.

Together, the book's five chapters address the tension between the attempt of the dominant social formations to exercise control in a "top-down" hegemonic order and the possible negotiations or contestations of the target groups in a "bottom-up" encounter with the established elite. Yet we advance no theory to account for the interaction of the (often totalizing) hegemonic with the (often infinite) negotiations of audiences. Rather, we look to concrete historical instances at a time of particularly pronounced transition and crisis using the quality films as an analytical tool for understanding more fully the mechanisms of a particular hegemonic order.

Responses to Cultural Crisis:
Political Domination and Hegemony

IN THE 1870s, the trauma of the Civil War barely behind it, the United States plunged into a cycle of economic boom and bust accompanied by acrimonious and violent labor disputes. Waves of immigrants from southern and eastern Europe and the pressures of rapid urbanization further exacerbated the tensions stemming from economic upheaval and earlier Irish and German immigration. Native-born Americans, ranging from the inhabitants of Fifth Avenue mansions to the farmers of the Great Plains, began to fear the unruly and alien mob, perceiving a threat not only to the very fabric of a capitalist society but to its fundamental cultural values as well. Organized working men sought to redress the balance of power between labor and capital, while socialists and anarchists advocated not ameliorating the social situation but revolutionizing it. Perhaps even more dangerous, however, was the profound cultural reconfiguration of the period. Newcomers brought with them the "foreign" values of their native lands, while the concentration of immigrants and workers in the cities permitted the flourishing of an urban popular culture, the growing prominence of which challenged established values. The emergence of a mass consumer culture that cut across all social formations further subverted the vested cultural authority of traditional tastemakers.

The supporters of the status quo responded to these pressures in two ways: first, by employing state agents (the army, the police, the militia) in an attempt to establish political domination; and second, by employing nonviolent means to secure assent to the existing distribution of power, in other words, to establish a hegemonic order. As we have pointed out, however, this hegemonic order was not a static entity but changed constantly as a result of both its defense and its contestation. Hence, the broad bifurcation between the advocates of political domination, whom we term the repressives, and the advocates of hegemonic incorporation, whom we term the assimilationists, masks underlying complexities to which we shall allude throughout the book.

Fears of imminent social dissolution initiated by the first general strike in United States history, the railway strike of 1877, crystallized around the Chicago Haymarket incident of 1886. At an anarchist-sponsored strike rally a bomb hurled by a still unknown assailant killed a policeman. His enraged comrades retaliated, killing four demonstrators and wounding many—and shooting several of their fellow officers in the process.[1] In the aftermath eight anarchists were tried and convicted for inciting to riot through their publications. Although some from the left side of the political spectrum rallied to the defendants' cause, the mainstream press coverage of the Haymarket "riot" and the subsequent trial invoked the frightening spectres of anarchy and revolution stalking the land.

The depression of 1893–97, entailing hundreds of bank failures and more than a hundred railroad receiverships, saw further violent encounters between labor and the henchmen of capital. The 1892 Homestead strike against Andrew Carnegie's steel corporation and the 1894 Pullman strike against the manufacturer of the railroad cars resulted in more labor deaths as well as federal government intervention through both court injunction and the United States Army. Anarchists remained in the public eye, one attempting to assassinate Carnegie's deputy, Henry Frick, another succeeding in his attempt against the president, William McKinley.

Some native-born Americans mounted virulent attacks upon the "foreigners," whom they associated with the decline of the nation. An official of the Grand Army of the Republic spoke of "foreign born rotten banana sellers, thieving rag dealers, Italian organ grinders, Chinese washmen and Bohemian coal miners, whose aspirations would make a dog vomit."[2] The clergyman Josiah Strong, author of the best-seller *Our Country*, believed that immigration, connected with many of the forces disrupting the status quo, was at the root of the nation's ills. "Immigration . . . has fed fat the liquor power. . . . Immigration is the strength of the Catholic Church. . . . Immigration is the mother and nurse of American socialism. . . . Immigration tends strongly to the cities, and gives them their political complexion. And there is no more serious menace to our civilization than our rabble-ruled citizens [in the cities]."[3]

Indeed, immigrants were intimately linked in the public mind with the myriad evils threatening consensual values: criminality, prostitution, intemperance, striking, violating the Sabbath, and so on. These, in turn, became inseparable from the problems of overcrowding, lack of sanitation, and moral decay attendant upon the growth of the cities. And of all cities, New York, the headquarters of the film industry, most resonantly symbolized what many feared might be the coming order of culture and society, for nowhere was the perceived link between immigration and the imminent collapse of the American way of life more "obvious" than in America's Gotham.

New York—with its corrupt, inept administration, with Ellis Island, the main point of entry for "the huddled masses yearning to breath free," with the appalling slums south of Fourteenth Street—epitomized all the problems of the newly industrialized, urbanized nation. Daniel Coit Gilman, president of the Johns Hopkins University, said that "New York is an example to all this land—a colossal object lesson . . . a sort of teachers' college where other cities may learn both what to do and what not to do."[4] The Buffalo members of the New York State Tenement House Commission took a less temperate view. "After several days of silent amazement, they exclaimed: 'New York should be abolished.' "[5]

Demographic data from the period document the magnitude of the "alien" presence in New York City. According to the 1910 census, the foreign-born constituted 47.9 percent of the population in the borough of Manhattan.[6] More important than the statistics were perceptions of New York as "the second largest German city in the world, the second largest Italian city, the largest Irish city, and by far the largest Jewish city in the world."[7] The period's discourse emphasized the magnitude of the alien presence, treating the Germans, Italians, Irish, and Jews as an undifferentiated block and often overlooking the fact that the various ethnicities exhibited profound dissimilarities in terms of their motives for emigration, attitudes toward religion, family structures, cultural exposures and expectations, and countless other factors. These differences among ethnicities were further compounded by differences within the ethnic communities with regard to class, education, prior occupations, and so forth.[8]

Although a few astute social workers were sensitive to these complexities, for the majority of native New Yorkers the inescapable presence of the newly arrived foreigners served as a constant reminder of the profound upheaval in their familiar social and cultural order. For Henry James, returning from a lengthy sojourn in the United Kingdom, the city's foreign populace produced culture shock. The writer characterized the influx of immigrants as an assault upon the body politic exceeding the self-imposed trauma of the circus sword- or fire-swallower. James lamented being forced "to share the sanctity of his American consciousness, the intimacy of his American patriotism, with the inconceivable alien." For several days after a visit to Ellis Island, James wandered the streets of Manhattan profoundly conscious of the "ghost in his supposedly safe old house." James felt constrained to accommodate his conceptions of patriotism and national identity to "*their* monstrous, presumptuous interest" powerfully manifested in "that loud primary stage of alienism which New York most offers to sight."[9]

James might have been even more appalled had he visited the slums south of Fourteenth Street rather than the relatively salubrious Ellis Island. In fact, the observations of a missionary on a midnight tour of New York's tenement districts would have confirmed his worst fears about the dissolution of his familiar society.

> A few steps out of Broadway, we came to the vilest dens of infamy. In one room, not more than ten by twelve, we came upon eighteen human beings, men and women, black and white, American and foreign-born, who there ate, slept, and lived. In that room we found a women of the highest refinement and culture with the faded dress of a courtesan upon her dishonored body; a former leader in the Salvation Army, a woman of sweet song, half drunk; a snoring, disgusting Negro wench; an opium-eating licentious Italian, et al.![10]

The horror here stemmed not so much from the wretched lot of these human beings but rather from the fact that their intermingling transgressed the rigid boundaries of gender, ethnicity, and class necessary for the maintenance of the social order. Note that two of the occupants of this tenement room, the woman of "highest refinement and culture" and "a former leader in the Salvation Army," were members of that class and gender often associated with the maintenance of traditional cultural values.[11] If this promiscuous intermingling of bodies and value systems could bring these women to such a sorry pass, what might be the effects on a national scale? This small space epitomized the corrosive and corrupting potential of the urban condition.

How, then, were the dominant social formations to respond to this social and cultural upheaval? The very words "Haymarket," "Homestead," and "Pullman" came to symbolize for some a nation teetering on the brink of a revolution that only forceful repression could avert. Many of the editorials appearing in the press verged on the hysterical in their calls for extreme measures. One of the nation's Christian journals urged most un-Christian violence. *The Independent* recommended employing the full arsenal of the modern military against the railroad strikers of 1877. "If the club of the policeman, knocking out the brains of the rioter will answer, then well and good; but if it does not promptly meet the exigency, then bullets and bayonets, cannister and grape . . . constitute the one remedy and the one duty of the hour. . . . Napoleon was right when he said that the way to deal with the mob was to exterminate it."[12] A prominent American, soon to be police commissioner of New York City, also gave his advice on handling such situations. Said Theodore Roosevelt, "My men [his ranchhands] . . . are Americans through and through. I believe nothing would give them greater pleasure than a chance with rifles at one of the mobs. . . . I wish I had them with me and a fair show at ten times our number of rioters. My men shoot well and fear very little."[13]

But physical force alone would not suffice, for the danger stemmed not only from strikers and rioters but from the even more insidious influence of contesting social and cultural values. The *New York Times*, editorializing about the "problem of vice in the tenement houses," suggested that "the present danger is from moral, not physical infection, and it requires a system of moral disinfection."[14] The moral infection which the *Times* identified, using a prevalent period metaphor of disease and contagion, could not be combatted by the police and militia. Many in the dominant social formations, taking their cue from Matthew Arnold, believed that the social and cultural crisis would be solved not through force but through the incorporation of the newcomers and the discontented into a shared value system that would link together all the members of an increasingly disparate society.

Faced with the political turmoil in England that had resulted from demands for working class suffrage, Matthew Arnold, in his influential *Culture and Anarchy*, first published in 1869, proposed a means of combatting moral infection through culture, which he defined as "a pursuit of our total perfection by means of getting to know, on all the matters which most concern us, the best which has been thought and said in the world."[15] This Arnoldian definition delimited the cultural to the realm of expressive forms traditionally identified with arts and letters and thus excluded the broader anthropological sense of culture as lived experience.[16] Arnold argued that this delimited sense of culture could constitute a set of shared values that would encourage reasonable— namely, nonviolent and nonrevolutionary—behavior. "The very principle of the authority which we are seeking as a defence against anarchy is right reason, ideas, light."[17] Arnold argued that the incorporation of all into culture as defined by the dominant social formations would ameliorate class divisions and thus civil strife. Culture "seeks to do away with classes; to make the best that has been thought and known in the world current everywhere; to make all men live in an atmosphere of sweetness and light."[18]

Although Arnold firmly grounded his analysis in the English political situation, discursive parallels indicate that his solution seems to have been taken up by many in the dominant social formations of the United States, who attempted to forge a cultural consensus that would incorporate rather than repress disruptive forces such as workers and immigrants by extending a vision of sweetness and light across the boundaries of race, gender, ethnicity, and class. For the purposes of this project, we work from the period's own sense of Arnoldian culture, defining the dominant culture as the expressive forms valorized and circulated by the dominant social formations.[19] But this dominant culture was by no means monolithic, the fin-de-siècle upheaval described above rendering it particularly fractured and unstable. Various educational, economic, and social elites, all members of dominant social formations, nonetheless contested among themselves the definition of the culture that was to be extended. And, in practice, this extension did not result in cultural egalitarianism, since even those seeking to forge cultural consensus did not intend to create a seamless monolith in which all citizens had precisely the same cultural exposures. Rather, as Pierre Bourdieu suggests, restrictions on the circulation of some cultural expressions resulted in the creation of hierarchies, which preserved necessary distinctions among social formations by enhancing the value of some kinds of cultural capital relative to other kinds. While some of these hierarchies were created de novo, others resulted from a reconfiguration of the existing cultural landscape, as dominant social formations appropriated expressive forms that had once belonged to popular culture.[20]

To exemplify the process whereby the dominant culture was constructed, we look briefly at two of the most important of the institutions of cultural reproduction during this period, public schools and libraries. Mandatory public education, regulated on a statewide level, became widespread in the United States around the turn of the century just as immigration from southern and eastern Europe swelled. In urban centers such as New York City the public schools constituted the first line of defense against the "alien invasion," charged with the responsibility for teaching immigrant children the language of their new country as well as its manners and morals. The rhetoric of key figures in education confirms that many perceived the schools as agents of assimilation that would help to avert the collapse of the dominant social and cultural order by building consensual values.[21] John Dewey, the philosopher and educational theorist, saw the schools as instilling the virtues necessary for social harmony. "When the school introduces and trains each child of society into membership within such a little community, saturating him with the spirit of service, and providing him with the instruments of effective self-direction, we shall have the deepest and best guaranty of a larger society which is worthy, lovely, and harmonious."[22]

Many considered that literature and history, embodying as they did the "best that has been thought and said," were the subjects best suited to the purposes of moral inoculation. New York City's Department of Education told its teachers that "every school study has a specific moral value. Literature and history embody in concrete form moral facts and principles . . . furnishing him [the child] with ideals and incentives, and molding his moral judgment."[23] *McGuffey's Fifth Reader*, a textbook widely adopted on the national level, also spoke of moral education as occurring through the teaching of literature and history. "Care has been taken to maintain the same high literary and ethical standard that has hitherto so distinctly characterized these books. Lessons inculcating kindness, courage, obedience, industry, thrift, true manliness, patriotism, and other duties and obligations form no small portion of the contents."[24]

A knowledge of literature and history, together with the other "civilizing" influences to which the schools exposed immigrant children, would result in a painless and almost unnoticeable assimilation into the American way, asserted those in power. A study funded by the Carnegie Corporation of the schooling of the immigrant concluded that

> Americanization has taken place through the schools, but it has been an unconscious byproduct. . . . There is very seldom designated in the elementary school weekly program . . . any subject entitled citizenship. . . . And yet Americanization and citizenship are the usual resultants of all school training. The child receives impressions, inspirations, and impulses from the pictures he sees in the classroom, from the stories he reads in his history, from the exercises he attends in the assembly hall, from the celebration of patriotic anniversaries and the salute of the flag.[25]

Although public libraries were not as pervasive as the schools, their proliferation does seem to have resulted from the same desire to assimilate rather than to repress. In fact, Andrew Carnegie, perhaps taking a hint from his good friend Matthew Arnold, redirected his activities from the violent repression of labor unrest to the funding of public libraries, giving more than $41 million for the erection of 1,679 library buildings. According to Carnegie, the choice of public libraries was based on "my belief, as Carlyle has recorded, that the true university of these days is a collection of books, and that thus such libraries are entitled to a first place as instruments for the elevation of the masses of the people."[26]

Others even more explicitly linked the public libraries to the cultural and social crisis. The American Library Association compared the upheaval of turn-of-the-century America to the decline of the Roman Empire. "Free corn in old Rome bribed a mob and kept it pacific. By free books and what goes in them in modern America we mean to erase the mob from existence."[27] But books would not only keep the mob pacific; they would also instruct the mob in civic virtue. An article appearing in the Library Journal in 1891 explained how the public library would fight moral infection. "The hope and safety of organized society depend upon the wide diffusion of intelligence and culture; and from no centers can such influences be so beneficently extended as from the generously supported and wisely-managed public libraries."[28] The library's dissemination of the "best that has been thought and said," asserted John Cotton Dana, an influential American librarian, would ensure the future stability of the country. "The coming generations . . . will speak more plainly; will think more clearly; will be less often led astray by the 'mere words' of false prophets of every kind; will see that all men are of the one country of humanity; and will, to sum it all, be better citizens of a good state."[29]

Although the interpretive community of librarians shared the belief that their institution of cultural reproduction should work to ameliorate the cultural crisis, they disagreed about tactics. The more didactically inclined avowed that public libraries should encourage the reading of nonfiction, some even demanding that patrons borrow a nonfiction book in addition to every piece of fiction. On the principle of making rabbit stew—first, catch the rabbit—others believed that libraries could use popular fiction to lure patrons in and then lead them to higher pursuits.[30] Individuals outside the interpretive community, particularly those at whom these "free books" were directed, discerned the hegemonic implications behind the growth of the public libraries. Some on the left, such as Eugene Debs, criticized Andrew Carnegie as a "philanthropic pirate" who built libraries with the profits wrested from his exploited workers. A Pittsburgh union leader, addressing a rally against the acceptance of a Carnegie library, asserted that he would "sooner enter a building built with the dirty silver Judas received for betraying Christ than enter the Carnegie library."[31] Despite these scattered protests, however, the assimilationist work of the public libraries proceeded apace.

Schools and libraries, together with other institutions of cultural reproduction, all joined in a concerted effort to create cultural consensus by making "the best that has been thought and said" available to the masses and, when possible, as in the case of schools, mandating its inculcation.[32] This effort at the forging of what Gramscians would term a hegemonic order stood in sharp contrast to the wish of Teddy Roosevelt and his hired guns to impose political domination but just as adamantly sought the control of the "lower orders." In a period when the moral infection of alien values seemed more pernicious than riots in the streets, some believed that literature, history, and religion might be more effective tools than bullets and bayonets for building a unified country.

Cheap Amusements: The Repressive Response

The Vice Commission of Chicago, in its investigation of the "Social Evil," that is, prostitution, reported that:

> Among the recreational conditions directly tributary to the increase of the victims of vice, are the privately managed amusement parks; dance halls, . . . candy, ice cream and fruit stores used as pleasure resorts; immoral shows, theatre plays and moving pictures; saloons where music, vaudeville performances, and other recreational attractions are accessory to the drink habit; drug stores, where gambling devices and the selling of cocaine and other drugs are accessories.[33]

The gathering of the masses in cheap amusement venues exacerbated the perceived threat to the nation's cultural fabric.[34] The spectre of laborers and immigrants liberated from the regimentation of the workplace and congregating freely to revel in crude, vicious and lascivious entertainments struck fear into the hearts of many respectable Americans, who saw little difference between a mob of strikers and the unruly patrons of the cheap amusements.

Members of dominant social formations may have seen these amusements as competing with the institutions of cultural reproduction and as subverting the creation of a carefully controlled cultural consensus. Yet strikes could be declared illegal and strikers violently suppressed, whereas making cheap amusements illegal and using force against their patrons posed constitutional problems. Difficult to regulate as they were, cheap amusements quickly emerged as the primary site of cultural contagion associated with the "lower orders." The fact that social reformers conducted at least fourteen major studies in various urban centers testifies to the extent of the concern.[35]

In 1896 *Scribner's Magazine*, one of the publications most strongly associated with the culture of the dominant social formations,[36] ran an article on Coney Island that testified to the anxiety cheap amusements provoked in some observers, terms such as "delirium," "panic," and "pandemonium" reflecting the writer's perception of the "lower orders" giving way to their "uncircumscribed propensities." The "masses" at this time frequented only a small section of Coney Island, tellingly labelled "the Bowery," "that which is cheap and yet pretentious, that which is loud, that which is beer-sodden, and that which is 'faked' or made-up or make-believed." The writer described the Bowery in terms redolent of James talking about the inconceivable alien. The Bowery was

> the seat of a delirium of raw pleasure. Physically, the place is a sort of Chinatown of little frame buildings set about, helter-skelter, like a cityful of houses in panic. Aurally, it is a riot of the noises of roller-coasters . . . of test-your-lungs and test-your-strength and test-your-grip machines . . . of razzle-dazzle rings that go all ways at once, like a ship's compass; of a band of howling Sioux; of the yells of the shouters in front of the freak museums; . . . in short, of pandemonium.[37]

The "Chinatown of little frame buildings" connects Coney Island with the alien and foreign, while "delirium" and the disorientation of the senses it implies further connects these amusements with the contagion of the tenements.

Just as late-twentieth-century media critics obsess about the harmful effects of television, their late-nineteenth-century counterparts alleged that cheap amusements exerted a deleterious influence upon the malleable and often underdeveloped minds of young people, uneducated laborers, and immigrants. Josiah Strong connected urban environmental conditions to the demoralizing cheap amusements that lured their patrons to destruction.

> Where there is a lack of nourishing food and of the tonic of pure air, debilitated nerves crave excitement; hence the large number of saloons, gambling hells, dance halls, and theatres in the most crowded portions of the city. The vaudeville or variety show which abounds and is largely patronized is generally poor and often vile. Coarse theatricals, promiscuous public dances, and drinking saloons prepare the way for easy ruin.[38]

Even when consumed in private, cheap amusements, such as "sensational" fiction, posed a serious threat to the social fabric.[39] Francis Parkman, an eminent historian, argued that the taste of immigrants and their progeny for the sensational press rendered universal suffrage problematic. "It may be doubted whether, as a general rule, the young Irish American is a better or safer citizen than his parent from Cork. He can read; but he reads nothing but sensation stories and scandalous picture-papers, which fill him with preposterous notions, and would enfeeble a stronger brain than his and debauch a sounder conscience."[40] Josiah Strong also complained about the lurid, sensational press. "Corrupt and corrupting publications profusely illustrated, have become well-nigh as ubiquitous as the vermin of an Egyptian plague. In addition to the sensational sheets which make a specialty of vice and crime, concerning which they tell the truth(?), the whole truth and much more than the truth, cheap fiction abounds. 'Blood-curdling' stories for boys and girls are a large part of this stuff."[41] Parkman's use of "enfeebling" and Strong's equating of corrupt publications to the "vermin of an Egyptian plague" show how widespread were the metaphorical connections among disease, infection, and cheap amusements.

In 1887 the Reverend Otto Peltzer, author of the biblical play *Moses and Pharaoh*, wrote an impassioned defense of the theatre, attempting to persuade his fellow Christians of the stage's moral potential. The popular melodrama, by contrast, came in for resounding condemnation.

> There is much room for argument against a certain class of production on the stage to-day. . . . It is to be regretted that, like the sensational scandal-and-criminal columns of the daily papers, these exhibitions are intensely gratifying to a certain class of patrons of the theatre. . . . The jargon of the swamp, the debasing lingo of the police reporter, the abounding epithets of tap-room frequenters, the colloquialisms of the street arab will come trippingly from the pens of these play-makers. Horrors intensified, grossness exaggerated, modern barbarity, the doings of swindlers, drunkards, beggars, thieves, the lowest form of degradation, scenes in the gambling halls and prisons . . . accidents, explosions and mangled limbs, are their leading features. . . . Plays with convicts for heroes; with plots made up of impossibilities and exaggerations . . . give no instruction—they are monstrosities that teach no lessons. They positively poison the minds of a young generation.[42]

The moving picture, the newest of the cheap amusements, rapidly became a primary focus for the advocates of both the repressive and assimilationist strategies for dealing with the cultural crisis. After all, the moving picture had the potential to become more pervasive and influential than the theatre, the libraries, or even the public schools. The medium's reliance upon technologies of mechanical reproduction, together with its evident popularity, enabled it

to disseminate, in a highly systemized fashion, texts and interpretations originating outside the realm of authorized interpretive communities and not
broadly circulated by other institutions of cultural reproduction. This ability
gave rise to perceptions of the storefront moving picture shows as among
the most rapidly growing and the most dangerous of the unregulated cheap
amusements pandering to the masses in their leisure time. These perceptions
were exacerbated by the content of the films, the location and character of the
exhibition sites, and the class and ethnic composition of the audiences. In the
earliest years of American cinema, "actualities"—short, nonfiction films that
appealed to the Victorian didactic instinct—had constituted the bulk of the
studios' output. By 1904 the studios had begun to produce primarily fiction
films, many of which derived their plots from the sensational press and the
lurid melodrama and thus declared their affiliation with the despised cheap
amusements.[43] John Collier, an assimilationist actively involved in the debate
over moving pictures, took a retrospective look at the film medium in 1910,
specifically connecting film's subject matter with the most reprehensible aspects of popular culture. Motion pictures "began, wanton, sensational, sometimes obscene, for that was what cheap amusements were expected to be in
those days."[44]

One of the earliest popular press reports on the new medium asserted that
nickelodeon audiences especially enjoyed films portraying criminal activities.
"Pursuits of malefactors are by far the most popular of all nickel deliriums. You
may see snatch-purses, burglars, and an infinite variety of criminals hunted by
the police and the mob in almost any nickelet you have the curiosity to visit."[45]
Such films, thought some, were certain to have the same negative effects on
their patrons as did other cheap amusements, with their demoralizing subject
matter. After reciting a litany of film-inspired suicides, murders, and robberies, a writer in the *American Review of Reviews* declared that "with young, formative, and impressionable minds the results are, of course, worse. Indeed,
the motion picture show is as widely suggestive to this class as the cheap
sensational novel used to be."[46]

Almost concurrent with the shift in film content was a shift in exhibition
sites. In 1895 Koster & Bial's Music Hall, one of the large vaudeville houses
on New York City's Thirty-fourth Street, first began projecting moving pictures, thereby ensuring the commercial success of the new medium. Until
about 1905 most viewers either saw moving pictures at vaudeville houses
such as this or at traveling shows that exhibited at fairgrounds or churches.
Around that time, however, the advent of the fiction film—in combination
with the founding of a film rental distribution system, the film exchanges—
permitted the emergence of theatres primarily devoted to moving picture
exhibition, the nickelodeons. These nickelodeons, concentrated in urban
centers, were often located in or within easy reach of working class and/or

immigrant neighborhoods, and thus attracted many of the inhabitants of these areas.[47]

Although the character of nickelodeons and their audiences obviously varied from location to location, no moving picture shows were as heavily publicized as those of New York City or so thoroughly excoriated. By 1908 New York rivaled Chicago for the greatest concentration of nickelodeons, estimates ranging between five hundred and eight hundred. A 1910 survey by a progressive civic reform organization, the Russell Sage Foundation, claimed that even after a period of consolidation there were 201 theatres in Manhattan alone, 71 located below Fourteenth Street.[48] Whatever the reality, however, period discourse established the same synecdochical relationship between New York's nickelodeons and the national menace of the moving picture as between New York's urban pandemonium and the national social and cultural crisis. As the author of the Sage Foundation report said, "The uptown conception of a moving-picture show was then [two years ago], as to a less extent it still is, a place of darkness, physical and moral."[49]

Journalists visiting New York's nickelodeons, although often favorably inclined toward the "nickel madness," still described audiences in terms that may have supported the negative association of moving pictures with cheap amusements and the "lower orders." Barton Currie, writing in August 1907 at a point when nickelodeons were just beginning to emerge as a major entertainment in New York, claimed that two hundred thousand people daily frequented the moving pictures. His article characterized audiences by describing a hypothetical pickpocket attempting to ply his trade in a New York nickelodeon.

> He has a choice of a dozen neighborhoods, and the character of the places varies little, nor does the class of patrons change, except here and there as to nationality. Having entered one of these get-thrills-quick theatres . . . let him look about him at the workingmen, at the tired, drudging mothers of bawling infants, at the little children of the streets, newsboys, bootblacks, and smudgy urchins. . . . The pickpocket who enters one of these humble booths for sordid motives must be pretty far down in his calling—a wretch without ambition.[50]

A 1908 visitor to a Bowery nickelodeon reported that he saw "Chinese, absorbed, taciturn, eager. There were Italians—mothers, often with sleeping bambinos in their laps. Fully a third of the audience was Yiddish—Russian and Austrian Jews."[51] Nickelodeon audiences in cities such as New York and Chicago were also characterized as heavily working class, as in the following from *Motography*.

> [The moving picture] has brought amusement to the door of the work-driven sweat-shop worker, the tired out, overworked, underpaid mechanic, the poor house slave of a mother whose family cares keep her drudging from early morn till

late, but who can manage to slip around the corner and see the five-cent picture show, the only amusement she has, the thousands of cheap laborers in every field who cannot afford the luxury of twenty-five-cent or fifty-cent theatres, but can get amusement for themselves and their families at five cents a head.[52]

The 1910 Russell Sage survey described the Manhattan nickelodeon audiences as 72 percent "working class," 25 percent "clerical class," and 3 percent "leisure class."[53]

Writing three years later and taking a retrospective look at the controversy over moving pictures, Maude McDougall pointed to the connection between the composition of New York nickelodeon audiences and anxieties about film content. "From twenty to twenty-five per cent of the patrons of moving-picture shows are children. And because the entertainment is inexpensive, and because it requires no translation, a very large percentage are immigrants. Immigrants and children! The entire raw material of future citizenship. No wonder the 'high-brows'—parents and teachers, legislators and entertainers—are concerned over the influence of these cheap shows."[54] Other estimates put the proportion of children in the audience at over 50 percent, while the Russell Sage report found that, of 1,140 children surveyed, 68 percent of the boys and 54 percent of the girls attended nickelodeons weekly, and 16 per-cent of the total attended daily.[55] In terms of the period's perceptions of moving picture audiences, then, it is understandable that the new medium was seen as posing a serious threat to the mission of the institutions of cultural reproduction.

The accuracy of these perceptions is another matter entirely. The rapid changes in the industry and in audiences that took place between 1907 and 1913 make it particularly difficult to discuss nickelodeon viewership with any accuracy. In addition, the haphazard nature and survival of empirical data, coupled with the biased reports of a trade press intent upon improving the industry's image and of the industry's opponents intent upon suppression, limit our ability to rely on period evidence. Moreover, nickelodeons and their audiences differed widely from neighborhood to neighborhood, even within New York City, rendering any overarching characterization suspect.[56]

But contemporary perceptions seem to have counted much more heavily than reality in responses to the problem of moving pictures.[57] Consider, for example, Dr. Howard D. King's summary of nickelodeon locations and audiences.

As is well known, the great majority of these theatres exist where the population is greatly congested, as in tenement districts and laboring settlements. The reason for this is obvious. It is the patronage of the poorer classes which makes the moving picture industry a paying proposition. These cheap theatres are usually located in old rookeries or poorly paying commercial sites, as abandoned shops of small tradesmen, etc.[58]

The industry's detractors found the rapidly proliferating nickelodeons, said to be springing up like mushrooms on every street corner, particularly vexatious. Many proprietors of the storefront theatres had no prior experience in show business, and, said critics, no conception of how to operate a safe, clean, and orderly house. Vincent Pisarro, chief investigator of the Society for the Prevention of Cruelty to Children, said that many exhibitors were drawn from the dregs of society. "The managers . . . are of an exceedingly low type. They are made up of the offscouring of the theatrical business, race track touts, cheap gamblers, and even of ex-criminals."[59]

Whatever the exhibitors' backgrounds, the converted storefronts they managed, with their inadequate seating, insufficient ventilation, dim lighting, and poorly marked, often obstructed exits, posed serious hazards for their patrons, as numerous police and fire department memos from the period confirm. Regular newspaper reports of fires, panics, and collapsing balconies undoubtedly contributed to the popular perception of nickelodeons as deathtraps. But catastrophic accidents aside, the physical conditions threatened the community in more insidious ways. A 1908 report on cheap amusements said of the nickelodeons: "Often the sanitary conditions of the show-rooms are bad; bad air, floors uncleaned, no provision of spittoons, and the people crowded closely together, all make contagion likely."[60] Medical authorities related these conditions to the same diseases that plagued the tenement districts. In an article on "Moving Pictures and Health," *The Independent* reported on the health problems associated with the nickelodeons and with their patrons' behavior, particularly their tendency to expectorate on the floor and seats.[61] The article drew upon Dr. King's article in the *Journal of the American Medical Association*, which concluded that "as a disseminator of tuberculosis the moving picture theatre ranks high and it will become necessary to enact special health laws to remedy the evil."[62]

Descriptions of the physical conditions inside nickelodeons bore a striking resemblance to depictions, so beloved by social reformers, of the crowded, dark, and ill-ventilated tenements among which the storefront theatres thrived. The promiscuous mingling of genders, classes, and ethnicities in these theatres, coupled with the "vicious" and "vulgar" nature of the films themselves, made the moving pictures a particularly visible target for those concerned with the maintenance of the cultural status quo. Tellingly, the metaphor of disease and contagion figured as prominently in the specific discussions of the impact of the moving pictures and the nickelodeons as it did in the discussion of the effects of the immigrant and working classes on the country at large. One Methodist preacher, the Reverend John Wesley Hill of New York's Metropolitan Temple, for example, explicitly used this metaphor in condemning moving pictures, claiming that they were "causing a spread of moral malaria throughout the community."[63] The burgeoning of nickelodeons nationwide, with audiences estimated at over 45 million per week by the start of 1909, suggested that the new medium was not simply a localized infestation but rather a plague of national proportions.[64]

How, then, to control this raging epidemic? Some advocated the use of state power to repress, or at least strictly regulate, both the sites and the content of moving pictures. In many localities, reformers called for official municipal censorship. As early as 1907 Chicago established a board of police censors that reviewed all the films shown within the city's jurisdiction and often demanded the excision of "offensive" material.[65] San Francisco's censors enforced a code so strict that it barred "all films where one person was seen to strike another."[66] In New York City, repressive reformers, arguing contra those who claimed that the industry itself could regulate film content, proposed at various times that the police or the Board of Education or the Board of Aldermen be given censorship powers. Some states, Pennsylvania and Ohio first among them, did in fact institute state censorship boards.

Many municipalities sought to require that nickelodeons meet the same stringent fire safety standards originally designed for legitimate theatres, even though the expenses entailed would have driven many proprietors out of business. Zoning laws were also used to prohibit the operation of nickelodeons near schools or churches. In addition to these thinly veiled attempts at suppression, other laws were aimed directly at the box office. Many state and local statutes forbade the admission of unaccompanied children, thereby depriving the nickelodeons of a major source of income. Granted, nickelodeon patrons undoubtedly encountered many physical hazards in their pursuit of amusement, as the frequent newspaper reports of fires and other accidents attest. Nonetheless, the ideological agenda behind the various attempts to ameliorate these conditions must be acknowledged. Requiring proprietors to adhere to a building code undoubtedly increased the patrons' safety, but it also increased the necessary capital investment, tending to drive out of business the more marginal immigrant entrepeneurs who operated some of the more "offensive" establishments.

The repressives also revealed their ideological agenda by invoking state and local blue laws to shut down the nickelodeons on Sundays, most wage earners' only day off and, not surprisingly, the best day at the box office. The implementation of the blue laws most clearly demonstrates the tensions between the native-born Protestant elite and the cultural values of the "lower orders," who were perceived as threatening the status quo. The Reverend Hill, author of the comment on "moral malaria," saw the violation of the Sabbath as a harbinger of anarchy. "Dr. Hill said the Nation was insidiously corrupted by the infringement of certain laws. The indifference of the managers [of the nickelodeons] and others to the existing laws, he asserted, was a step toward anarchy. . . . 'We hear of the blue laws of Puritanism, but much more might be said of the red laws of riot, carnival, and immorality. Our destiny would be surer for our respect of the blue laws.' "[67] After listening to Dr. Hill's sermon, "most of the congregation walked east through Fourteenth Street ... where they saw a string of nearly three hundred persons waiting in line to see the moving picture show."[68]

The Interdenominational Committee of the Clergy of Greater New York for the Suppression of Sunday Vaudeville, one of several similar lobby groups among the Protestant clergy, attempted to pressure city government into enforcing the laws on the books that prohibited certain kinds of Sunday entertainments. In a letter, the Reverend A. B. Churchman, treasurer of the committee, urged New York's Mayor George B. McClellan, Jr., to use the blue laws to close nickelodeons on Sundays. The committee asserted that Sunday shows encouraged the gathering of idle workers. "The especial point we would like to make against Sunday opening would be that, being a holiday, the rougher element of the neighborhood would be idle, and much more likely to congregate than upon any other day."[69]

But the committee went beyond its self-declared purview to list a litany of complaints about the general operation of the moving picture shows, illustrating the perceived connections among several fears—of immigrants, of their cheap amusements, and of the overall moral turpitude of the cities. The nickelodeons supposedly not only attracted loiterers on Sundays but, even more damagingly, encouraged workers to be idle during the work week. Churchman related the story of a father in "great distress" because "of the very fact that his boys had become so infatuated with the moving picture show that they are not willing to give attention to their daily work." Perhaps most tellingly, the committee's comments reflected widespread fears of "aliens." "It [the nickelodeon] is on the very block where several Black Hand outrages have occurred. The houses are crowded with Italians. Groups of men are almost always to be found upon the sidewalks, and anything like a show which would encourage further loitering would be a menace."[70]

In the clearest instance of the success of the repressive strategy, Mayor McClellan summarily revoked the licenses of all the city's nickelodeons on Christmas Eve of 1908.[71] The previous day the mayor had hurriedly convened a hearing to take testimony about the physical conditions of the nickelodeons and the moral effects of the films. Opponents and proponents of the moving pictures alike fought to define the medium's cultural function, in the process addressing many of the issues we have discussed above. The *New York Herald* summed up the debate. "Clergymen and officers of societies to prevent crime ... condemned the nickel theatre as a moral sinkhole and physical deathtrap, and ... those interested in the business ... defended them as places necessary for the amusement of the poor and for their moral and educational uplifting."[72] Members of the clergy, representatives of children's aid societies, and other "public-spirited" citizens denounced the nickelodeons as dens of iniquity harboring criminal elements from pickpockets to prostitutes. Their atmosphere also encouraged lascivious behavior on the part of the more respectable clientele, said E. Fellowes Jenkins, superintendent of the Society for the Prevention of Cruelty to Children. "The darkened rooms, combined with the influence of pictures projected on the screens, have given opportunities for a new form of degeneracy."[73] Canon William S. Chase, who became a lifelong opponent of the new medium, denounced exhibitors who ran Sunday shows as having "no moral scruples whatever. They are simply in the business for the money there is in it." Bishop Greer, of the Protestant Episcopal diocese, was unable to attend the hearings but sent a letter instead. He said he had been informed that "many of these pictures are of an indecent character, and are largely patronized, especially on Sunday, by the youth of the city; and exerting upon them a demoralizing influence. Whatever tends to contaminate or degrade the youth of the city is degrading and lowering [to] the tone of its future citizenship."[74]

Mayor McClellan also released to the press evidence that he had gathered concerning the varieties of moral contagion emanating from the city's picture shows. The New York Daily Tribune reported that "McClellan has received data from Police Commissioner Bingham and various city magistrates showing that the rapid growth of the picture business and the reckless disregard of the law by some of the proprietors had developed a class of disorderly women who confine their activities to the moving picture shows."[75] The article further implied that the nickelodeons afforded a haven for child molesters, a view promulgated by E. Fellowes Jenkins. The mayor cited a city magistrate's report regarding "an arrest of an Italian and a little girl at a moving picture show when the lights were unexpectedly turned on." They were both sent to the workhouse, even though the Italian's attorney had provided a "plausible explanation."[76] The mayor also claimed to have received more than a score of letters from citizens, all attesting to "the fact that many of the places tend to degrade morals."[77] Citing both the moral and physical dangers of the moving picture shows, Mayor McClellan revoked the licenses of over five hundred New York City nickelodeons.

Cheap Amusements: The Arnoldian Response

New York exhibitors sought legal relief, and the nickelodeons were back in operation almost immediately. The most blatant attempt at outright suppression through political domination had failed, although many still called for punitive measures against moving picture operators who showed "indecent" films on unsafe premises conducive to "degeneracy." But the debate over the moving picture shows and other cheap amusements continued between the forces of repression and the forces of assimilation. In sharp contrast to the Reverend Hill and his ilk, who wished to regulate leisure by using state power to eradicate cheap amusements, progressive reformers of an Arnoldian bent wished to provide equally attractive yet "morally superior" alternatives to these amusements, thereby incorporating their erstwhile patrons into the cultural mainstream.

New York City's Committee of Fifteen, a group of prominent citizens who conducted a vigorous investigation into prostitution, specifically connected cheap amusements with the "Social Evil." While calling for the suppression of such perverse pleasures as dance halls and ice cream parlors, the committee noted the necessity for

> the furnishing . . . of pure and more elevating forms of amusement to supplant the attractions of the low dance-halls, theatres, and other similar places of entertainment that only serve to stimulate sensuality and to debase taste. . . . If we would banish the kinds of amusement that degrade, we must offer to the public in this large cosmopolitan city, where the appetite for pleasure is keen, some sort of suitable alternatives.[78]

Altruism alone did not necessarily motivate the desire of the dominant social formations to provide "suitable alternatives." Counterattractions would address the cultural crisis by instilling common values, but they would also ameliorate the social crisis, precluding agitation by filling workers' leisure hours with less harmful pursuits. A lawyer involved in drafting an ordinance to regulate New York City's nickelodeons argued that moving pictures, properly controlled, could benefit the dominant social formations. "If we want these people to be normal, content, cheerful workers, we must provide them with ordinary opportunities for recreation, and if we do not we can expect nothing more than an abnormal class, exaggerating their grievances and constantly dissatisfied. Hence it is just as important to make the workingman satisfied with his lot as to make his lot satisfactory."[79] Charles Sprague Smith, the managing director of New York City's People's Institute, put the matter even more succinctly, pointing to the alternatives that he believed the United States faced at the turn of the century. "The fact is clear that in time organization either for good or for evil must come to these lower classes. It is either revolution or evolution."[80] His institute, together with others both in New York City and across the country, attempted to ward off revolution in favor of evolution by, among other things, the supplying of counterattractions.

We shall now look more closely at three New York City institutions of cultural reproduction that provided counterattractions: the People's Institute, the Educational Alliance, and the Bureau of Lectures. All three attempted to use "the best that has been thought and said" to overcome the differences that separated "man from man and class from class," in ways that would complement the related activities of institutions such as public schools and public libraries. Several factors motivate our discussion of these uplift organizations. Both their overt articulation of the policy of counterattractions and their proximity to those social formations perceived as most susceptible to the ill effects of the cheap amusements made these organizations particularly suitable role models for the film industry as it attempted to position itself within the mainstream of American culture. As we will show in the next chapter, both the subjects of the quality films and the industry's rhetoric about culture and uplift echoed the discourse of these and other institutions of cultural reproduction. Moreover, the People's Institute became actively involved with the moving picture medium, forging an alliance of sorts with the industry. In addition, because these organizations targeted social formations often marginalized through the hegemonic inflection of historical evidence, an examination of their activities provides us with one of the relatively few indices of the possible cultural exposures of nickelodeon audiences.

The People's Institute, founded by Charles Sprague Smith in 1897, aimed to bring about the mutual understanding of "the classes" and "the masses." As a strong advocate of progressive civic reform, the institute encouraged an informed and active electorate, holding frequent "People's Forums" at which citizens could debate and vote on pressing issues of the day, such as the traction trusts. The institute also sponsored a thrice-weekly lecture series on topics ranging from personal hygiene to electrical engineering to Dante. The emphasis, however, was on social science, reflecting Smith's desire to "assist in the solution of social problems."[81]

There was a curious conjunction between the institute's vaguely social democratic political agenda and its very conformist cultural agenda that fully embraced the concept of counterattractions.[82] Smith, in advocating the strategy of counterattractions to deal with the "saloon problem," clearly articulated Arnoldian sentiments.

> You have asked me, looking out upon a field where only tares grow, if the sole way to extirpate the weeds is to cut them down. I reply, give me the share to cut deep into that field and turn up fresh soil. Let me then drop into the open furrows grains of wheat. And by and by, Nature will come to my assistance, and working with me will destroy the tares.[83]

Smith went on to enumerate the grains of cultural wheat that would destroy the cheap amusement weeds, listing the activities of the social settlements, the Board of Education's free lectures, and the People's Institute's instruction in ethics, social science, and history.

Literary topics, of the right kind, were another important component of the institute's lecture series. "Literature," said Smith, "has been studied mainly for its ethical and social stimulus and experience is leading us to confine our courses here to the supreme works and the greatest writers."[84] These lectures often filled the Great Hall of the Cooper Union, which seated sixteen hundred people, a great many immigrants and laborers among them. The institute's Department of Drama and Music produced plays with casts drawn from institute members, staged professional performances at the Cooper Union, and established a reduced-price ticket program that enabled wage earners, schoolteachers, and schoolchildren to attend professional theatrical productions.[85]

In Smith's view, these theatrical activities substituted for "the cheap, often meretricious, melodrama and vaudeville, commonly accessible to those of limited means, the best that the theatre affords, thus making good drama a source of pleasure and uplift to a multitude of lives."[86]

Administered by the New York City Department of Education, the Bureau of Lectures, one of the first continuing adult education programs in the United States, extended the counterattractions of the public schools. In the spring of 1887 a *New York World* editorial proposed a lecture series for the working men and women of the city, which the New York legislature authorized to begin shortly thereafter. The offerings of the Bureau of Lectures, publicly funded as they were, lacked the specific social focus of many of the People's Institute lectures and thus ranged over a greater subject area. Mari Ruefhofer of Columbia University, speaking at the Bureau of Lectures' annual reunion in 1908, characterized the organization's diverse offerings. "Just to glance over the lecture menu for the coming year is a liberal education. Here rambles may be had from classic Hellas to Kimberly, to high life in Congo land, to a bicycle trip to the moon, all for the coming. Instruction may be had on Roentgen rays, on the authenticity of a Rubens, on history from Adam to Charlemagne, on Napoleon, on literature from the Koran to Kipling, from Shakespeare to Sherlock Holmes."[87] Whereas the People's Institute lectures were given only in English, the Bureau's speakers delivered lectures in German, Yiddish, and Italian as well.

The supervisor of the Bureau of Lectures, Henry M. Leipziger, stated that the "object of our work" is "to culturize the masses."[88] Leipziger again extolled the attractions of the public lecture series in Arnoldian terms, arguing that the lectures appealed to those who toiled long hours and desperately sought for "sweetness and light" in their limited leisure time. "There were found hundreds who responded to the yearning call for the higher life, who trudged willingly as pilgrims to the fountain of truth."[89] The "fountain of truth" would greatly enrich the lives of these humble pilgrims, felt Leipziger, by exposing them to culture they might otherwise not encounter. But it would also have beneficial results for society as a whole.

> If men and women follow the things that are pure and good and of high repute;
> if they come in contact with noble literature; if they read good books; if they
> become acquainted with the lives of noble men; . . . if they are put in touch with
> the great problems of history . . . surely such men and women must be better
> equipped for democratic citizenship than those to whom these opportunities are
> denied or who fail to take advantage of them.[90]

Leipziger boasted that the public lectures served as successful counterattractions, luring people away from the cheap amusements. "Thousands of young men and women, who probably pass their evenings at cheap shows, or even less elevating occupations, are gradually acquiring the lecture habit."[91]

The Educational Alliance, organized in 1889 with financial support from the German Jewish elite of New York City, including such financiers as Jacob Schiff, Felix Warburg, Henry Morgenthau, and Isidor Straus, established a large settlement house in the heart of the lower East Side.[92] The German Jews, who feared that the influx of Eastern European Jewish immigrants would cause an outbreak of anti-Semitism from which they would not be exempted, visualized the alliance as a means of rapid assimilation.[93] The Educational Alliance aimed "to aid the recently arrived Jewish immigrant, so as to enable him to comprehend the spirit of American institutions."[94] Or, as its *Thirteenth Annual Report* bluntly stated, " 'Americanizing immigrants' are the two words which come nearest expressing the reason for which we exist."[95] This "Americanizing" took the form of a multitude of activities, including cooking classes, instruction in personal hygiene, and physical education.[96] The Baron de Hirsch School, the most publicized of all the alliance's activities, taught English to newly arrived immigrant children to prepare them for the public schools.

The alliance's literary clubs, English literature classes, theatrical performances, and free lectures constituted one of the most extensive arrays of counterattractions in New York City. The *Thirteenth Annual Report* openly connected the alliance's stage presentations to the strategy of counterattractions.

> There is not an English theatre on the East Side pretending to a high standard; melodrama and vaudeville are the only source of amusement for the young man and woman who speaks and understands English. We propose to reach this class and have given them an opportunity to share in the thought of the master minds and their lofty conceptions, as formulated in the real drama.

As the report went on to say, the alliance's theatrical endeavors specifically targeted recent immigrants, hoping to prevent them from "falling a prey to the vicious tendencies of cheap drama, appealing to them on all sides."[97]

These three institutions of cultural reproduction approached the problem of cheap amusements differently from those who advocated the use of state power for suppression or strict regulation. Together with a broader array of forces involved in the process of cultural reproduction, these organizations believed that the provision of constructive and uplifting alternatives would wean the patrons of cheap amusements away from vicious and vulgar fare and initiate them into a shared set of cultural values predicated upon the "best that has been thought and said."[98] Significantly, these uplift organizations all eventually distinguished film from other cheap amusements and even incorporated moving pictures into their counterattraction offerings.

The People's Institute involved itself most systematically with the new medium and in fact provides the most explicit example of an alliance between an institution of cultural reproduction and the film industry. Charles Sprague Smith was one of the industry's most vocal defenders at Mayor McClellan's

1908 hearing, asserting that "the city should investigate certain conditions that foster a good deal more rottenness than moving picture shows" and that the moving picture is "a force that can do much good if properly conducted."[99] According to the *Daily Tribune*, a prolonged outburst of applause followed Smith's statement, and McClellan issued a stern rebuke.[100]

Smith spoke with authority, basing his opinion on the findings of an investigation of cheap amusements conducted earlier that year by the People's Institute and the Woman's Municipal League. The report on the investigation noted that nickelodeons were

> in some sections of the city . . . assuming a social character, being attended largely by families including the children. While some of these places are objectionable many are commendable, and, provided influence is brought to bear upon the central film agencies, and in some other ways, they offer an opportunity for educational influence. Efforts are being made for the improvement of the character of these shows and for securing better legal and sanitary regulation.[101]

While the report warned that the moving picture shows certainly needed improvement, John Collier, secretary of the People's Institute, argued that "the moving picture show is a constructive influence, meeting a genuine need in the people, and pointing the way to an important opportunity for schools, settlements, churches and educators generally."[102] Moreover, such shows had the potential to be a source of benefit among the vast audience they reached. "All the settlements and churches combined do not reach daily a tithe of the simple and impressionable folk that the nickelodeons reach and vitally impress every day. Here is a new social force, perhaps the beginning of a true theatre of the people, and an instrument whose power can only be realized when social workers begin to use it."[103] The institute was making the fairly radical suggestion that social reformers should no longer group the nickelodeons with the penny arcades and dance halls but rather employ the new medium to fight the cheap amusements, to serve, in fact, as a counterattraction.

The survey's positive assessment of film led to plans for further involvement with the medium, which Michael Davis, chair of the investigating committee, put forth in a letter to Howard Mansfield, the chairman of the Board of Trustees. "The potentialities of the moving picture have impressed us all greatly, and we have felt that there is a great opportunity to exploit these potentialities. This can be done in part through pressure upon managers of existing shows, but only in fullness through a show over which we have control."[104]

Davis, in effect, suggested two plans for exploiting the beneficial potential of the moving picture. In a magazine article summarizing the findings of the cheap amusements survey, the institute publicly proposed one of these plans, the establishment of a model moving picture show.

The investigation committee, which is to be perpetuated as a sub-committee of the Drama Committee of the People's Institute, will in all probability start up one or more model nickelodeons, with the object of forcing up the standard through direct competition, of proving that an unprecedently high class of performance can be made to pay, and perhaps, in the event of success, of founding a people's theatre of the future.[105]

The institute's nonprofit status prohibited it from following up on this scheme.[106] But the institute did implement its other idea. As a direct result of the nickelodeon closings, the institute, together with the New York Moving Pictures Exhibitors' Association, which had been formed to seek legal redress, created the National Board of Censorship, composed of members of various progressive civic organizations. With the industry's full cooperation, the board reviewed films prior to their release, often demanding the excision of scenes felt to transgress the bounds of good taste. By March 1909, with the cooperation of the Motion Picture Patents Company (to be discussed in the next chapter), the board was exercising its censorship powers over the majority of films, both domestic and foreign, released in the United States. The Board of Censorship assured that institutions of cultural reproduction, such as the Bureau of Lectures, the Educational Alliance, and the public schools, would have a steady supply of suitable films, should they decide to integrate film into their activities.

The formative role of the People's Institute in the National Board of Censorship (later the National Board of Review) has received more than adequate attention.[107] Beyond its formative role in the National Board, however, perhaps the most significant interaction between the institute and the motion picture industry took the form of Charles Sprague Smith's tireless advocacy of the new medium. In lectures, newspaper articles, and public testimony, Smith and his associates countered the attacks of repressives who sought the medium's strict containment by repeatedly asserting its power to uplift the masses.

But Smith did more than simply talk about film. He encouraged key individuals in institutions of cultural reproduction to watch moving pictures, hoping to persuade them to adopt the new medium. In 1910, the year of his death, Smith arranged through the Board of Censorship a special series of film programs for religious and educational leaders. One hundred persons, including the superintendent of schools, Dr. William H. Maxwell, Dr. Henry Leipziger, and numerous district superintendents and principals, attended a showing at the Board of Education. A few days later a group of prominent clergymen and churchworkers also attended a film program. The industry, cognizant of Smith's contributions, eulogized the professor following his death in 1910. "Professor Smith's services in behalf of the motion picture have been exceedingly valuable, and his death at this time is a great loss to the cause of educational pictures, in behalf of which he had prepared elaborate plans for their introduction to the educational authorities of New York."[108]

Charles Sprague Smith and his People's Institute most clearly epitomize those progressive reformers who, sensitive to the new medium's potential, sought to tame rather than destroy it. In its early years the American film industry had to decide between fighting the forces of repression through legal means, as it had done in the case of the nickelodeon closings, or allying with assimilationists such as Smith and emulating their counterattractions strategy, thereby gaining not only cultural acceptance but potentially a broader market. In the next chapter, we discuss how the film industry took its place within the mainstream of American culture.

The Film Industry's Drive
for Respectability

AS LATE AS 1912 *Motography* still perceived the need to counter the various accusations against the film medium, even though the industry had constantly proven its bona fides.

> It seems absurd that we must go on fighting these charges over and over again. . . . Acquittal of the charge, and conversion of the complainant, seems but a signal for new Quixotes to rise and fight the windmills they imagine they see whirling about our heads. Does a clergyman but express approval of a picture, and a hundred other churchmen are instantly up in arms, ready to prove a condition they have never seen and know nothing of.[1]

This chapter details the strategies that the film industry employed in attempting to reposition itself in American society as a mass entertainment acceptable to all social formations rather than a cheap amusement. First, we show how the industry forged a discursive alliance with the institutions of cultural reproduction. Second, we discuss how signifying practices were brought into line with those of "respectable" entertainments. Third, we discuss the production of the quality films. Although the subject matter of these films reflected the cultural offerings of institutions of cultural reproduction, they were sufficiently polysemic to ensure a wide audience. The quality films thus constitute one of the clearest instances of the massification of high culture attendant upon the film industry's full incorporation into American society.

Taking its lead from those investigating cheap amusements, the industry attempted to distinguish itself from these entertainments while at the same time claiming to serve as an active agent in their downfall, inasmuch as the moving picture habit could substitute for the vastly more offensive saloon, dance hall, or penny arcade habit. A Russell Sage report on New York City leisure activities asserted the superiority of the moving picture shows to other pastimes associated with the lower classes. "The motion picture is now offering to the public a more positively desirable form of entertainment than can be found at any other type of indoor commercial recreation."[2] John Collier, of the People's Institute, said that the nickelodeons not only provided better fare than the cheap amusements but actually lured away their patrons. Motion pictures "gained the favor of the wage earning and immigrant classes, drove the penny arcades out of business through competition, decimated through competition the old-style burlesque and melodrama houses and one-night stands throughout the country, and swept thousands of patrons from the galleries of the standard theatres of all kinds."[3]

The industry, which had long been saying the same thing, happily reported any utterance distinguishing film from cheap amusements. The *Views and Film Index* summarized the results of the 1908 People's Institute survey, particularly stressing the contrast between "good" nickelodeons and "bad" penny arcades and saloons. The penny arcades

> were found to be places of an entirely distinct character and not always a pleasant one. Attended largely by children, they showed in numerous cases a tendency to offer vicious pictures. It was the only way, apparently, in which they could compete with the larger, more extensive pictures of the cinematograph shows. Even so, it was found, the penny arcades were not holding their own. Their numbers are diminishing; their owners are in many cases making them over into the more desirable nickelodeons.[4]

Stephen Bush of the *Moving Picture World* reiterated the necessity that the industry distance itself from debasing pastimes. To "gain the sympathy and recognition of the best and highest elements in our civilization" film makers must reject "cheap comedy and cheap melodrama."[5] In the same issue of the *Moving Picture World*, an anonymous author remarked, "Public intelligence and education . . . have laughed and scorned the melodrama to death and it can scarcely be revived via the moving picture route. It is altogether too unreal to please this wise and inquisitive generation."[6] Entertainments even more dangerous than the melodrama gave way before the salubrious influence of the nickelodeon, claimed the trade press. In one of many articles on the topic of film versus the saloon, *The Nickelodeon* reported that, "Saloon keepers have protested excitedly against its [the nickelodeon's] permanent establishment as a menace to their trade. The saloon has lost its hypocritical and pious cloak as the workingman's club. The nickelodeon now beckons to the saloon's former patron with arguments too strong to be withstood."[7]

A *Motography* article, "Motography as an Arm of the Church," claimed that the moving picture's supplanting of more degrading amusements had ingratiated the industry with the churches. "The American people have the moving picture habit. Its spread has sounded the death knell of [cheap] melodrama, and it is driving the vicious burlesque out of business. Some of the pictures have inclined toward vulgarity and viciousness, but the present attitude of so many churches insures that all pictures in the future will be just a little cleaner than they have been in the past."[8]

Mere distancing from cheap amusements, however, would not suffice. As Stephen Bush suggested in 1908, the industry had actively to position itself with the forces of righteousness in the struggle over the cultural order. "The motion picture, the greatest factor in the future instruction and amusement of mankind, must range itself with the forces that make for good, that mean progress and spell advancement."[9] What better model to emulate than institutions of cultural reproduction such as those discussed in the previous chapter? Sympathetic observers described the film industry in terms remarkably similar to those applied to these institutions. Consider the appellations given to the People's Institute, "a practical school of democracy," the Bureau of Lectures, "a university for the people," and the Educational Alliance, "the breadwinners' college."[10] Similar phrases were often employed in reference to the film industry: "academy of the workingman," "the poor man's elementary course in the drama," and "the poor man's grand opera."[11]

Stephen Bush also asserted that moving pictures could actually have a more profound and beneficial impact on workers and immigrants than the institutions of cultural reproduction working among them. "No university settlement or extension work can do more for the education and amusement of the masses than the moving picture theatre."[12] In 1910 the *Moving Picture World* suggested that reformers might achieve their ends more readily through motion pictures than through the tactics they were currently employing.

> There is no greater opportunity open to-day for broadening and raising the standard of popular intelligence, of bringing to the heart of the masses, draped in color, action and interest, the meat of literature, drama, science and current events than the nickelodeon. Nothing, indeed could be a more advantageous addition to school and college methods. . . . How eminently more practical and reasonable, instead of building new reading rooms for toil-worn bodies and brains, adorning seething tenements with the irony of a porcelain bath . . . to build a few plain motion picture theatres on the borderland of the wolf's domain and give two or three free day performances a week with titles and postscripts of the subjects given verbally for the unschooled. . . . And no more simple or available application of this opportunity lies open to-day than the two or three day a week plan for a new Carnegie or Smith nickelodeon in the east ends of our crowded cities.[13]

In the opinion of the *Moving Picture World*, then, instead of ameliorating tenement living conditions with bathtubs and reading rooms, social reformers should build nickelodeons tellingly named after Andrew Carnegie and Charles Sprague Smith. Moving pictures had, according to this somewhat biased source, become a more effective means for achieving Carnegie's and Smith's goals than the public libraries and lecture series these gentlemen had supported. Moving pictures would thus supplant not only the cheap amusements but all the counterattractions offered by institutions of cultural reproduction. The well-known pundit, Elbert Hubbard, who later professed to be a "moving picture fiend," summed up much of this discourse when he said that the moving picture is "one of the things that is helping to make this old world over into a better and happier place."[14]

The film industry sought not only to distance itself from cheap amusements but also to align itself with more "respectable" entertainments such as the Broadway stage. The pre-Hollywood cinema has recently been the subject of intensive investigation.[15] We can thus draw on the latest research in early film history in outlining the various strategies the film industry employed to affect a shift in its perceived status in American society. Although this research ranges from close textual analysis to detailed studies of particular production companies, our primary interest lies with works that concern the industry's changing status during the transitional years from 1907 to 1917, most particularly those that focus on film's emulation of more respectable entertainments. Before turning to the most explicit of counterattractions, the quality films, we will briefly consider industry organization, site regulation, writers, stars, performance and narrative structure.[16]

Only a week before the nickelodeon closings on December 24, 1908, the most powerful elements of the film industry, headed by the Edison and Biograph studios, had formed the Motion Picture Patents Company, a trust intended to regulate distribution and exhibition and to respond to increasing pressure on the industry from public and private critics.[17] By the end of 1908 the film exchanges (middlemen distributors) and the nickelodeons were threatening to seize control of distribution and exhibition, and were even moving into production. Led by the Edison and Biograph companies, the producers thus attempted to redress the balance by forming the Motion Picture Patents Company, or, as it was popularly known, the Trust.[18] The MPPC derived its powers from pooling patents on film stock, cameras, and projectors. Film exchanges, which had to meet the MPPC's standards, were now obliged to rent films rather than buy them outright, and only licensed exhibitors, who paid the MPPC a weekly royalty on their patented projectors, could rent Trust films from the exchanges. Ironically, however, the Trust's attempt to control the industry gave rise to a quite vigorous group of so-called independent producers, who supplied products to the many nickelodeons not licensed by the MPPC.

This struggle within the film industry, both among film producers—the Trust versus the independents—and among producers, distributors, and exhibitors, complicates our use of the term the *film industry* and necessitates careful consideration of trade press evidence. With regard to the film industry, unless otherwise specified, we will use the term to refer to Trust producers, and in particular to the Vitagraph Company of America. With regard to the trade press, we have found that a virtual consensus exists on the subject of uplift and the quality films among the various trade papers, regardless of the provenance of any particular journal. Yet we should note that some of the journals on which we rely had very strong ties to certain producers. For example, the *Film Index*, jointly owned by Vitagraph and Pathé, seems to have been controlled by a committee of the MPPC.[19] Even supposedly neutral papers such as *Motography* and the *Moving Picture World* were subject to pressure from the producers, who used advertising as leverage to produce favorable publicity. The members of the MPPC often threatened to withhold their advertising from various journals, and, in the case of the *Moving Picture World*, did so on two separate occasions for fairly lengthy periods.

Such strong-arm tactics were at variance with the sweetness-and-light rhetoric that the industry disseminated to the public. While the members of the MPPC hoped to redistribute profits by redressing the balance of power among producers, distributers, and exhibitors, they also wanted to improve the industry's overall profits by allaying their critics' fears. At Mayor McClellan's hearing, Vitagraph's J. Stuart Blackton spoke of the MPPC and "told of a meeting held last week in the home of Thomas A. Edison, whereat it was agreed that hereafter no film of an unproper character will be made in America or allowed to come into America and be used."[20] As for film content, the MPPC boasted that the industry had already made inroads into the cheap amusements and would continue to do so, provided it produced films of the right kind.

> Already the picture show has killed off the cheap melodrama. The fact that the new films treat of historical, geographical and educational subjects gives an idea of the marvelous possibilities of the motion picture, and is in itself a justification of the Patents Company's determination to absolutely eliminate all matter that does not possess either educational or cleanly amusing value.[21]

The Patents Company also paid attention to exhibition venues, announcing that site inspections would ensure the "absolute safety and decency of all licensed theatres" and briefly sponsoring fire and accident insurance for its licensees.[22] The MPPC's obvious concern with the upgrading of exhibition venues once again indicates that, whatever the reality, both those within and without the industry perceived nickelodeon conditions and locations as a major problem. The Trust may also have tried, however, to garner favorable publicity concerning the existing conditions in order to change negative public perceptions. In January 1909, right on the heels of the nickelodeon closings and the MPPC's formation, the *New York Times* ran a feature article—

obviously penned by someone favorably inclined toward the industry—that stressed the upgrading of the exhibition venues. "An average investment of $4000 for each 'store show' was considered conservative. The cheapest of them cost $500, the more pretentious $25,000. The finest 'store show' properties in the city included one in Harlem, costing $30,000, and another in Fourteenth Street representing an investment of $80,000."[23]

The trade press repeatedly agitated for improved theatres with higher admission prices in upscale venues. "Americans of means want surroundings that are congenial, and are willing to pay the price without haggling. Millions of them are barred from picture theatres now because of the discomforts of the smaller houses."[24] As early as 1908 the New York Dramatic Mirror lauded the advancement from "roughly fitted up store" shows to the "handsomely decorated and well equipped little theatres." According to the Mirror, many of these "better houses" adopted the "ten-cent scale, catering to a better class of audience."[25] The Moving Picture World, which admittedly had a vested interest in the matter, rejoiced in reporting the replacement of "the cheap old store fronts" located in "cheap thoroughfares" with "better, larger and more expensive theatres" in the "best shopping districts, and even the fashionable residential areas."[26] "Men and women of refinement and discrimination," said the World, would become picture fans "wherever suitable arrangements for their comfort are provided."[27] Ultimately, these "suitable arrangements" required duplicating the milieu of the first-class Broadway houses. "Won't somebody open . . . a moving picture house showing the best work with luxurious surroundings and with orchestral accompaniments? If that . . . were done . . . we should be reaching the apotheosis of the moving picture . . . it would become so respectablized that the censorship would no longer be required, and the manufacturers would be fighting for the sources of the best writers, producers and photographers in America."[28]

Calls for the best writers often accompanied demands for the uplift of the industry. The trade press urged the motion picture industry to legitimate itself by producing scenarios penned by well-known writers of fiction and drama. In 1908, for example, the New York Dramatic Mirror ran an article by a "moving picture enthusiast" who strenuously advocated "a higher class of authorship in the construction of plots or stories." As opposed to the "crudest kind of drama" and "the lowest kind of slapstick comedy," which had hitherto dominated, stories produced by higher-class authors would appeal to the "more intelligent class of spectators."[29] As Kristin Thompson has shown, the studios soon followed this advice, obtaining scenarios from the numerous free-lance writers of novels and short stories, as well as from the less numerous free-lance playwrights.[30] The studios also took much material from authors both living and dead, often foregrounding the films' sources in their advertisements. Thus, for example, in 1908–09 the Biograph Company released The

Devil (Ferenc Molnár) and *The Call of the Wild* (Jack London), whose titles recalled the two famous authors. The company also released *The Barbarian Ingomar* (Friedrich Halm; 1908), *The Song of the Shirt* (Thomas Hood; 1908), *Ramona* (Helen Jackson; 1910), *The Unchanging Sea* (Charles Kingsley; 1910), and *The Sands of Dee* (Charles Kingsley; 1912), in these instances mentioning the authors in the *Biograph Bulletin*.

The emulation of the theatrical star system also served to link the moving picture industry with respectable entertainment. Richard deCordova dates the development of the star system to late 1909 and early 1910. At this time, according to deCordova, a discourse about the "picture personality," such as Florence Lawrence or Mary Pickford, began to appear in the trade press. In addition, members of the MPPC began to hire well-known theatrical actors to appear in their films. In 1909, for example, Edison engaged the French panto-mimist Pilar-Morin for a series of films.[31] By 1911 the discourse on the "picture personality" included a listing of an actor's prior credits, both cinematic and theatrical, a tactic that, deCordova states, served to "legitimize film acting, *in general*, by associating it with the acting of the legitimate stage."[32]

During this transitional period, cinematic acting began increasingly to re-semble the acting of the Broadway stage, rejecting the codified conventions of an older performance style that had come to be associated primarily with the cheap melodrama.[33] The trade journals' professed abhorrence of the melo-drama necessarily entailed disdain for the broad, stylized, and exaggerated gestures of the melodrama's actors. Here again, the moving picture had an opportunity to educate the benighted masses, weaning them away from cheap amusements. "Take the veriest dyed-in-the-wool lover of tank melodrama, who never saw a real play in his life—make him attend a motion picture theatre daily and see capable companies doing faithful, honest work, and it would be a good safe bet that the next time he saw a heroine rant or a hero clutch at his vitals and roll his eyes, he would laugh instead of applaud."[34]

The emulation of stage performance style coincided with a transition to narratives that centered around a psychological approach to character.[35] As Tom Gunning argues, "The approach to characterization in the *narrator-system* asserts its hold on *story* through an expression of *psychology*, by which I mean the portrayal of interior states, such as memories or strong emotions, which are then seen as motivation for the action of characters."[36] In Gunning's view, the emergence of the narrator system coincided with the industry's efforts to upgrade its status. "It is in terms of attracting the middle class to films that the *narrativization* of filmic discourse takes on economic significance. It was be-lieved that films which could deliver experiences similar to the socially re-spected narrative arts of the novel and theater (and which in fact would often be adaptations of classics in those genres) would appeal to the 'better classes.' "[37]

An excerpt from an exhibitor's letter to the *Moving Picture World* indicates that those within the film industry were well aware of the need to emulate respectable entertainments. The exhibitor touched on many of the issues that concern us: the class of the audience, the intertextual associations of signifying practices, and the importance of the proper subjects.

> No doubt if our manufacturers keep on the line of serious improvements, they will reconcile the better classes, and show them that moving pictures are not only the cheap amusement of the poor, but a pastime and an educator for all. The day that manufacturers elevate their work or reject all that is low, indecent, badly acted, badly staged, etc., and offer only good clean subjects produced with all the care given to theatrical plays, we shall see a new boom. Show houses will not only be found on the Bowery or on the East Side, but in the more refined sections of the city. When this day arrives, we will have a new public able to understand historic films and admire good work. As there is much pleasure felt by the cultured class in reading a book from the pen of a good author, there will be the same pleasure on the part of the better class in following the motions of a good film.[38]

Clearly, changes in many signifying practices, including editing, lighting, and set design, could be linked to the overall transition of the film industry during this period. An excellent overview of these developments has been provided by Kristin Thompson in *The Classical Hollywood Cinema*. We, however, are primarily concerned with the increased production of films devoted to literary, historical, and biblical subjects during the transitional years, since these films constitute one of the industry's most obvious attempts to ameliorate negative perceptions and to attract the "better classes." The quality films composed a relatively small, albeit highly publicized, percentage of the industry's total output. They nonetheless afford one of the most striking examples of the film industry's efforts to establish an alliance with institutions of cultural reproduction.

The Quality Films

Frank Dyer, the vice president of the MPPC, said of film in 1910, "The producing men . . . realize [the potential for] the ultimate development of the art to a position of dignity and importance. When the works of Dickens and Victor Hugo, the poems of Browning, the plays of Shakespeare and stories from the Bible are used as a basis for moving pictures, no fair-minded man can deny that the art is being developed along the right lines."[39] A representative of the National Board of Censorship asserted that the medium had already exposed the multitude to uplifting cultural fare. "Through motion pictures more people have been acquainted with Shakespeare in five years than have seen Shakespeare on the stage in the century preceding. The great episodes of the Bible . . . have been carried to more people than attend the Sunday-schools of the country."[40] The trade press repeatedly stressed that films with biblical, literary, and historical subjects would serve to improve the position of the film industry in American society and to attract a better class of spectators. In speaking of "high class educational pictures," the *New York Dramatic Mirror* asserted "that a more general use of pictures of this class in all picture houses can have only one effect, and that is an elevating influence and a much needed improvement in the general repute in which moving pictures are held by the public. This matter of repute is a vital one for house managers, as well as film makers and renters. It is the foundation on which the future permanency of moving pictures must be built."[41] This article appeared on December 26, 1908, two days after Mayor McClellan's nickelodeon license revocations.

Of course, more pecuniary considerations may have motivated the producers. Presumably, the reliance of these films on widely circulated texts would to some extent sell them in advance to exhibitors and audiences, who would both have preexisting knowledge of the subject matter. Given their referencing of texts circulated by institutions of cultural reproduction, the quality films may also have been expected to have a longer market life than other films. In fact, the Motion Picture Patent Company's distribution arm, the General Film Company, founded in 1910, established an educational unit. Its catalogue lists, among other films, biblicals (*The Life of Moses, Saul and David*, and *Jeptha's Daughter*, all Vitagraph films), literaries (*Julius Caesar, Twelfth Night, A Midsummer Nights Dream*, all Vitagraph films, along with *The Taming of the Shrew*, by Biograph), and historicals (Vitagraph's *Napoleon*, and Pathé's *The Young King of Rome, Napoleon in 1814*, and *Washington Relics*).[42] The desire to appeal to a European market may also have caused some filmmakers to choose subjects whose strong intertextual resonances gave them appeal even outside the United States. In addition, the *Ben Hur* copyright infringement case provided a strong incentive for producers to adapt familiar material that was in the public domain, such as Shakespeare. Such material had the advantage of being well known but not the disadvantage of legal protection. Although these factors certainly bear investigation, we are presently concerned with illuminating the conditions of production for the quality films, particularly by reference to the alliance between the film industry and the institutions of cultural reproduction discussed in the previous chapter.

As is evident from studio publicity and the trade press, the film industry had apparently reached a vague consensus concerning the definition of "classic," "artistic," or "quality" films. "On Filming a Classic," the most extended attempt to characterize these films we have found, appeared in *The Nickelodeon* in 1911.

"Classic" is here used in a rather loose and unrestricted sense, as it generally is used by adherents of the photoplay, meaning vaguely a kind of piece that is laid in a bygone era and one which aims to evoke some kind of poetic and idealistic illusion differing from that illusion of mere reality with which photoplays are ordinarily concerned. "Costume play," "historical piece," "poetic drama," variously convey a similar idea. Often the subject is one that is already known to the drama and universally admired, or it may be an adaptation from some story of poetry or fiction, or taken from the pages of history or the Bible. . . . It is needless to say that such subjects are the hardest kind to present. They demand an expensive outlay of costumes and scenic effects, deep and careful research into the manners and customs of the era depicted . . . faultless photography, and above all a Producer . . . who shall . . . possess the eye of an artist and the mind of a poet."[43]

We can hardly improve upon this definition, although we prefer to distinguish more clearly among literary, historical, and biblical films.[44] Literary films are adaptations of canonized literary texts.[45] Historical films are not merely set in a past era but deal with particular historical personages. Biblical films illustrate characters and incidents from the Bible, as opposed to dealing with religious or inspirational topics generally. The producers' discourse about these films foregrounded intertextual resonances, setting the quality films significantly apart from other films. As will become apparent in the following chapters, the referencing of texts that were circulated and valorized by institutions of cultural reproduction situates the quality films within the dominant culture as defined in chapter 1.

The heaviest American production of quality films coincides with the transitional years of 1907 to 1913, yet the popularity of foreign "qualities" prior to 1907 indicates an established market demand for films of this kind. In 1906 the *Views and Film Index* listed fifty subjects from the past five years that "had a pronounced success and which have marked a distinct stage in the business." Among the films were *The Prodigal Son* (Pathé), *Joan of Arc* (Méliès), *Robinson Crusoe* (Méliès), *Marie Antoinette* (Pathé), *Napoleon Bonaparte* (Pathé), and *Faust and Marguerite* (Méliès). The list included no American productions.[46] Other European quality films popular in the United States before 1907 included Pathé's *Passion Play* and *Joseph and His Brethren* and Gaumont's *Life of Christ*.

During the transitional years, the American film industry released numerous quality films, various studios exhibiting different production patterns. Although we can find no official announcement of a quality films policy, the Trust does implicitly seem to have encouraged its members to produce these uplifting subjects. Frank Woods, of the *New York Dramatic Mirror*, concluded that the Trust had realized that "business can be increased only by improvement in character and quality of subjects. To this friendly rivalry we owe the artistic Pathé films d'art; the Vitagraph Napoleon pictures, with others to follow of the same character, the remarkably strong and ably acted Biograph dramatic and comedy subjects."[47]

As Frank Woods indicates and film historians have shown, the Biograph Company seems to have concentrated more on bringing cinematic signifying practices into line with those of respectable texts than upon producing quality films.[48] The same issue of the *Mirror* that featured Wood's comments on the Trust also contained an article about the Biograph Company lauding the studio for the good example it provided to other American manufacturers. "Biograph subjects may not always be as big in a spectacular way as some of the others, but there is a certain strength and high literary merit to the character of nearly all of their film stories and an artistic finish to the settings and acting that has not yet as a general rule been attained by the other American producers."[49] The few Biograph quality films tended to be literary adaptations: in 1908, *After Many Years* (Tennyson), *The Taming of the Shrew* (Shakespeare), and *A Fool's Revenge* (Hugo); in 1909, *Resurrection* (Tolstoy), *The Cricket on the Hearth* (Dickens), *The Sealed Room* (Balzac), *A Fair Exchange* (Eliot), *Leather Stocking* (Cooper), *Pippa Passes* (Browning), and *The Golden Supper* (Tennyson); in 1911, *Enoch Arden* (Tennyson) and *A Blot in the 'Scutcheon* (Browning).

By contrast, the Edison Manufacturing Company foregrounded its historical films, in 1911 planning a series that would show "the most important events in American history from the discovery of America by Christopher Columbus to recent times."[50] Learning, however, that the Selig Company had already embarked on filming Columbus's discovery and "subsequent events," Edison decided to "begin our series with the events immediately preceding the Revolutionary War and carry it to the present day."[51] Qualities filmed by the Edison Company include, in 1908, *Nero and the Burning of Rome*, *The Devil*, and *The Midnight Ride of Paul Revere*; in 1909, *Les Misérables* (Hugo) and *The Attack on the Mill* (Zola); in 1910, *Love and the Law* (adapted from a portion of Dickens's *David Copperfield*), *The House of the Seven Gables* (Hawthorne), *A Christmas Carol* (Dickens), *Faust* (Marlowe), *Frankenstein* (Shelley), and *The Star-Spangled Banner: A Life of John Paul Jones*; in 1911, *His First Commission: A Story of Abraham Lincoln*, *The Price of Victory: A Story of Napoleon Bonaparte*, and *The Cardinal's Edict* (about Cardinal Richelieu); and in 1912, *Martin Chuzzlewit* (Dickens), *The Charge of the Light Brigade* (Tennyson), *Prisoner of War* (Napoleon at St. Helena), *Lady Clare* (Tennyson), *A Day That Is Dead* (Tennyson), and *The Bells* (Poe).

The Motion Picture Patents Company's failure to license one-half to one-third of the country's nickelodeons served as a stimulus to the so-called independent studios to supply unlicensed exhibitors and eventually to compete with the Trust for the patronage of even the licensed exhibitors. Despite the ongoing and intense competition between the Trust and the independents, for the most part the latter produced films similar to those of the former. This similarity extended to the production of quality films: *Jane Eyre* (Thanhouser,

1910); *The Winter's Tale* (Thanhouser, 1910); *The Scarlet Letter* (IMP, 1911); *Gunga Din* (Powers, 1911); *A Doll's House* (Thanhouser, 1911); *David Copperfield* (Thanhouser, 1911); *Romeo and Juliet* (Thanhouser, 1911); *Hiawatha* (IMP, 1910); and *Star of Bethlehem* (Thanhouser, 1912). As this list of titles indicates, the Thanhouser Company was the independent producer most heavily committed to quality filmmaking.

Foreign companies, particularly the Italian and French studios, turned out a great many literary, biblical, and historical films, some of which seem to have had a direct influence on American manufacturers. The most extensively publicized of these quality films were the subjects produced in France by the Pathé Company under the rubric of film d'art. In 1908 the Pathé Company had begun to produce films either based on literary works or written by well-respected authors and featuring well-known theatrical stars. One of the first of the films d'art to reach the United States, *The Assassination of the Duke du Guise*, was written by Henri Levedan of the Academie Française and recounted a famous historical incident from the reign of Henry II.

The Assassination was reviewed in the *New York Daily Tribune* upon its Paris premiere, at a time when reports of moving pictures in the newspapers usually dealt with nickelodeon disasters.[52] Further articles on the film d'art movement appeared in the mainstream press, while the film trade press asserted that these films d'art inspired American producers to new heights. "In America, in particular, the finished work of the Pathé films d'art both in a photographic and a dramatic sense have spurred producers to greater efforts in the direction of better results. The films d'art . . . have been closely watched and studied by the more intelligent American producing forces, and to this is due in a great measure the remarkable improvements made all along the line."[53] The exceptional coverage accorded film d'art outside the trade press may indeed have served as an incentive for American filmmakers to emulate the Pathé productions.

Companies such as Ambrosio, Milano, Film d'art Italiana, and Gaumont also exported quality films to the United States, as the following list, with U.S. release dates, illustrates: *Charlotte Corday* (Pathé, 1909); *Kiss of Judas* (Pathé, 1909); *Oliver Cromwell* (Pathé, 1909); *The Hostage* (based on Schiller; Ambrosio, 1909); *Don Quixote* (Gaumont, 1909); *Nero, or the Burning of Rome* (Ambrosio, 1909); *Macbeth* (Cinès, 1909); *The Marriage of Esther* (Gaumont, 1910); and *Christopher Columbus* (Gaumont, 1910).[54] Foreign manufacturers may have had a particularly strong motivation to produce quality films for export to the United States market. The trade press often complained that many imported films dealing with contemporary topics, particularly those from France and Italy, did not accord with dominant American values. The *Moving Picture World* asserted that "imported films have got a bad name," pointing to their "gilded obscenity and veiled indecency." But the *World* praised Ambrosio's *Nero, or the Burning of Rome* in contrast to these objectionable imports, comparing it to legitimate stage productions and alleging that "in work of this kind, the independent import reaches the very high water mark of film production."[55] While the manners and mores of contemporary foreign films may have caused concern and, worse yet, had the potential to reinforce the "alien" values of immigrant audiences, the literary, biblical, and historical subject matter of the quality films accorded well with the consensus-forging mission of institutions of cultural reproduction.

The titles listed above suggest the subject matter of the quality films but do not, of course, address their deployment of signifying practices, to which we now briefly turn. We have said that the producers' foregrounding of their textual sources distinguished the quality films from other films of the transitional period. We have also said that the signifying practices of the quality films seem more directly related to specific intertexts than do those of other films. Granted, intertextuality determines the conditions of production and reception for all films, so that the intertextual relationships of the quality films should be seen as a matter of degree. As we have argued, other films of the period did reference texts, such as novels and the theatre, in terms of the broad contours of representation. The quality films, however, directly invoke *specific* texts—a famous painting, a well-known Broadway production, a particular biography—in ways that other films generally do not. In 1911 James B. Crippen, writing in *Motography*, argued that explicit intertextual references would greatly enhance a film's appeal.

> There are almost as many opinions in regard to a film as there are people who see it. . . . The only films which can be depended on to win anything like universal admiration are those which bear evidence of great cost, those which have a patriotic or religious tendency, those which portray a famous classic. . . . In other words the film must enjoy a prestige that is extrinsic. It is admired largely for a merit that comes from without.[56]

Crippen seems to imply that the quality films are admirably suited to a strategy of uplift since their intertextual frames structure audience reception to a greater degree than would be the case for other films. As we will show, however, the industry's critics occasionally balked at even the most intertextually structured films, such as *Julius Caesar*, fearing that the exhibition sites permitted too great an interpretive latitude. We will also argue that viewers could bring to bear intertextual frames derived from less respectable intertexts than the films' foregrounded sources, lending to the quality films a greater polysemy than some may have suspected or desired.

The quality film's intertextual referencing is most apparent with regard to acting, narrative structure, and visual signifying practices. The overall trend in performance style during the transitional period was toward a verisimilar code intertextually derived from contemporary theatrical acting and associated with a degree of psychological realism. Generally, however, the actors in cos-

tume and historical dramas tended not to employ this verisimilar code but
rather used the histrionic code derived from an older theatrical acting style.
Even in those quality films made during 1909 or 1910, when the shift in
performance style was well under way, actors still used the histrionic code.
The producers conceivably chose to use a "classical" performance style associated with theatrical productions of historical and biblical drama.[57]

Consistent with the maintenance of the older performance style, the quality
film narratives tended to be less centered around psychologically individuated
and internally motivated characters than were many films of the transitional
period. Narratives structured around individuated characters were principally
driven by these characters' actions, producing a causal chain of events, or a
syntagmatic narrative. By contrast, quality film narratives, structured around
characters well known from extracinematic intertexts, tend toward the para-
digmatic. Given the assumed familiarity of the story, a film's producers could
chose among a number of key events without having to connect one event to
the other through the elaboration of the character's motivations.[58] This does
not mean that quality film characters were not to some degree psychologized.
But psychologization was not the linchpin of their narrative structure as it was
in the classical Hollywood cinema.

Given that narrative structure is integrally related to the combination of
visual signifying practices, one can discuss the latter without reference to the
former only for heuristic purposes. Indeed, the editing patterns of the quality
films seem somewhat retrograde in comparison to the period's overall movement toward the conventions of spatial-temporal continuity that characterized
classical Hollywood cinema's construction of a transparent reality. *The Nickelodeon*'s observation that the quality films aimed "to evoke some kind of poetic
and idealistic illusion differing from that illusion of mere reality with which
photoplays are ordinarily concerned" suggests that the quality films deployed
signifying practices in a distinctive fashion, although we have not undertaken
the extensive and detailed analysis necessary fully to establish the ways in
which their editing patterns differed from those of the period's other films.
Moreover, the fact that the films we focus on all date from 1907 to 1910, a
period when the tremendous fluidity of visual signifying practices rendered
everything potentially anomalous, would make such a comparative analysis
inconclusive.[59]

Aside from their subject matter, the mise-en-scène of the quality films provides the strongest instance of the intertextual referencing that distinguishes
these films from other films of the period, the sets, costumes, and even the
actors' poses all tending to reference specific extracinematic intertexts. These
references accorded with mainstream society's sense of the "correct" depiction
of literary, biblical, and historical characters and events, a correctness that the
producers' publicity foregrounded.[60]

The above discussion considers the quality film primarily in terms of the industry's forging of an alliance with cultural arbiters, but the motivations for the production of such films are rather more complex, indeed, overdetermined. The industry's desire to join in the project of top-down social control did not necessarily constitute the sole or even the primary factor in the conditions of production. Many studios, both domestic and foreign, produced literary, historical, and biblical films with strong intertextual resonances, but it was the Vitagraph Company that specialized in the qualities. The following section outlines some of more proximate conditions of production for this particular studio's "high-art moving pictures."

Vitagraph and the Quality Films

So well known was Vitagraph for its quality output that trade press overviews of studio production patterns often mentioned the company's literary, historical, and biblical films. In 1911 *The Nickelodeon* ran an article entitled "The Old Lady in the Audience," in which a fictional Mother Squeers "gossips" about the various studios. About Vitagraph, Mother Squeers commented: "It releases these fancy films every now and then, biblical and classical subjects—you know the kind. Some of these have been of highest merit and some have not (at least I didn't like some of them), but they all showed ambition and went to swell the Vitagraph prestige. You may remember how well they were boosted in advance. Vitagraph knows how to advertise."[61] The following is a representative, but by no means complete, list of Vitagraph quality films made from 1908 to 1913, not including the five films we will focus on: *A Comedy of Errors, The Reprieve: An Episode in the Life of Abraham Lincoln, Salome,* 1908; *Saul and David, Judgment of Solomon, Oliver Twist, Richelieu, or The Conspiracy,* 1909; *Twelfth Night, The Martyrdom of Thomas a Becket,* 1910; *A Tale of Two Cities, Vanity Fair,* 1911; *Cardinal Wolsey,* 1912; and *The Pickwick Papers,* 1913.[62]

Although other American studios produced quality films during this period and although quality films constituted a relatively minor proportion of Vitagraph's overall output (most of which resembled the comedies and melodramas cranked out by the other studios), the company foregrounded these productions in its publicity and promotion, using them to distinguish their studio to a greater extent than did any other American producer. Publicity took the form of the *Vitagraph Bulletin* (later, *Vitagraph Life Portrayals*), which was intended for exhibitors, and advertisements in the trade press, while promotion took the form of film reviews, film synopses, and feature articles, again in the trade press. While we prefer to separate promotion from publicity, the symbiotic relationship between the studios and the trade press makes the

1910 Vitagraph advertisement in the *New York Dramatic Mirror* illustrating the
studio's differentiation strategy.

distinction hard to maintain. More often than not, the trade press simply replicated, or perhaps slightly recast, material emanating from the studios, as was
most evident in the case of the *Film Index*, jointly owned by Vitagraph and
Pathé.

Since it is the relationship between the studio's discourse and the cultural
position of the quality films that concerns us, however, we should emphasize
that this is *not* a history of the Vitagraph Company.[63] Nonetheless, the quality
films should be contextualized within a studio's overall operations. Why, for
example, might Vitagraph have chosen to produce literary, biblical, and historical films? We have considered the general preconditions for these films but
now wish to consider circumstances unique to Vitagraph that may have related to their quality film output: Vitagraph's position in the European market,
the studio's organization, the role of James Stuart Blackton, and the use of
quality films for the purpose of studio differentiation. We shall also look
briefly at Vitagraph's discourse concerning the marketing of the qualities.

Relative to the best-documented and most intensively researched of all pre-
Hollywood American studios, the Biograph Company, we know comparatively
little about Vitagraph's operations. We do know, however, that there was a

marked contrast in production resources between Biograph and Vitagraph.[64] Whereas Biograph occupied a modest brownstone studio on Fourteenth Street, Vitagraph's Brooklyn facilities included three newly built studios, with two more under construction by the end of 1908. The company also had offices in Paris, London, and Berlin. Vitagraph claimed that "the constantly increasing demand" for Vitagraph films "throughout the World" had necessitated this studio expansion.[65] The scale of Vitagraph's operation during this period thus substantially exceeded Biograph's, Vitagraph boasting over twice as many directors and a far greater output of films. In 1908 Vitagraph turned out "more new subjects each week than any other American concern."[66]

Perhaps the most important distinction between the two studios, and one of the most influential factors in the conditions of production for the quality films, was Vitagraph's prominence in Europe. For Vitagraph, the leading American film exporter prior to World War I, the desire to do well in the European market would have provided a strong motivation to produce quality films that could be readily understood by foreign audiences. Vitagraph opened its main European offices in Paris in 1906 and by 1908 had built a complete film laboratory, from which it sent prints to distribution offices in Italy, England, and Germany.[67] Vitagraph actor James Morrison claimed that the Paris office approved film subjects before they went into production to ensure their suitability for a European market.[68] Surprisingly, however, even nationalistic films did well in Europe, at least according to Vitagraph, which said of its George Washington series, "On the walls of the Vitagraph offices [in Italy] there hang a series of posters made for these releases. They are not unlike the posters you saw here, but they bear an Italian imprint as testimony to the widespread interest these films excited across the Atlantic."[69]

Studio organization also set Vitagraph apart from other American producers. Vitagraph moved earlier toward a system of "autonomously functioning in-house departments," presaging the division of labor of the Hollywood studios.[70] Charles Musser argues that Vitagraph first instituted "new organizational structures that more clearly favored vertical rather than horizontal methods of organization. Modern tools of management were implemented that assured clearer hierarchy and accountability." By 1907, Musser tells us, management had become centralized to the point that James Stuart Blackton acted as the overall producer, overseeing three units headed by directors who reported to him.[71] Blackton served as head of production throughout Vitagraph's existence, while his partner, Albert E. Smith, handled the business side of the operation.

The paucity of evidence about Vitagraph's studio operations makes it difficult to detail the production of the quality films, but the above, in conjunction with studio publicity, at least provides the grounds for educated guesswork. The large number of films produced by Vitagraph would have permitted, and perhaps even demanded, a higher degree of internal product differentiation than was necessary at, for example, Biograph. The division of labor, with special resources potentially available for the quality films, may have facilitated this particular strategy for product differentiation.

Vitagraph publicity does support the inference that the scale of the studio's output, together with greater resources and more intensified division of labor, facilitated production of the quality films. In 1910 the *Vitagraph Bulletin* self-servingly reported, "Looking about the Vitagraph Company's plant, we were impressed with the efficiency of its scenic department both in numbers and skill, which accounts for the wonderful and the beautiful results both in their interior scenery and exterior backgrounds. We doubt if any studio in the world has such a large scenic department so well equipped."[72] Apparently, this scenic department was often called on to make special efforts in the production of quality films. "Three paint frames form a part of the scenic equipment of the Flatbush studio, and for the past month all three have been in constant use, for there are the five special releases of *The Life of Moses* to be done in addition to heavy scenic productions of *Twelfth Night* and other films deluxe."[73]

There is thus some evidence to indicate that the studio's organization, as described above, encouraged the production of quality films. Vitagraph's own publicity, however, often claimed that the production of these films did not conform to the studio's standard operating procedures. Heralding the about-to-be released *Twelfth Night* (1910) as "the best of all" its Shakespearean dramas, the *Vitagraph Bulletin* claimed,

> Most elaborate preparations are being made. . . . A Shakespearean player of country-wide fame is one of the Vitagraph producers and he has been given absolutely a free hand in the selection of special players. If the Vitagraph could announce the cast of characters on the sheet you would be astonished at the display of familiar names.[74]

No further reference to this "Shakespearean player of country-wide fame" appears in either the *Bulletin* or the trade press, leading us to suspect that the publicist may have stretched the truth a little. But Vitagraph more credibly claimed to have gone outside the studio in search of production personnel for *The Life of Moses*. "The entire series . . . was supervised by the eminent divine and lecturer, Reverend Madison C. Peters, D.D., and will stand the closest criticism of biblical students."[75] Beginning with *The Life of Moses* in 1909, Peters served as consultant for many of Vitagraph's biblical subjects, and Vitagraph publicity suggests that he may have directed some films. For historical films, Vitagraph allegedly created an entire department, although we have found nothing to substantiate their claim. "The Vitagraph Company announces the establishment of a special editorial and production department for the presentation of the series of Leather Stocking Tales and other historical and semi-historical tales of American history. This department . . . will concern itself entirely with historical productions, made insofar as possible in the actual locations wherein the original scenes took place."[76]

Information concerning studio organization in conjunction with biographical data may provide us with another explanatory paradigm for Vitagraph's
quality film production. Although one would not wish to bank too heavily on
biographical history, it would be equally problematic to ignore such a factor
altogether, and thus to neglect James Stuart Blackton's role in the production
process. In his study of the Vitagraph Company, Anthony Slide asserts that
Blackton must "be given credit for Vitagraph's policy of filming the classics in
the early years of its existence."[77] Blackton had lower-middle-class English
origins but definite upper-class aspirations.[78] Although he had emigrated to
the United States at the age of ten, he claimed to have attended Eton, and
he rejoiced when his yacht club bestowed on him the title of Commodore
Blackton. Marion Blackton Trimble reported in her biography of her father
that not long after Vitagraph opened its Brooklyn studios in 1905 and began
primarily to produce fiction films,

> My father and A. E. [Smith] remembered a vow to "uplift the masses," and the
> filming of the classics was undertaken in earnest. The works of Tennyson, Shake-
> speare and Milton and many of the better known Greek tragedies were scenarized,
> the scripts consisting of little more than a few notes tucked between the pages of
> the originals. And if, in telescoping these profound works into one reel of film,
> something of the full value was lost, the essence, the power and the spirit re-
> mained, so that many a housewife and her plumber spouse . . . achieved, through
> their visits to the local nickelodeon, at least a nodding acquaintance with Lancelot
> and King Arthur, with Julius Caesar and Lady MacBeth, with Elektra and Aga-
> memnon. If the deeper implications of the plot baffled the moviegoers, the human
> passions, the loves and griefs, and killings-in-revenge were plain enough to
> them.[79]

Blackton, whose own daughter at times characterizes him as a nouveau
riche social climber, had economic capital but lacked cultural capital. His
alliance with the discourses and activities of institutions of cultural reproduction may have been designed to improve his own, as well as his industry's,
status. The subject matter of the quality films does seem particularly suited to
the enhancement of Blackton's social status. Two of the Vitagraph qualities we
focus on, *Francesca di Rimini* and the Napoleon films, were linked to the Dante
and Napoleon fads that had been in vogue among cultural and economic elites
at a slightly earlier date. But as Trimble's words suggest, Blackton's adaptations ensured that the quality films would be polysemic enough to please all
comers, as would be appropriate for "high culture" texts seen in "low culture"
venues.

The extent to which Blackton was instrumental in Vitagraph's production
of quality films may be debatable, but we do know from Vitagraph publicity
that these films constituted an important part of Vitagraph's studio differentiation practices. Indeed, we suspect that Vitagraph's need to distinguish its
product from that of other studios may have been among the strongest moti-

vations behind the quality films. In announcing its 1908 expansion, the company said that the new facilities would "even further improve the quality and enhance the quantity of its output in the United States." Vitagraph chose to inaugurate its enhanced production schedule with a quality film, "a grand spectacular reproduction of Shakespeare's RICHARD III a magnificent subject surpassing in every detail all previous efforts in this line."[80] A Vitagraph publicity pamphlet from about 1911 similarly foregrounded the quality films in its description of the studio's output. Referring to *The Life of Moses, Lancelot and Elaine, Vanity Fair, A Tale of Two Cities, Battle Hymn of the Republic, Lincoln's Gettysburg Address,* and *As You Like It,* the pamphlet remarked that, "The Vitagraph Company is noted for its elaborate feature films, sparing no amount of pains and expense in their production. . . . Some of these productions involved an expenditure of twenty thousand dollars and it was money well employed, when the amount of pleasure extended and the good accomplished is considered as compensation."[81]

The trade press often asserted that the quality films not only distinguished Vitagraph from other studios but in fact formed the most laudable portion of its productions. Said the *Film Index*: "While turning out its quota of ordinary good and entertaining subjects, the best work of the Vitagraph Company is to be found in the big picture productions of historic character. . . . The Vitagraph producers undertook the visualization of popular literary masterpieces and events in history. . . . The result has been shown in the splendid Washington and Napoleon pictures, Victor Hugo's Les Miserables, Sir Walter Scott's Kenilworth and many other equally noteworthy."[82]

The emphasis on the quality films in Vitagraph's publicity indicates that these films were part of a product differentiation strategy that may have contributed to the studio's reputation among both exhibitors and audiences. During the period in question, the programs of fifteen-minute films, or one-reelers, shown in the nickelodeons changed daily. Films were primarily identified by studio name, and patrons returned to their neighborhood picture shows expecting to see more of their favorite Biograph or Vitagraph films. Given that studios vied with each other to lease or sell prints to the film exchanges, each studio had to find some way to establish the strong brand recognition required to persuade exhibitors to keep renting its films from the exchanges.[83] In this context, one could view Vitagraph's prominent advertising of the quality films as a rhetorical ploy designed to appeal to the exhibitors' sense of and need for uplifting entertainment. Although Vitagraph doubtless leased far more comedies and melodramas than qualities, the sustained publicity awarded to the qualities suggests some level of consistent public endorsement. Ideally, this conclusion could be substantiated by empirical evidence, but unfortunately we have no information whatsoever concerning the number of prints made of the quality films or their lease and box-office revenues.

Certainly, though, Vitagraph publicity constantly asserted the potential popularity of the qualities, even, at this early date, suggesting exploitation strategies to exhibitors. While *The Life of Moses* was in release, the *Vitagraph Bulletin* offered exhibitors several suggestions for promoting this and other quality films so as to increase box office receipts and woo a new clientele to the new medium.

> There are numerous ways in which you can use Vitagraph subjects, such as the Life of Moses series, the various Shakespearean subjects, the Jean Valjean films, and the many other Vitagraph masterpieces, to create new patronage for your houses. . . . Did you ever try using extra supplies of posters? . . . Order extra lithograph posters for the big Vitagraph features such as we have mentioned—the more posters the better. Have them hung or posted liberally where they will do the most good, with date strips pasted at the bottoms telling when and where the public can see these particular films. . . . Do your billing some days ahead, just as the big shows do, and you will surely be surprised at the result.
>
> But posters are not the only means of building up business with Vitagraph feature subjects. . . . Small bills are employed by many exhibitors. When used rightly and distributed carefully, they have immense drawing power. These bills can be printed at small cost and should contain the stories of the feature films which you can copy from these bulletins. Be sure to announce on the bills the dates when you will have the particular subjects you are advertising. This is most important, as it is the new patrons you are most desirous of attracting to your house. Your regular patrons will come anyhow. Each new one that you secure adds that much to your receipts and if you get him for one visit you may hope to keep him coming regularly.[84]

Far from wishing to alienate its old audiences in the quest for a better class of patron, Vitagraph publicity repeatedly insisted that the quality films had a broad appeal and were, in fact, all things to all people. The industry's own discourse points to the crucial position of the quality films in an emerging mass culture that would provide similar cultural commodities to a range of social formations whose members were equipped to use them in different ways. Of *Vanity Fair*, *Vitagraph Life Portrayals* said, "This supremely magnificent Vitagraph portrayal is incomparably dramatic, scintillating with flashes of satiric comedy and deep grasps of pathos and keenest of character studies, depicting society and incidentally the great battle of Waterloo with all its thrilling and historic interest."[85] Whatever "grasps of pathos" may be, the company clearly intended *Vanity Fair* to please all comers. Moreover, Vitagraph quality subjects, according to the studio, appealed not only to all parts of the audience but to all the higher parts of the body: heart, mind, and soul. Declared a full-page Vitagraph advertisement in the *New York Dramatic Mirror*: "Vitagraph films are so strong, so powerful, so gripping, so elaborate, so entertaining, so beautiful, so popular that no picture program is satisfactory without them. YOU MUST HAVE VITAGRAPH FILMS. Vitagraph dramas stir and thrill the heart. . . . Vitagraph historical subjects educate and entertain the mind. Vitagraph religious films inspire and captivate the soul."[86]

Vitagraph publicized the quality films even more stridently. The hyperbole sometimes verged on the hucksterish and, as one might expect from Hollywood's precursors, stressed the pecuniary attractions of these films for exhibitors. About *Vanity Fair*, "produced from William Makepeace Thackeray's celebrated novel of the same name," Vitagraph said, "*This is what the people are shouting for. Do a little shouting yourselves and your doors won't be big enough to let them all in.*"[87] *Elektra* was also touted as a crowd pleaser. "You have heard of the great opera of 'Elektra.' Well, the operatic production 'has nothing on' our production. . . . It is a film that will stand 'billing like a circus.' " The copy minced no words: "You want big audiences: you want big returns. 'Elektra' is the biggest thing yet in moving pictures. It catches them big."[88]

Nothing here indicates that *Vanity Fair* or *Elektra* formed part of a deliberate campaign to change the film industry's image. Indeed, this hucksterism may seem somewhat incompatible with a wish to ally with institutions of cultural reproduction, although it does attest to the producers' own perceptions of these films' polysemy. But uplift sentiments also abounded in discourse concerning the quality films. Speaking of *Richelieu*, the *Moving Picture World* commented that "the influence of such pictures is beneficial. They stimulate interest in important historic events and they graphically present the beauties of literary masterpieces. Under their influence public taste will improve and the artistic and literary impulses will be cultivated and become stronger. It is one important feature of the diffusion of artistic and literary education through the medium of the motion picture."[89] The *Film Index* praised the Vitagraph Company for its uplifting effect upon the entire film industry. "The greatest contribution of the Vitagraph Company to the picture industry is its efforts to dignify the character of the subjects offered to the public and to raise motion pictures out of the commonplace as an amusement feature."[90]

In 1913 a reporter for the *New York Dramatic Mirror*, undoubtedly aware of Vitagraph's identification with uplifting quality films, asked J. Stuart Blackton, "What is the educational value of the film of the future?" Although Blackton did not specifically invoke the quality films in his answer, he spoke precisely to their expected impact, indeed dating the beneficial influence of the moving pictures to the year in which Vitagraph began to produce fiction films, the literaries, historicals, and biblicals among them. "To my mind, future is not the right word. The picture *to-day* is the greatest educational factor in the entire world and has been for the last seven or eight years. It has been the greatest educational factor the world has ever known up to the present time. It is a universal language understood by the entire world, civilized or uncivilized."[91]

Vitagraph not only employed the proper rhetoric about uplift but actively tried to persuade individuals engaged in the dissemination of culture to view the quality films in the hopes that they would then encourage others to attend the nickelodeons. The *Vitagraph Bulletin* suggested that exhibitors should try to interest schoolteachers in their historical film, *Benedict Arnold*. "The student of history who sees that reel will know more about the Arnold-Andre incident than he ever would through book study. He sees flesh and blood men enacting [the story]. . . . It is a lesson in history and patriotism . . . and if you could send a neat notice to your teachers with perhaps an invitation to come themselves, it would work to your advantage."[92] The *Bulletin* suggested similar tactics for *The Life of Moses*, in this case pitching the film to "newspapermen, . . . clergymen, educators and cultivated people generally."[93]

Capitalist enterprise that it was, Vitagraph obviously did not make the quality films to drive away the current patrons of the nickelodeons, claiming on the contrary that biblicals, literaries, and historicals would perform well at the box office. The company also hoped that this uplifting fare would attract a new clientele, in the process transforming the nickelodeon's image from cheap amusement to respectable entertainment. But whether desiring to retain old patrons or to lure in new ones, Vitagraph had to worry constantly about its viewers. Would the old patrons understand and enjoy the quality films enough to keep coming back to the nickelodeon for more Vitagraphs? Would the hypothetical new patrons find these films sufficiently in accord with their cultural values to think that they were adequate and even pleasing representations of familiar material?

Conclusion

This chapter has looked at the range of techniques employed by the film industry as it attempted to shed its association with cheap amusements and enter the respectable mainstream. In keeping with the cultural focus of this book, we have characterized the quality films as the industry's most explicit response to the period's cultural crisis, while also addressing such other factors as foreign markets. As a more detailed consideration of the conditions of production for the quality films will reveal, the producers sought explicitly to associate their films with certain interpretations and certain modes of representation of the cultural figures or texts featured in their films. The quality films thus embody the visions of culture endorsed and circulated by the film industry at a moment of cultural reconfiguration.

An exclusive focus on the conditions of production might suggest the conclusion that the quality films were simply part of a top-down attempt to reinforce a contested hegemonic order. Extending the analysis to the conditions of reception challenges this conclusion. In fact, as we suggested above, although the producers themselves foregrounded the "high culture" intertextual associations of the qualities, they were well aware of the need to retain their old audiences and thus publicized the quality films as polysemic enough to appeal to a broad spectrum of viewers. The following three chapters, which explore the conditions of reception for these films, will show that these polysemic texts could have been read not only through the explicitly referenced "high culture" intertexts but through a wide variety of other texts as well, including elements of that popular culture from which the industry purportedly sought to distance itself. This consideration of the conditions of production *and* reception reveals the operation of the period's taste hierarchies and so prevents us from privileging the readings derived from the producers' explicitly referenced intertexts. The quality films thus serve as one indicator of the period's overall cultural reconfiguration.

Literary Qualities:

Shakespeare and Dante

ON DECEMBER 1, 1908, the Vitagraph Company released *Julius Caesar*. Three weeks later, on December 23, New York's Mayor McClellan held his hearings on the moving picture shows. Surprisingly, given the Vitagraph film's eminently respectable derivation, some of the industry's critics denounced this film as emblematic of the evils of the medium. J. Stuart Blackton served as the motion picture industry's spokesman at McClellan's hearings, where he defended his film from further charges of immorality. "The sweeping assertion that lewd, lacivious and immodest pictures were shown seems to simmer down . . . to the fact that poor old Julius Caesar wore a skirt that was a little too short, but I am not mistaken, skirts were worn quite short in Julius Caesar's day and we have to be correct in staging and costuming our pictures."[1] William Fox, president of the Moving Picture Exhibitors' Association, shared Blackton's surprise at the attacks on the Shakespearean adaptation. Speaking at a meeting held on Christmas day by several hundred New York City exhibitors, Fox said, "At the hearing on Wednesday one of the clergymen said a show was immoral because on the screen when he saw the show was a picture of an actual scene in Julius Caesar. I love my profession for its artistic side. The Mayor says, because a scene of Julius Caesar was shown, that I am mixed up in an immoral business."[2]

The Roman emperor continued to haunt the proceedings. Many of Fox's fellow exhibitors referred ironically to the censorship of *Julius Caesar*, unable to believe that anyone could possibly find filmed Shakespeare immoral or objectionable. The "morality joke" became a running gag as "they cheered the great Julius time and again and altogether had a merry Christmas time of it." They pointed to *Julius Caesar* as a primary example of film's contribution to culture. "Several of the orators appealed to the shade of Julius Caesar to acclaim the moving picture as an artistic triumph of the century, a triumph which no devotee of the liberal arts could ignore and every true artist must celebrate." The exhibitors also referenced the film's theatrical antecedents, as if to gain respectability through this alliance. "The shades of old William Shakespeare, of Booth and of Barrett, of Davenport and several others were called upon to witness 'this blasphemous libel upon their royal selves and of the character they set forth.' "[3] Indeed, the players in the Vitagraph film were alleged to have been garbed in the very costumes worn by their theatrical predecessors.[4]

The defaming of Caesar remained a cause célèbre among the moving picture folk well after the brouhaha surrounding the nickelodeon closings had subsided. The trade press responded to attacks on the film, *The Nickelodeon* implying that even the moving pictures' uneducated and immigrant clientele knew Shakespeare well enough to resent censorship of the film. An article quoted "an Italian" as saying, "The Romans—they killed Julius Caesar. Then show it—all of it. Why not? It took place. For what is the censorship board—to give us skimmed milk and spoil art? In Rome they wore the *toga virilis* to the knee. Now they show it long and clumsy. For why? Would they put corsets on the 'Venus of Milo'? Bah."[5] Whereas some prominent New Yorkers merely complained, the Chicago police board of censors had actually demanded the excision of the film's assassination scene.[6] Three years later Blackton was still voicing his disgust, claiming the same protection for his medium as that accorded a more acceptable institution of cultural reproduction, the theatre. "They cut out the killing of Julius Caesar. Ye Gods! Imagine a couple of brawny policemen walking on the stage of a New York theatre and (not) politely ordering E. H. Sothern to 'cut out the murder part, cull.' "[7]

Although Shakespearean texts had been tailored previously to fit Victorian sensibilities, Blackton's amazement at the censoring of his Shakespearean adaptation seems quite genuine. It also points to one of the strongest incentives for the production of these films. By the turn of the century, Shakespeare had emerged as a primary component in the consensus-building efforts of institutions of cultural reproduction. A remarkable consistency prevailed in the representations of Shakespeare circulated by these institutions, many of the texts taking a "reduced" form that simply referenced well-known phrases and key scenes. (Indeed, we will argue that Vitagraph's *Julius Caesar* conformed so perfectly to prevailing representations of Shakespeare that contemporary viewers did not complain about a fifteen-minute, silent compression of a complex written text.) The circulation of this reduced Shakespeare unified social formations usually distinguished by their differential access to and familiarity with fuller and more complex textual expressions. The consensus established through the reductionist approach valorized the Bard as cultural icon and referenced the plays, but it did not necessarily demand widespread and intimate familiarity with Shakespeare's texts. Members of all social formations, recognizing key phrases and scenes, could thus participate in the overarching appropriation of Shakespeare for the purposes of consensus building. In asserting the consensual function of Shakespeare, we differ from Lawrence Levine in his analysis of the place of the poet in nineteenth- and twentieth-century American culture. Levine argues that Shakespeare was once popular and well-known among members of all social formations but was appropriated by dominant social formations in order to increase their perceived distance from the masses. While we agree to some extent with Levine's notion of "sacralization," our evidence suggests a greater continuity of Shakespeare's presence among all social formations, as well as a greater complexity in the social uses of Shakespeare, than Levine acknowledges.

In contrast to Shakespeare, Dante, who was never popular and never "sacralized," served primarily a hierarchizing function in turn-of-the-century American culture, Dante texts circulating mainly in restricted social formations. Dante texts enjoyed no reduced consensual form, providing instead sites for the display of interpretive competence, demonstrations of which reinforced preexisting distinctions among social formations. Whereas a nodding familiarity with the Bard gained from exposure to his ubiquitous presence established membership in the consensual project, acquiring distinction through Dante required referencing a more delimited and less accessible set of intertexts.[8]

Considering their textual circulation patterns reveals the respective cultural functions of Shakespeare and Dante during this period, the former serving as consensus builder and the latter as distinction maker. This chapter will examine how the Vitagraph *Julius Caesar* coincided with the most widely circulated and convergent textual expressions of Shakespeare, while at the same time incorporating signifiers that connoted a more restricted, or distinctive, Shakespeare. The cultural position of this film will then be contrasted with that of *Francesca di Rimini*.[9] Since Dante lacked any overarching congruence among intertextual referents and served the project of cultural distinction through diverse, rather than consensual, interpretations, we will examine the intertexts on which the producers may have drawn to make the film and the intertexts viewers may have used to make meaning of the film. These two sets overlap to some extent. Yet viewers with no exposure to producer-referenced texts, or indeed with no exposure to any Dante texts, could have made sense of Vitagraph's *Francesca*.

While these films in many ways make an ideal pair for our purposes, we must nonetheless offer two provisos before proceeding. Their textual bases crucially distinguish these films from each other. The Vitagraph *Francesca di*

Rimini ultimately derives from a short passage in canto 5 of Dante's *Inferno* that was subsequently retold in elaborated versions by numerous authors. Although not all editions of *Julius Caesar* are precisely alike, all circulate as "Shakespeare's *Julius Caesar*" and retain a certain uniformity, whereas the versions of the Francesca story circulate under the names of their various authors (Boccaccio, Leigh Hunt, George Boker) and exhibit great disparities in plot and characterization. *Francesca* thus encourages a level of interrogation not necessary with *Julius Caesar*, since viewers may have had available much wider ranging intertextual frames to make sense of the text.

Despite these differences in the *Ur*-texts, both films ultimately derive from "history," which complicates their literary status. Shakespeare's *Julius Caesar* was but one of many recountings of the fate of the Roman emperor, while Dante is said to have based the Francesca passage on a lesser-known historical incident. Although some viewers may have known of Julius Caesar primarily through historical texts not directly related to the Shakespeare play, we will focus only on Shakespearean intertexts. And although a viewer's prior knowledge of Francesca da Rimini probably stemmed from Dante-related texts, one should not discount the possibility of a reading of the film through historical texts.

Industry Discourse on Shakespeare

Despite Caesar's contentious reception in New York and Chicago, the industry persisted in turning out yet more Shakespeare films. From 1908 to 1913 the American film industry produced at least thirty-six fifteen-minute Shakespearean films, while importing a great many more foreign Shakespeare productions. Among the plays most frequently filmed were *Julius Caesar*, *King Lear*, *Hamlet*, *Macbeth*, *The Merchant of Venice*, *Romeo and Juliet*, and *A Midsummer Night's Dream*. Additionally, films such as *Comedy of Errors* (Solax, 1913) used Shakespearean titles but not plots, while other films such as *A Village King Lear* (Gaumont, 1911) presented versions of the plays in contemporary settings. Variant American titles along these lines included: *A Modern Portia* (Lubin, 1912), *Taming Mrs. Shrew* (Rex, 1912), and *A Galloping Romeo* (Selig, 1913).[10] Many studios foregrounded the Shakespearean connections of these films, as, for example, did a publicity release for *Indian Romeo and Juliet* (Vitagraph, 1912): "It is far more Shakespearean than Shakespeare."[11]

Film industry rhetoric stressed the uplifting and educational effects of the Shakespeare films. The industry's own discourse thus not only tends to privilege a particular construction of the conditions of production but also constitutes an element of the conditions of reception, one that points to the film industry's desire to ally itself with the hegemonic agenda promoted by institutions of cultural reproduction. The industry's failure to articulate other possible motivations for the production of Shakespearean adaptations reveals the discursive strategy of cultural alliance that was behind the repeated assertions of the beneficial potential of these films.

Yet the industry had several good reasons to produce these particular films at this historical juncture. First, Shakespeare, although an English poet, was so revered in the countries of the European export market that adaptations of his works were guaranteed to sell. Second, in the wake of the 1907 *Ben Hur* copyright decision, studios were acutely aware of whether material was in the public domain and knew that Shakespeare was not only respectable but free. Third, as we will demonstrate, Shakespeare may have been far more accessible to a diverse spectrum of viewers than a late-twentieth-century perspective might suggest. Fourth, Shakespeare provided as many thrills—duels, illicit romances, murders—as the rankest cheap melodrama. And fifth, if critics accused filmmakers of the excessive depiction of duels and other unsavory material, the industry could feign outraged innocence and wrap itself in the Bard's cultural respectability. Yet trade press utterances and publicity copy never mentioned any of these motivations. Instead, they focused on the uplifting qualities of Shakespeare, while at the same time assuring exhibitors that this noble fare would not drive away their present clientele.

Despite the diverse motivations for the production of Shakespearean films, then, industry discourse constantly reinforced the equation of Shakespeare and respectablity, an equation we might be tempted to take for granted since Shakespeare has formed a part of the literary canon for so long. But, as Stuart Hall reminds us, "the abstraction of texts from the social practices which produced them" obscures

> how a particular ordering of culture came to be produced and sustained: the circumstances and conditions of cultural reproduction which the operations of the "selective tradition" rendered natural, "taken for granted." But the process of ordering (arrangement, regulation) is always the result of a concrete set of practices and relations. In constituting a particular cultural order as "dominant," it implied (though this was rarely examined) the active subordination of alternatives—their marginalization and incorporation into a dominant structure.[12]

Certainly, the very term *respectability* indicates the pervasive ideological assumptions regarding Shakespeare's work that were operative during the period: Shakespeare's "greatness" was so natural, so "taken for granted," as to brook no dissent concerning either the necessity for studying his works or the beneficial effects such study would have. We cannot even attempt to adumbrate the canonization of Shakespeare in English and American culture.[13] But we can look beyond this simple equation of Shakespeare and respectability through the examination of the contemporary utterances of cultural arbiters, from Andrew Carnegie to immigrant uplift organizations, all of which point to a more particular appropriation of Shakespeare at a time of intense cultural contestation.

In 1903 Carnegie addressed the Educational Alliance, stressing the assimilationist possibilities of the playright's works, an emphasis particularly appropriate in light of the alliance's efforts to Americanize the thousands of Eastern European Jewish immigrants pouring into New York City. "But, ladies and gentlemen, language makes race. You give me a man who speaks English and reads Shakespeare. . . . You give me that man, or that young woman, and I don't care where he was born, or what country he comes from."[14] Carnegie was not alone in his assessment of Shakespeare's Americanizing potential. In 1886 Thomas D. Weld advanced several reasons for the inclusion of Shakespeare in school curricula, one of which was a thinly veiled nativist stance. "Nothing would so withstand the rush into our language of vapid, foreign dilutions as a baptism into Shakespeare's terse, crisp, sinewy Saxon."[15] Obviously, Shakespeare, the "greatest" poet of the English language, proved powerfully attractive to those seeking to acculturate the non-English-speaking immigrant as well as the illiterate working man. James Hamilton, head worker of the University Settlement, one of several private immigrant aid centers in the tenement districts, wrote to the People's Institute supporting its plans for a People's Theatre and mentioning the recent Shakespearean productions at the Educational Alliance.

> No intellectual tonic could be finer or more stimulating. A good percentage of the audiences have not long been masters of the English Language. They have scarcely crossed the threshold of our literature. What a grand and inspiring entrance was here provided for them—the best English Literature ever cast in dramatic form.[16]

Perhaps the clearest and most oft-cited expression of Shakespeare's hegemonic function stems from an address delivered at the dedication of the Folger Shakespeare Memorial Library in 1932. Joseph Quincy Adams, the library's director, spoke of the mobilization of Shakespeare to counter the threat posed by the massive immigration of the previous decades.

> About the time the forces of immigration became a menace to the preservation of our long-established English civilization, there was initiated throughout the country a system of free and compulsory education for youth. In a spirit of efficiency, that education was made stereotyped in form; and in a spirit of democracy, every child was forced by law to submit to its discipline. . . . Not Homer, nor Dante, nor Chaucer, nor Spenser, nor even Milton, but Shakespeare was made the chief object of their study and veneration.[17]

While accepting the culture's general valorization of the Bard, spokesmen for institutions of cultural reproduction believed that productions of Shakespeare's works had precise and instrumental benefits: they would keep people from cheap amusements, teach them moral lessons, and generally improve them. In short, they had "educational and inspirational value."[18] Thomas Davidson, who lectured at the Educational Alliance, remarked on the moral lessons Shakespeare teaches. "How we hate hypocrisy after reading "Measure for Measure"; reckless ambition, after reading "Macbeth"; indecision, after reading "Hamlet," and so on!"[19] Henry Leipziger, supervisor of the Bureau of Lectures, defended his department against proposed budget cuts by claiming that poetry in general and Shakespeare in particular contributed immeasurably to man's existence and should be available not just to cultural elites. Speaking of his political antagonist, Leipziger said,

> His theory seems to be that the lowbrowed citizens who people this great city . . . merely because of lack of opportunity in early training, are entirely unworthy of or unfit to enjoy such highbrow things as poetry. Mr. Mayor, I am astonished and grieved. What has Robert Burns been to the world? What has Shakespeare been to the world? Eliminate poetry from the world, pluck the love of it from the hearts of the human race and life would be like a bush without its roses, like the trees without their leaves, like the meadows without their verdant green.[20]

Leipziger's statement epitomizes the pervasive acceptance of Shakespeare as transcendent, natural, and essential to a civilized society.[21]

Many studios, such as the Vitagraph Company, which accounted for the bulk of the American Shakespearean productions, made specific reference to the films' uplifting associations and benefits, thus echoing the sentiments of institutions of cultural reproduction. In reviewing the Vitagraph Company's *Twelfth Night* (1910), the *Moving Picture World* said,

> It elevates and improves the literary taste and appreciation of the greatest mass of the people, performing in this way a service which cannot be measured in material terms. Such work is the nature of an educational service which is deserving of the heartiest support of all who are working for the improvement of humanity.[22]

Clearly, Vitagraph and other film producers counted on the fact that the "taken for grantedness" of Shakespeare would resonate with those whom they wished to placate. But they also claimed that their Shakespearean films were, like the rest of the quality films, all things to all people. The desire to build a mass audience made it necessary to assert that different groups of viewers could activate these polysemic texts in different ways. The industry thus emphasized different aspects of their productions for different segments of the audience.

Studio publicity and trade press discourse implied that whereas some viewers came to the nickelodeon with a detailed knowledge of the Bard and his plays and could enjoy the films by virtue of this intertextual frame, others may have not have come thus equipped. The *Vitagraph Bulletin* accordingly emphasized the dual appeal of *A Midsummer Nights Dream* (1910). "Students of the great dramatist's works will thoroughly enjoy the careful pictorial presentation of the many scenes, while the whole play is so clearly portrayed that it will not fail to delight the spectator who is not familiar with the works of Shakespeare."[23] As this statement implies, the industry felt it necessary to make the story accessible to viewers lacking previous exposure to the Bard.

Shakespearean adaptations were not the only films requiring clear exposition, but they did pose special problems. As many scholars of early cinema have pointed out, a general crisis occurred in film narration during the years 1907 and 1908, which witnessed a move from extratextually dependent to internally coherent narratives.[24] Yet, unlike other films of the period, Shakespearean films by their very nature continued to draw heavily upon extratextual references, as did all the quality films. In response to this problem, the industry used two main strategies to ensure narrative comprehension: lectures and highly simplified plots. Speaking of the need for lectures to accompany literary adaptations, *The Nickelodeon* said:

> No doubt a film subject that is so clear it does not need explanation is really most desirable. But it must be admitted that some of the moving picture reproductions of the old masters of literature would be better understood by the unread public if they were carefully explained. . . . Obviously, if we cannot get pictures that are perfectly comprehensible to the average patron, we will have to explain them to him or lose his interest.[25]

Intertitles would serve to recall plots and well-known scenes for viewers familiar with Shakespeare, while lectures would ensure that Shakespearean films would delight viewers with no such previous exposure. "Even with the short explanatory titles the plays have been enjoyed by all who ever had any acquaintance with Shakespeare at all, and many persons who had never read a line of Shakespeare have come away delighted after seeing the pictures and hearing them competently explained."[26]

Successful streamlining sometimes produced a narrative whose coherence, claimed the filmmakers, transcended that of the original source. The *Biograph Bulletin*, promoting *The Taming of the Shrew*, boasted that its adaptation resulted in "one of the snappiest, funniest films of the kind ever made . . . only the stirring, interesting portions of the play are depicted; at the same time the story is clearly, though concisely told."[27]

The *Vitagraph Bulletin*'s reference to *A Midsummer Nights Dream*'s "careful pictorial presentation of the many scenes" indicates that the industry considered spectacle a compelling part of the appeal of its Shakespearean adaptations, particularly among viewers suspected of lacking the requisite intertextual frame for narrative comprehension. Reviewing Vitagraph's *Anthony and Cleopatra* (1908), the *New York Dramatic Mirror* mentioned both clarity and spectacle. Comparing the film to the favorably received *Richard III* (1908), the reviewer said, "It is clearer in telling the story, and even more elaborate in the spectacular features. The costumes and scenic effects are of the finest."[28]

"Palladium," a columnist for the *Moving Picture World*, summarized the various sources of appeal the industry articulated.

> Shorn of intricacy of language, transposed into simply worked synopses at frequent intervals, abridged by rapid action, but retaining all their dramatic interest, "Hamlet," "Macbeth," "Merchant of Venice," "Richard III," "Othello," etc., became absorbing epitomes of human interest within the comprehension and appreciation of all who saw them. Emotion and temperament are the sole requirements to hold the interest of the poorest and most ignorant to the simplified dramas of Shakespeare."[29]

Vitagraph expected that, like the other quality films, Shakespearean adaptations would expand the audience. The *Vitagraph Bulletin* said of *Twelfth Night*: "This release will attract Shakespearean students and dramatic societies. . . . It will help you in making regular patrons out of casual vistors."[30] But attracting new viewers most certainly did not entail excluding old ones. Instead, the film industry depicted itself as performing a public service by making Shakespeare available to the masses. The *Moving Picture World's* review of *Twelfth Night* echoed Vitagraph's sentiments, as well as those of the institutions of cultural reproduction that advocated a counterattractions policy. "It brings to many who really enjoy this drama an opportunity to see it adequately performed and at a nominal cost."[31]

The recurrence of a widely circulated anecdote concerning the "Herr Professor" testifies to the film industry's cognizance of the discursive centrality of Shakespeare in the cultural consensus project. An alleged Heidelberg University graduate and former Bowery bum, the Professor ran a nickelodeon on Avenue B on the lower East Side that specialized in Shakespeare and other quality films. Montrose Moses visited this establishment in 1908 and wrote of his experience in an article for the *Theatre Magazine* entitled "Where They Perform Shakespeare for Five Cents."

> The Herr Professor is anxious to make of his five-cent theatre an educational center among the children and grown people of the lower East Side, and to judge by the manner in which the crowds are flocking through the gaily painted entrance, and by the overflow left standing on the sidewalk waiting for the next performance, there is no doubt that the Herr Professor is meeting with success.[32]

In a speech to the Women's Forum, John Collier, secretary of the People's Institute, pointed to the Herr Professsor's nickelodeon as an exemplary use of the moving pictures.

> Why, one of the most popular picture shows in the city is conducted by a man—a Heidelberg graduate—but he got down in the world and became a regular Bowery

bum. Then he got hold of this picture place and began showing good pictures—things from Shakespeare, things from the Bible, and accompanied them with the lectures which his education enables him to give. The place has proved his salvation, and it is simply thronged with people. Oh, the people don't want bad amusements but often they can't get anything else.[33]

Two years later, the *Moving Picture World*'s "Palladium" wrote of the by-now legendary Herr Professor, mentioning "the early days of the motion picture in New York" when "a broad-minded public-spirited Jew . . . first varied the regular order of the usual melodramatic program by putting on Shakespeare's plays for the benefit of school and college students. To his surprise the change became immensely and universally popular and he established it as a regular one day a week program."[34]

Despite the alleged success of the Herr Professor, not everybody made a go of Shakespeare on the lower East Side. The *Film Index* spoke with the manager of another East Side nickelodeon, where the announcements and posters were in "Hebrew." This manager claimed that none of his clients liked Shakespeare. "We have the same people day after day, and we find out what they want and give it to them. The most elaborately produced Shakespearean plays don't appeal much to them; they don't understand them."[35] Complaints in the trade papers echoed those of this exhibitor: not everybody liked Shakespearean films. While some exhibitors, such as the Herr Professor, could profit handsomely from them, others avoided them out of necessity.

Industry discourse would lead one to draw several inferences about the Shakespearean films. The subject matter seemed intended to appease institutions of cultural reproduction and accord with their hegemonic agenda, as well as to draw in new viewers. The emphasis on spectacle and streamlined narratives probably resulted from the need to adapt lengthy and complex verbal texts into fifteen-minute silent film versions that could be enjoyed by all viewers, even working-class and immigrant audiences. The industry seems to have assumed that the more affluent and better-educated viewers whom it wished to attract with the Shakespearean films would be drawn in by the narratives, while the spectacular elements would appeal to the nickelodeon's old clientele. But culturally contextualizing industry discourse within a fuller array of evidence will further illuminate both the conditions of production and the conditions of reception for the Shakespearean films, thereby permitting us to test these inferences.

Shakespearean Circulation in the Broader Culture

Writing in 1904, L. Ralston Irving claimed that *Julius Caesar* was the most popular of Shakespeare's plays. "Perhaps 'Julius Caesar' has been played oftener and to more mixed audiences than any other of Shakespeare's plays. May not that be because the subject and the incidents of the play are familiar to a vast number of people?"[36] Our research reveals that turn-of-the-century Americans may well have encountered *Julius Caesar* in many widely circulating and diverse textual expressions. But the cultural circulation of this particular Shakespearean text must be contextualized within the broader cultural circulation of all Shakespearean texts.

While Shakespearean texts were pervasive at the turn of the century, contemporary commentary indicates that knowledge of Shakespeare, across social formations, was for the most part limited to familiarity with famous phrases, speeches, and scenes. Laments concerning the lack of real regard for Shakespeare abound. "We read about Shakspere, listen to lectures about Shakspere, talk about Shakspere, quote Shakspere; but not one in ten thousand of us can really read common passages of Shakspere intelligently."[37] In a piece entitled "Is Shakespeare Popular?" the editor of the *North American Review* summarized the Bard's place in early-twentieth-century culture.

> If one were to assert that Shakespeare is an unpopular author, little read, and that the average man has but a slight and intermittent taste for him, one would doubtless be met with flat contradiction. The ever-multiplying editions would be pointed to, and the fact would be cited that every household of pious intent and respectable tendencies supplies itself with Shakespeare immediately after it buys the family Bible. It is incontrovertibly true that everyone of average education has been piloted through two or three plays while in the high school; and college graduates can usually claim a bowing acquaintance with two or three plays, *plus* some volume of textual criticism. . . . But is this a test of popularity? The great question is, What does the tired man read when he comes home from business, and what does the worn-out mother of the family read when she has time to fold her hands and sit still? And the truthful answer is that he reads the evening paper, and she reads the advertisements in the back of the magazines to see what she *would* buy if only she could pay.[38]

Yet in their preferred evening papers and advertisements, the "tired man" and the "worn-out mother" could not have escaped the Bard, whose cultural presence extended even to these venues. The very congruences among institutions of cultural reproduction, ranging from schools to advertising, testify to Shakespeare's role in the building of cultural consensus. To adumbrate the incredible pervasiveness of Shakespearean images and phrases in late-nineteenth- and early-twentieth-century America, we look first at one of the most important of Shakespeare's manifestations—public school curricula. We then briefly discuss a selection of Shakespearean ephemera dating from the period. Finally, we look at the Shakespearean activities of New York City organizations involved in uplifting the city's immigrants and wage earners, focusing particularly on a comparison of their theatrical offerings with the Shakespeare of the "legitimate" stage.

Exposure to Shakespeare in public schools, for a certain age cohort, would have been systematic and widespread, since attendance through the eighth grade was legally required in most locations. Such exposure probably constituted the clearest instance of the Bard's function as a builder of cultural consensus, particularly in New York City's public schools, where substantial resources at the time were devoted to Americanizing the children of newly arrived immigrants. A common culture was manifested in the key scenes and key speeches that constituted much of the Shakespeare covered in the classroom.

New York City curricular guides mandated Shakespeare at every level, beginning with the memorization of Ariel's song "Where the Bee Sucks" in grade 2B. By Grade 8B students read "This was the Noblest Roman of Them All," as well as *The Merchant of Venice*, *Julius Caesar*, and Charles and Mary Lamb's *Tales from Shakespeare*. The *New McGuffey Fifth Reader*, widely adopted in public schools, included both "Under the Greenwood Tree," from *As You Like It*, and "Antony's Oration over Caesar's Dead Body." The catalogue of books for public school libraries in the boroughs of Manhattan, the Bronx, Brooklyn, Queens, and Richmond recommended *Shakespearean Comedies* for eighth graders, Imogene Clark's *Will Shakespeare's Little Lad* for seventh graders, and the Lambs's *Tales from Shakespeare* for both seventh and eighth graders. Shakespearean adaptations for children, of which *Tales from Shakespeare* was the best known, enjoyed considerable popularity, although Walter Field, in his *Fingerposts for Children's Reading*, recommended that children read the full text of *Julius Caesar* at age ten.[39]

The above tells us that students were expected to memorize and read Shakespeare but does not tell us how they were taught or what they might have learned. Although intended for college teachers, the study outline for *Julius Caesar* printed in the journal *Education* gives some notion of how educators approached this play. The outline recommends three readings of the play: a first for narrative comprehension, a second for dramatic qualities, and a third for broader cultural resonance. Included in the outline for the third reading is a list of "the most striking scenes of the drama": "Caesar and his train; the thunderstorm; the midnight meeting; Brutus and Portia; Portia on the Ides of March; the assassination; over Caesar's body; the tent scene; the parley; the ghost of Caesar appears to Brutus."[40]

While teachers, as members of an authorized interpretive community, may have wished to encourage an endorsed reading that fit within the bounds of cultural consensus, contemporary comments indicate that, as one would expect, reception was incredibly diverse. What might students actually have learned? Not much, asserted a *Harper's Weekly* column. "Nearly everyone in the educated class who was questioned had read one or two plays, usually at school, but nearly all held mistaken ideas about what they had read, and had a most superficial knowledge of the construction of the plays, the significance of the characters, and the points of preeminent excellence."[41] A short piece in the *Atlantic Monthly*, stitched together from "several examination papers lately presented at an academy in Pennsylvania," confirmed this impression. "Then Caesar reached the Senate safe, but Cascada stabbed him deep and Brutus gave him the most kindest cutting, which made the tyran yell, Eat, too, Brutus?"[42] Although educational institutions of cultural reproduction strove to structure reception and produce uniform interpretations, ample space for negotiation obviously still existed.

The pervasive Shakespearean cultural ephemera both reflected and reinforced Shakespeare's central place in the dominant culture and attested to widespread familiarity with his work. Of course, income, reading habits, consumption patterns, and the like would have determined variant exposures to these ephemera, as was not the case for the state-mandated educational exposures. Moreover, the institutions of cultural reproduction that circulated Shakespearean ephemera lacked any means for structuring reception, ensuring an even greater latitude of interpretation than existed in the schools. Relatively inexpensive versions of Shakespeare proliferated. For example, *The Ariel Shakespeare*, a forty-volume edition of the complete works, sold from $15 to $35 for the set, depending on the binding, with individual volumes also available for purchase. Shakespearean references even surfaced in the popular penny press. For example, in 1889 the *New York World* issued a complimentary city guide. Included in it was a short piece, "The National Game," about baseball that listed twenty-seven Shakespearean quotes meant to "convince one that the game is of remote origin." Among them: "A hit, a palpable hit" (*Hamlet*) and "Let me be umpire in this" (*Henry VI*).[43] A 1911 cartoon in the other major yellow press newspaper, Hearst's *American*, referenced the gravedigging scene in *Hamlet*, showing New York City Mayor William Gaynor as the gravedigger and Tammany boss Charles Murphy as Hamlet, holding a skull labelled "The Taxpayer."[44] Images of Shakespeare himself appeared in stereographs of his statue and grave as well as on the covers of writing tablets.[45] Shakespearean characters surfaced in a variety of textual expressions. For example, a writing tablet showed a bust of Shakespeare on a pedestal, along with Macbeth and Banquo confronting the witches. The text reads: "Stay, you imperfect speakers, tell me more."[46] Postcards, statuary, stereographs, calendars, and even card games similarly featured images of Shakespeare and Shakespearean characters or actors, often accompanied by short quotations from the plays. One social survey reported that families in New York's Hell's Kitchen decorated their homes with inexpensive pictures (obtained from Sunday papers, from street peddlers, or with tobacco coupons), including representations of "Romeo and Juliet" and "The Moor and Desdemona."[47]

Rather than attempt to enumerate innumerable ephemera, we give several examples specifically related to *Julius Caesar*. In 1902 New York's Eden Musee, a multifaceted amusement center offering everything from films to waxworks,

added the following tableaux to its World of Wax exhibit: The Death of Caesar, Marc Antony's Oration, and Brutus and Cassius Leaving the Forum.[48]
N. K. Fairbanks and Company, lard refiners, issued a series of trade cards
(circa 1880–90) featuring "familiar quotations" from the Bard. One shows a
pig in a rendering vat. The quote under him reads "Let me have those [sic]
about me that are fat, sleek headed chaps [sic], and such as sleep o'nights."[49]
A trade card for Libby, McNeill and Libby's Cooked Corned Beef shows carica-
tures of a plump toga-clad Caesar and Brutus conversing about a slim Cassius
lurking in the background. Caesar complains, "Yon Cassius has a lean and
hungry look, [. . . .] would he were fatter," whereupon Brutus suggests feeding
Cassius the advertiser's product. A card for Barker and Company Coal shows
Brutus and Cassius in Roman military costume with the caption, "Away, slight
man"—a verbatim quotation.

The *Albany Times* issued a holiday greeting containing parodies of well-
known literary and historical characters. In one of these, toga-clad Romans sit
reading a newspaper. Caesar's assassination is depicted in the smoke rising
from a lamp. An insert shows a newspaper article about the assassination.
Among the several headlines: "Great Caesar's Ghost," "Butchered to Make a
Roman Holiday" [Byron, "Childe Harold"], and "Imperial [sic] Caesar, dead
and turned to clay, may [sic] stop a hole to keep the wind away" [*Hamlet*,
V.i].[50] Probably either the newspaper staff's own ignorance or their dim estimation of their readers' knowledge of Shakespeare accounts for the fact that
none of the three quotations comes from *Julius Caesar*.

The slight misquotings and elisions on the trade cards and in the almanac
perhaps reflect the way in which such "familiar quotations" became common
parlance, as Shakespeare traveled from the structured reception of state-mandated institutions of cultural reproduction to the greater interpretive latitude
of the commercial sphere. The illustrations also suggest one means by which
visual representations of Shakespearean characters became fairly standardized. The trade cards show the play's characters in the proper attire for the
quoted scenes, the images reflecting and reinforcing a sense of correct period
detail. At the same time, the caricatured and parodic nature of the images, in
combination with their hucksterish purpose, makes it clear that Shakespeare
was no sacred cow. The commercial use of these scenes and phrases additionally attests to a widespread recognition of Shakespeare across economic divisions, since products such as lard and corned beef were doubtless consumed
by members of diverse social formations.

Whereas school lessons and cultural ephemera had the potential to cross
social formations, some institutions of cultural reproduction specifically directed Shakespeare at the immigrant and working classes associated with the
nickelodeons and other cheap amusements. Organizations such as settlement
houses, the YMCA, the Ethical Culture Society, the New York City Department of Education's Bureau of Lectures, the Educational Alliance, and the

People's Institute all sponsored lectures, classes, clubs, and theatrical productions that centered around Shakespeare's plays and characters. The Bureau of Lectures offered some presentations in foreign languages. In 1909, for example, E. San Giovanni gave a lecture on Shakespeare in Italian, while Josef E. Eron lectured on "Shakespeare and His Works" and "The Merchant of Venice" in Yiddish.[51] Ten years earlier the same Mr. Eron conducted a Shakespeare class at the Educational Alliance. "The work consisted of lectures, supplemented by readings and discussions of Shakespeare, his age, his work, and his influence. This class has been remarkably successful."[52]

One may be tempted to hypothesize that these organizations provided this fare to an unengaged clientele indifferent to the Bard. But the organizations' rhetoric suggests otherwise. Granted, this rhetoric was to some extent self-serving, since it was often aimed at current or potential funders. Nonetheless, these institutions consistently stressed the eagerness with which their offerings were embraced. An Educational Alliance annual report stated:

> There is no necessity in the East Side to create a taste for the fine and elevated in literature. The taste is there. All that is necessary is to guide its development. The classes in Shakespeare and in English literature serve as barometers of the literary atmosphere permeating such part of the lives of the working people of the community as is not taken up with earning their daily bread. To show the demand for higher studies among men and women, who are frequently underestimated as to their intellectual calibre, it may be pointed out that during the year there was in the Shakespeare class at each weekly session an average attendance of 159, while in the Class on English literature there was an average attendance of 192.[53]

Just as students may have rejected an endorsed reading, so might the clientele of these uplift organizations. Our evidence on this point, while scanty, is nonetheless suggestive. A *New York Tribune* reporter who attended a People's Institute lecture wrote about the "peppery" exchange between lecturer and auditor.

> "Didn't Shakespeare create bad women?" "Yes, but there were so many good ones—" "What?" interrupted the questioner. "Name one." Everybody looked astonished and Mr. Martin replied: "This isn't a Shakespearean catechism, but here are Portia and—" "But Portia wasn't a good woman; she wore men's clothes and so did Rosalind; they paraded as men, and all the good they did came from masculine qualities." This nearly broke up the meeting, but the questioner continued assailing the Shakespearean women. "Ophelia," he said with a sneer, "was nothing but a crazy lunatic."[54]

Some members of the "lower orders" may not have negotiated Shakespeare, rejecting his invocation as pretentious. The famous George Washington Plunkitt of Tammany Hall, the ward boss of Hell's Kitchen some of whose constituents hung Shakespeare pictures on their walls, advised young politicians to eschew the Bard. "Another thing that people won't stand for is showin' off your learnin. That's just puttin' on style in another way. If you're makin' speeches in a campaign, talk the language the people talk. Don't try to show how the situation is by quotin' Shakespeare. Shakespeare was alright in his way, but he didn't know anything about Fifteenth District politics."[55] Yet even Plunkitt's outright rejection of a Shakespeare whom he associated with the upper classes is one more marker of a widespread familiarity with the Bard across diverse social formations.

The above evidence concerning Shakespeare's circulation indicates that, contrary perhaps to late-twentieth-century expectations, Shakespearean textual expressions were in fact culturally pervasive. While the demonstration of pervasive circulation does not equal the demonstration of pervasive exposure, we can reasonably infer that most Americans, both native-born and immigrant, would have been exposed to Shakespeare in some form, although their enthusiasm for the Bard may have varied widely and some may well have perceived the ulterior motivations behind the dispensing of this "uplifting" fare. Much of our evidence, institutionally inflected and derived as it is, would support Levine's thesis of sacralization, showing that members of certain social formations favored the top-down transmission of Shakespeare throughout the culture. A *Boston American* reporter's criticism of this dynamic, however, reveals an awareness of the implications of top-down Shakespeare. "Why should theatrical benevolence always take the form of Shakespeare? Apparently because Shakespeare is safe, and is supposed to be good for the blood."[56]

Certainly, for purposes of fund-raising alone, organizations such as the Educational Alliance had to assert that their efforts met with success and indeed attracted enthusiastic crowds. But one should not for this reason simply discount their assertions. Reading this institutional evidence against the grain, as it were, complicates Levine's sacralization thesis, inasmuch as it supports the inference that the social formations at whom this top-down culture was directed may have had preexisting intertextual frames conducive to a favorable response to the Shakespearean offerings of institutions of cultural reproduction. This "against the grain" reading can be augmented by the scattered evidence that directly relates to the indigenous Shakespearean exposures and expressions of these social formations. For example, a columnist for *The Outlook* reported that "there is not another district of the same restricted area in the whole of Greater New York that supports so many book-stores as the . . . lower East Side." A customer at one of these stores stated that "they have translations of the best books in all literatures into Yiddish and Hebrew," Shakespeare among them.[57] The native-language Italian and Yiddish theatres in this neighborhood presented Shakespearean plays as well.

One can imagine a range of probable responses to Shakespearean texts. Given Shakespeare's centrality in the dominant culture, immigrants and workers may correctly have associated knowledge of his works with the possibility of upward mobility. And even those who resisted assimilation may have been familiar with Shakespeare within the context of their native cultures. And we certainly would not wish to discount the possibility that immigrants and workers received a noninstrumental pleasure from Shakespearean offerings, as the thriving Yiddish and Italian theatres attest.

This widespread exposure, coupled with the possible range of responses, helps to account for the popularity of Shakespearean films during the early silent period, when the industry sought to attract new viewers, retain old ones, and placate cultural arbiters. A closer look at the production patterns of the Shakespearean textual expression most closely related to film—the theatre—helps us to move beyond the simple statement that the film industry made Shakespeare films for all comers to a more complex analysis of the film industry's particular, and perhaps class-inflected, Shakespearean staging practices. We will see that Shakespeare's consensual function did not preclude distinctions among social formations that were predicated upon different modes of representing his plays. And we will examine the role these differences played in the conditions of production and reception for Vitagraph's *Julius Caesar*.

The Shakespearean Theatre

Obviously, the theatre represented a particularly important interpretive community and institution of cultural reproduction with regard to Shakespeare. During this period dramatized Shakespeare had the potential to reach members of most social formations. Moreover, theatrical productions provided the most proximate intertextual frame for the signifying practices of cinematic Shakespeare. For these reasons, New York City's Shakespearean theatrical scene is worth discussing at some length.

The People's Institute supplemented the Bard's inclusion in their lecture series with ongoing Shakespearean recitals at the Cooper Union, located near the heavily Jewish lower East Side and the heavily Italian Greenwich Village. At first these recitals took place in a lecture room, but they attracted so many auditors that they were soon transferred to the Cooper Union's Great Hall, which seated sixteen hundred people. By 1905 these recitals had become so popular that five hundred to one thousand people were turned away each night during the Christmas week performances.[58] The *New York Evening Mail* described an audience at what had become the traditional Christmas recital.

> Their attention was close, their eyes eager, their faces full of intelligent appreciation. There was no clapping of applauding hands because someone else did so. There was no someone else to them save the characters portrayed by the man on the platform before them. The applause, given with appreciation quite as much for the literary passages as for the emotional dramatic climaxes, burst like waves on the shore from all parts at once.[59]

The success of these recitals led Charles Sprague Smith to consider the building of a "People's Theatre" that would offer Shakespearean drama to the clearly appreciative denizens of the surrounding neighborhoods. The recitals' success, said Smith, "clearly indicates that a People's Theatre, where standard plays should be presented, at prices similar to those of our symphony concerts (10 cents), would meet a distinct and large need. What a lever for civic education and inspiration might not such a People's Theatre become!"[60] Although Smith never realized the People's Theatre scheme, he did make arrangements for the progressive English actor-manager Ben Greet and his company to perform in the Great Hall of the Cooper Union. Greet was one of the primary exponents of the Elizabethan staging movement that rejected the Victorian theatre's lavishly spectacular Shakespeare, preferring instead to foreground the plays' verbal components. Greet's company thus suited Smith's needs both in terms of financial considerations and in terms of his emphasis on Shakespeare's language. In May 1904 the Greet Company gave three performances at the Cooper Union, two of *The Merchant of Venice* and one of *Twelfth Night*.[61] The performances, including a special matinee for schoolchildren, sold out and generated a good deal of favorable publicity for the People's Institute.[62] Over the next few years the Greet Company continued to give numerous performances of Shakespearean plays under the auspices of both the People's Institute and the Educational Alliance.

Since New York City's theatrical licensing laws prevented the continued use of the Cooper Union facilities, Smith and the People's Institute implemented a program that enabled students, teachers, and wage earners to purchase reduced-price tickets to legitimate theatrical productions, many of them Shakespearean, such as Robert Mantell's *Julius Caesar*. As had the recitals, this form of "people's Shakespeare" also met with public approbation and even, claimed the People's Institute, gave Shakespeare a new theatrical lease on life.

> A few years ago, Beerbohm Tree, the English tragedian . . . proposed giving some performances of Hamlet, but the theatre manager, fearing rows of vacant seats, flatly rejected the proposal. But now, since the People's Institute has brought the purveyors of the drama to the once neglected "common people," Shakespeare is no longer a scarecrow, and any theatre manager in the city would consider the production of one of the old classics tomorrow if the modern show at present on the boards of his theatre should prove a failure.[63]

Although, as always, evidence of the actual audiences reception is elusive, Ben Greet himself forcefully argued that the people "below Fourteenth Street" supported Shakespearean productions far more enthusiastically than their uptown counterparts. Greet believed that his proposed Shakespeare Memorial Theatre should be located downtown "within easy reach of the mass of the people. For it is among 'the people,' in contradistinction from 'society,' that Shakespeare is most appreciated. . . . Among the people of simpler life . . . the loving appreciation of Shakespeare is as fresh as if the man were the greatest living playwright of the most modern day."[64]

In a proposal to develop a theatre on the site of the old Astor Library near the Cooper Union, a People's Institute spokesman made much the same argument concerning the relative merits of uptown and downtown audiences, pointing to the latter's eager and informed engagement with the theatre.

> It is evident that the patrons of these [Yiddish, Russian, and German] theatres in the lower east side district attend them for more than mere amusement; they are looking for and expect good dramatic art, as well as enlightenment and education, in customs, speech, manners, history, etc. In short they seem to approach the theatre in a very different spirit from that displayed by the constituents of the Broadway audiences, which are largely migratory i.e. made up for the most part of out of town people who come here from all over the country. . . . Added to these we have the proverbially "tired businessman" from Wall Street who wants AMUSEMENT and no tax upon his tired brain; of such is the Broadway audience.[65]

Not only did the patrons of the ethnic playhouses approach the theatre in a very different spirit, they probably approached it more often. Despite their economic hardships, the clientele of the Yiddish theatre spent a considerable amount on theatrical entertainments. A cashier at the Thalia told John Corbin of *Harper's Magazine* that "there are many poor Jewish families that spend sometimes three, four, five dollars a week here at this theatre." As Corbin pointed out, "A brief calcuation will show that, compared with their earnings, this represents a patronage of art infinitely beyond that of the families uptown who parade their liberality in supporting the Metropolitan Opera House."[66]

These poor Jewish families may have encountered Yiddish versions of Shakespeare quite frequently.[67] A leading playwright of the Yiddish theatre, Bernard Gorin, related an anecdote that attests to the pleasure these audiences took from the Bard, even if they had no prior exposure to his work.

> 'Hamlet' filled the house to suffocation, although the audience had no idea of the author's identity. On the night of the first performance of 'Hamlet' the public rose like one man, and with deafening applause demanded that Shakespeare should appear before the curtain. When the manager, Mr. Heine, came out and explained that Shakespeare had been dead for some centuries, but that the translator, Mr. Seifert, was present, the audience shouted, 'Bluff! Bluff! Shakespeare! We want Shakespeare'![68]

Empirical evidence reinforces these impressions about theatrical attendance among the "lower orders." In 1907 and again in 1909 progressive reformers conducted detailed surveys of the standard of living of New York City's wage-earning classes.[69] In 1907 the Greenwich House Committee on Social Investigations asked two hundred Greenwich Village families with incomes ranging from $250 to $2,556 to respond to detailed questions about their consumption habits.[70] In 1909 the Russell Sage Foundation conducted a citywide survey of 391 families earning between $500 and $1,000 a year.[71]

Although the surveys concentrated mainly on expenditures for necessities such as food, fuel, and lodging, they did include some questions designed to gauge the consumption of cultural commodities, including the theatre. The 1909 survey found that 25 percent of the families in the $600 to $700 range went to theatres (which included nickelodeons) and 66 percent of these families went on excursions to anywhere from city parks to Coney Island. Of families in the $900 to $1,000 range, 51 percent went to theatres and 87 percent on excursions.[72] The frequency of theatre attendance among some of the respondents startled the 1907 investigators. "Yet the amount which some of the more prosperous families spend on the theatre is surprising. Some of the women go regularly every week all winter to Proctor's, Weber and Field's, or the Fourteenth Street Theatre, but rarely to an uptown theatre. They buy fifty-cent seats."[73] While the wage earners and their families may have primarily patronized the vaudeville theatres clustered around Fourteenth Street, the empirical evidence of the surveys, coupled with period observations, suggests that the people below Fourteenth Street were active theatregoers and may well have attended Shakespearean productions, at least occasionally.

Evidence about Shakespearean and other productions in New York City further illuminates the theatrical exposures of the various social formations. A 1909–10 survey of amusements in Manhattan shows that early-twentieth-century Broadway theatre exhibited a remarkable similarity to its late-twentieth-century counterpart. Many complained that Broadway catered only to the proverbial "tired businessmen" or to out-of-towners, both of whom sought only light entertainment in the form of musicals and comedies. The National Board of Review papers contain the following reflection on the theatrical scene prior to the advent of moving pictures.

> What was the theatre as it existed ten years ago? . . . The "standard" theatre, whether a drama, comedy, or extravaganza, was then, as now, dominated by New York City. Then, as now, the standard theatre of New York City was mainly influenced by the travelling public and the comparatively well-to-do people of whom the father of the family was a businessman, whose work consumes his vitality, and the mother a social women with interests superficial on the whole. The wage-earning public—the mass of the American people—has never been the determining factor in deciding what kind of production—artistic or moral—the American theatre should offer.[74]

The musical comedies *The Chocolate Soldier* and *The Dollar Princess* each ran for 240 performances in the 1909–10 season. In the same season no Shakespeare play performed at the high-price or so-called standard theatres made the list of successful, long-running performances. Indeed, plays such as *Hamlet* and *Macbeth* ranked at the bottom of the list of the shortest-running plays, with five and four performances respectively. Curiously enough, in that season, out of a total of 121 plays, only nine Shakespeare productions appeared on the boards of the "standard forty," whereas nine out of the sixty-four plays presented by the lower-priced theatres were Shakespearean, almost twice the proportion of Shakespeare at the higher-priced venues.[75] The neglect of Shakespeare by the higher-priced theatres was not new. In fact, more than twenty years earlier, a critic had complained that "all these exhibitions of idiocy and horse play [are] patronized by thousands, while Lawrence Barrett's "Francesca Da Remim" [sic] and anybody's "Shakespeare" barely pays expenses."[76] By the turn of the century the phrase "Shakespeare spells ruin" had become a commonplace among theatrical producers, who often feared mounting productions of the Bard's works despite their cultural status.

In a 1904 article, "Why Shakespere Languishes," James L. Ford observed that "the works of Shakespere and the serious dramatists are neglected, while too great consideration is shown to . . . light musical or farcical entertainments." Ford, however, did not agree with those who "wail over the degeneracy of the popular taste" that the neglect of Shakespeare supposedly indicated, claiming instead that the modern businessman's money-making toils incapacitated him for serious intellectual engagement during his leisure hours. "The fact that the men who are doing the real work of the world should find themselves in a mood for melodious tomfoolery, rather than for such an intellectual diversion as the representation of *Hamlet*, argues not that their brains are defective, but that business is brisk."[77]

Although opinions remained divided over Shakespeare's potential for profitability—some asserting that Shakespeare did not, in fact, spell ruin—comments on the theatrical scene indicate that conforming to the nineteenth-century trend toward ever more elaborate and spectacular staging offered the only hope for profitable Shakespearean productions at the higher-priced theatres. "The sum . . . expended in the production of one play of Shakespeare on the current over-elaborate scale would cover the production of two or three pieces mounted with simplicity and a strict adherence to the requirements of the text. We are told, however, that a very small public would interest itself in Shakespeare's plays if they were robbed of scenic upholstery and spectacular display."[78] Yet while the majority of the uptown theatres adhered to the spectacular tradition throughout the century's first decade, others, such as Ben Greet, argued for a minimalist staging akin to the practices of Shakespeare's own time. Production patterns suggest that a rough correspondence existed between these two major staging practices and the attendance patterns of certain social formations. Thus, whether by design or not, the spectacular model Vitagraph chose to emulate resonated with the intertextual frames of its desired, rather than its current, audience.

The spectacular staging tradition, initiated as early as the 1830s by Charles Macready, was predicated on Victorian didactic values, in particular those relating to the teaching of history and an obsession with archaeology. Productions regularly copied items from museum collections, solicited the expert opinions of historians of fabric and architecture, and otherwise sought authenticating sources for their sets and costumes. These spectacular productions frequently made explicit reference to widely circulated paintings, as in Tree's *Henry VIII*, in which the actor playing the title role appeared in a costume identical to that shown in the famous Holbein portrait. The producers also staged familiar images from the many popular pictorial Shakespeares, such as the *Henry Irving Shakespeare* (1887–90), illustrated by Gordon Browne, and *The Comedies of Shakespeare* (1896) illustrated by Edwin Abbey. Martin Meisel, drawing upon period usage, has termed this practice of bringing famous pictures to life *realization*, that is, "literal recreation and translation" of the images "into a more real . . . vivid, visual, physically present medium."[79] As we shall see, realizations helped to foreground the intertextual referencing of many of the Vitagraph quality films.

So great was the passion for spectacle that productions staged incidents that occurred offstage or not at all in the Shakespearean texts. For example, an 1885 *Comedy of Errors*, at the Star Theatre in New York, included an elaborate musical interlude showing Antipholous and Ephesus in the villa of the courtesan Phryne. This was an example of what Michael Booth refers to as "an elaborate interpolation of the kind so popular with Victorian managers and audiences, an illustration of a line or two of a speech, a realization of a historical moment, an extension and filling-in of the text."[80] Accommodating non-Shakespearean material and all this scenic splendor necessitated drastic cuts in the original texts. When Beerbohm-Tree staged his *Henry VIII* in 1910, for example, he cut 47 pecent of Shakespeare's text. Contra this love of elaboration, some few argued that since Shakespeare was, after all, an Elizabethan writing Elizabethan drama, his plays should be staged in accord with the fashion of their time, namely, with minimal sets and costumes. But the spectacular representation of Shakespeare remained dominant even through a period of critical reappraisal at the turn of the century, despite the arguments of opponents of spectacle such as William Poel and Ben Greet calling for an alternative staging practice closer to that of the Elizabethan theatre.

With the exception of those who could obtain the People's Institute's reduced-price tickets to the spectacularly staged uptown productions, most people who lived below Fourteenth Street got a very different Shakespeare than did the uptown crowd. As we have mentioned, the People's Institute made an annual tradition of Shakespearean recitals—perhaps the starkest possible mode of representing the plays in live performance. The Shakespearean plays specifically produced for the clientele of the People's Institute or the Educational Alliance were staged by the Ben Greet Company in the Elizabethan fashion. Greet believed that his minimalist staging methods enhanced the audience's appreciation of the texts, rather than obscuring Shakespeare's words with unneccessary clutter. "The plays as I have given them," Greet said, "do not depend upon the spectacular attraction which is so large an element in the appeal of the conventional Shakespearean production of our time, with its dependence upon richness of scenic effect, and its consequent sacrifice of the poetic and dramatic integrity of the text."[81] We do not, of course, wish to imply that the workers and immigrants of the lower East Side would have rejected free or inexpensive spectacularly staged productions or not have attended the uptown productions had they the money. In the absence of these alternatives, however, solo recitals and starkly staged productions necessarily constituted their primary exposure to Shakespeare.[82]

What accounted for the above attendance patterns? To explore this question in detail would go beyond the scope of this book, since the associations of the two modes of representation with particular social formations are overdetermined, but we can suggest some answers. Economic determinants provide one obvious explanation. The People's Institute and the Educational Alliance had neither the financial nor the theatrical resources to present an elaborately staged Shakespeare. The need to maintain social distinctions also factors in. Those who could afford high-priced tickets were entitled to rub shoulders with their peers while enjoying lavish productions and basking in the knowledge that others had access only to the less expensively staged Elizabethan versions. Another explanation might cast the difference in modes of representation in ideological terms. Perhaps the advocates of the Elizabethan mode believed that its emphasis on the linguistic aspects of the text permitted more direct access to the plays' moral messages, whereas spectacular staging might obscure these lessons. As Charles Sprague Smith said when discussing the need for a theatre to present Shakespearean productions, "An important agent in the crusade against vice and ignorance was being neglected or rather perverted to ill use" by the spectacular staging of the uptown theatres.[83] Whatever the reasons for the presentation of a highly verbal Shakespeare to the "lower orders," staging practices reveal that Shakespeare could function to maintain cultural hierarchies as well as to create cultural consensus.

The Vitagraph *Julius Caesar*

A late-twentieth-century viewer unacquainted with the circulation patterns of Shakespearean texts in the early part of the century might ask the following questions about the Vitagraph *Julius Caesar*. Why would Vitagraph make a film that presumably only the educated and cultured classes could understand or appreciate? And how could a fifteen-minute silent rendering of Shakespeare's lengthy and complex written text possibly appeal even to the educated and the cultured? Contra the implicit assumption underlying the first question, our evidence shows that Shakespeare was, in fact, culturally pervasive. Shakespearean texts circulated through a variety of institutions of cultural reproduction—schools, advertising, the theatre, and so on. These multiple sites of circulation may well have resulted in multiple and overlapping sites of exposure for any one member of most social formations, and particular social formations as a whole most certainly would *not* have had a monopoly on an elaborated Shakespearean intertextual frame.

Contra the implicit assumption underlying the second question, we have shown that although people may have encountered Shakespeare on all sides, they seemed most familiar with those key scenes and key phrases that circulated in reduced texts rather than with the entire texts of the original plays. School lessons for the most part concentrated on the reading and memorization of selected passages from the best-known plays. Ephemera such as trade cards of necessity presented a very minimalist Shakespeare. And most productions of the plays themselves emphasized lavish visual pleasure at the expense of the full presentation of the written texts.

Our intertextual evidence thus reveals that, in reducing the verbal elements to key scenes and phrases and accentuating visual pleasure and spectacle, Vitagraph's *Julius Caesar* was fully consonant with most contemporary Shakespearean texts. Phrases such as "only the stirring, interesting portions," "clearly though concisely told," and "clearer in telling the story" indicate that the film industry shared the expedient approach to Shakespeare seen in textual expressions as diverse as waxworks and trade cards advertising lard. At the same time, phrases such as "careful pictorial presentation" and "more elaborate in the spectacular features" show that the industry—not surprisingly, given the nature of the medium—referenced the spectacular staging tradition and valued the pictorial over the written.

Before proceeding with our analysis, we should provide a description of the film for those who have not seen it. In keeping with our decision to rely where possible upon period discourse rather than impose our own readings, we will quote Vitagraph's own description.

> Scene 1 — Street in Rome. Casca and Trebonius upbraid the citizens for praising Caesar. Scene 2 — The Forum. A soothsayer bids Caesar "beware the ides of March." Scene 3 — Mark Antony wins the race and "thrice he offers Caesar a crown." Scene 4 — Cassius tempts Brutus to join the conspiracy against Caesar. Scene 5 — Brutus' garden. Meeting of the conspirators. Scene 6 — Caesar's palace. Calphurnia [sic] tells Caesar of her dream and begs him not to go to the senate. The conspirators enter, laugh at his fears, urge and get his consent to go. Scene 7 — Street near Capitol. The soothsayer again warns Caesar. Scene 8 — The Capitol. The assassination of Caesar. Scene 9 — The Forum. Brutus addresses the mob. Antony enters with Caesar's body. Scene 10 — Brutus' camp

Vitagraph production still from *Julius Caesar*. The key phrase, "Beware the Ides of March!"

near Sardis. Cassius upbraids Brutus. Scene 11 — Brutus' tent – quarrel – Caesar's ghost. Scene 12 — Plains of Philippi. Armies of Mark Antony and Octavius Caesar, and Brutus and Cassius. Scene 13 — The Battle. "Caesar, thou art revenged even with the sword that killeth thee." Scene 14 — Brutus slays himself. "Caesar, now be still. I killed not thee with half so good a will." Scene 15 — Brutus funeral pyre. "This was the noblest Roman of them all."[84]

The *New York Dramatic Mirror*'s review of the film testifies to its consonance with standard representational practices, namely, the selection of key scenes and the use of impressive sets.

In some respects this is the best of the Shakespearean adaptations the Vitagraph Company has yet produced. . . . But the chief points for praise are the intelligent manner in which the adaptation is managed, and the fine scenic settings that are supplied. By selecting only the vital scenes and inserting comprehensive explanatory titles in the film the story of the play is rendered fairly free from obscurity— the greatest obstacle to overcome in doing Shakespeare in moving pictures.[85]

The film, which was shot on painted theatrical sets in the standard tableau style of the period, compresses the Shakespearean text, the fifteen shots omitting six of the play's seventeen scenes. As we have said, the theatrical practice of radically cutting the plays as well as the widespread circulation of "reduced" texts would have rendered audiences familiar with such compression. Vitagraph's description indicates that the film contained four direct quotes and one paraphrase of some of the play's best-known lines. Just as the film thus features key phrases, it also features key scenes. The college study outline mentioned above enumerated the ten "most striking scenes of the drama," eight of which appear in the Vitagraph film. The scenes omitted from both the outline's list and the film deal with Marc Antony and his co-rulers, perhaps indicating a cultural preference for narrative simplification.

The costuming and architecture in the film accord with the images circulated on Shakespearean ephemera, such as the trade cards we have described, as well as with the spectacular staging tradition. Recall J. Stuart Blackton's defense of his film from charges of immorality through invoking the very historical accuracy that formed such a major component of the spectacular tradition. Newspaper accounts of his testimony further connected the Vitagraph film to this theatrical tradition by implying that the costumes worn in the film had been used in famous stage productions. Period critics such as Stephen Bush also pointed out that some of the sets reproduced well-known paintings, such as Gérôme's assassination of Caesar.[86] The on-screen depiction of offstage action again illustrates Vitagraph's adherence to contemporary theatrical practice. In Act I, scene ii of the play, Marc Antony thrice offers Caesar the crown offstage, while onstage Brutus and Cassius listen. The film's third shot, preceded by the intertitle "Marc Antony three times offers Caesar the crown," shows Caesar seated in a grandstand, surrounded by a crowd of extras. While Caesar watches the race that Shakespeare's Casca only describes, Marc Antony presents the crown to him. The film's eleventh shot uses a cinematic device, superimposition, to emulate a moment of theatrical spectacle: the appearance of Caesar's ghost to Brutus at Philippi.

Placing the Vitagraph *Julius Caesar* within the circulation patterns of Shakespearean texts in turn-of-the-century America, together with elucidating the conditions of production and reception for this particular text and, more generally, for the Shakespearean films produced by Vitagraph and the rest of the film industry, permits us to reframe our late-twentieth-century assumptions. Our intertextual evidence confirms film industry discourse in one regard: the industry's expectations that such films would placate its critics seem well-founded, despite the objections to *Julius Caesar*. The pervasiveness of Shakespeare that we have documented further confirms the industry's discourse. Given the widespread familiarity with the Bard, the industry quite reasonably assumed that these films would appeal not only to cultural elites but to "the greatest mass of the people," thereby accomplishing the goal

Vitagraph production still from *Julius Caesar* realizing Gérôme's *Death of Caesar*.

Lithograph after Gérôme's *Death of Caesar* (1867).

of attracting new audiences while retaining old ones. Yet our evidence leads us to question the industry's assumption that clearly and simply told stories presented in spectacular fashion were aimed at viewers with little or no knowledge of Shakespeare. As we have shown, the Shakespearean films were in fact consonant with a culturally prevalent mode of Shakespearean representation that would have been familiar to members of most social formations.

This last point, which speaks to the industry's perceptions of audience reception, illustrates the mutual inflection of conditions of production and reception. Our intertextual evidence demonstrates a pervasive exposure to Shakespeare that helps to account for the industry's production of these films. Had a taste for Shakespeare not already existed among potential audiences, it is unlikely that the film industry would have persisted in its endeavor. Vitagraph and other studios were not pioneering purveyors of Shakespeare for the "masses," many of whom had probably encountered some form of Shakespearean textual expression. The industry, however, may have provided some viewers with their first exposure to a dramatized Shakespeare. After visiting the Herr Professor's nickelodeon, Montrose Moses concluded that people too poor to afford even discounted theatrical admissions enjoyed moving-picture Shakespeare. "In numbers measuring over two hundred thousand throughout New York City, this kinetoscopic clientele is composed of people who cannot afford to go to the theatre, even though such an organization as the People's Institute strive to reduce for them the theatre prices along Broadway."[87] But the pervasive exposure that formed an important element of the conditions of production should not be interpreted as an undifferentiated exposure across social formations, since viewers' diverse intertextual frames would have constituted an equally important element of the conditions of reception. For example, proponents of Elizabethan staging may well have resented the films' emulation of the spectacular tradition, while those who had experienced Greet's free productions may well have missed the engagement with the written text.[88]

The recognition of the variegated conditions of reception attests to the complexity of cultural construction and engagement. We nonetheless wish to underscore that, at this historical moment, the uniform recognition of Shakespeare as cultural icon overarched specific interpretations, whether oppositional or not. This assertion may surprise those readers familiar with recent scholarship on audience reception, which asserts an unlimited possibility for the production of negotiated and/or oppositional readings. While we certainly acknowledge this possibility, particular *readings* do not concern us, a point that perhaps requires brief explication.

During the period in question, the booming Shakespeare criticism industry, driven by authorized interpretive communities and institutions of cultural reproduction, ensured the ongoing production of endorsed readings. At the same time, Shakespeare's pervasiveness undoubtedly ensured the production of a multiplicity of marginalized readings, readings not produced by authorized interpretive communities and circulated by institutions of cultural reproduction. Yet the overarching appropriation of Shakespeare for the purposes of cultural consensus ensured that *all* readings, endorsed or marginalized, served ultimately to enhance his centrality. No matter how various readers or social formations either encountered Shakespeare or interpreted the plays, their very engagement with these texts contributed to the perception of a unified society with shared cultural references. This perception doubtless served the needs of those who advocated an Arnoldian response to the current social/cultural crisis. It also formed an important factor in the conditions of production and reception for Vitagraph's *Julius Caesar*. But Shakespeare's iconic status should not be seen solely as the product of the Arnoldians' efforts to forge cultural consensus, since his preexistent pervasiveness made him more suitable for this kind of appropriation than any other cultural figure. And the residual traces of his popularity among marginalized social formations serve to counter a monolithic, top-down model of social control.

Vitagraph's invocation of a central cultural icon and *Julius Caesar's* congruence with prevalent modes of representation may have placated some of the industry's critics, but it clearly distressed others. Although Vitagraph sought to participate through its Shakespeare adaptations in the forming of a cultural consensus, the initially puzzling complaints of censors in New York City and Chicago hint at contestation among cultural producers as the film industry struggled to elevate its status. Since no mechanisms existed to regulate content, audiences, or exhibition venues, film was initially not as constrained as media such as the theatre. This situation was exacerbated by the nature of film's audiences. The critics suspected that workers and immigrants required a far more structured presentation of Shakespeare than the cinema afforded, which led to the objections from the Chicago police and the New York mayor to the depiction of an "actual" scene of assassination and to the clergy's complaints about costuming that bared men's knees.

The religious objections, although extreme, were actually in keeping with the puritanical attitude of some Protestant denominations, particularly the Methodists, toward the theatre, an attitude that dated to the regime of Oliver Cromwell. Theatrical adaptations, no matter how seemingly inoffensive, would not have recommended themselves to this constituency. But, in general, Victorian society was satisfied to protect its offspring from the Bard's earthier aspects, permitting them to read the full texts only at an older age or in the classroom under strict pedagogical supervision. Shakespeare was a good tonic for everyone, although some required a diluted form. Theodore Weld, advocate of Shakespeare as purveyor of "terse, crisp, sinewy Saxon," praised those Shakespearean editors who produced a G-rated version of the Bard.

On the . . . principle of discretionary selection and omission, Bowdler's *Family Shakespeare* was long since compiled. Near twenty years ago, Prof. Hows of Columbia College, New York City, published his *Shakespearean Reader* as a school text book. . . . More recently, Rev. Henry N. Hudson of Boston has published his *School Shakespeare*, an admirable text book for advanced classes. And still more recently Mr. W. J. Rolfe, AM, and the Clarendon Press Editors have printed their carefully and judiciously expurgated editions.[89]

Since newly arrived and unassimilated immigrants were often viewed as childlike, some may have felt that dramatized versions of the texts intended for the "lower orders" should also be carefully censored. Unlike Shakespearean films, most Shakespearean texts circulated in venues that closely structured reception and sought to restrict textual polysemy. School lessons and textbooks most certainly attempted to narrow the range of students' readings, teachers' manuals and other instructors' aids valorizing some interpretations over others. The standard theatre likewise had mechanisms for controlling both audiences and interpretations. Admission price regulated audience composition, and certainly limited the attendance of unaccompanied children, while newspaper reviews policed content and provided interpretive guidelines.

In the wake of the nickelodeon closings, the *New York Daily Tribune* specifically recognized the potential polysemy of moving pictures, arguing that they required censorship even if the theatre did not. "Public safety on the moral side is, moreover, no better provided for, there being practically no supervision of the character of the [moving picture] shows given, and the need of censorship being very different from that in the case of theatres, where the press keeps the public informed of what is being presented."[90] True, films were on occasion accompanied by lectures, but for the most part film had none of the theatre's control mechanisms. The exhibitors neither regulated audience composition nor attempted to structure reception, while the daily program changes precluded popular press reviews. Francis Oliver, the chief of the New York City Bureau of Licenses, made a very revealing statement about the difference between *Julius Caesar* as play and as film. "Scenes of crime and depravity on the stage, which are witnessed by the most respectable people in the land, seem to be too violent and harmful in their effects upon the minds of the young to be permitted in show houses. . . . Brutus must not murder Caesar in the presence of our children."[91] A mere seven years after Leon Czolgosz had assassinated McKinley, it was perhaps preferable that Brutus not murder Caesar in the presence of immigrants either. Hence, the objections against Vitagraph's *Julius Caesar* seem to have been cast in terms of the film's probable deleterious effects upon its vulnerable audience of children, workers, and immigrants. One might also hypothesize that the overarching appropriation of Shakespeare sanctioned by Carnegie, Hamilton, and their ilk required an engagement with the written text that the silent film of course precluded. A fifteen-minute, fifteen-shot silent Shakespeare, no matter how congruent with culturally prevalent modes of representation, did not afford much opportunity to learn either a new language or new values.

Despite desires for a Shakespeare tailored to particular audiences or suitable for consensus building, Shakespeare's position as universally valorized and transcendent cultural icon did indeed permit New York City's showmen to have a merry Christmas time of it, the sheer absurdity of objecting to *Julius Caesar* weakening the arguments made by the industry's opponents. Shakespeare's cultural pervasiveness rendered him practically a sure bet for the fledging medium. This was not necessarily the case with Dante, however, as the reaction to Vitagraph's *Francesca di Rimini* reveals.

Dante's Cultural Circulation and *Francesca di Rimini*

As we said at the outset of this chapter, we chose to compare *Julius Caesar* with *Francesca di Rimini* because of the differences in the respective positions of Shakespeare and Dante in turn-of-the-century America, the former pervasively circulated and appropriated primarily for consensus building, the latter circulated in restricted fashion and appropriated primarily for purposes of distinction. Since Vitagraph's *Francesca* does not circulate widely either, we will provide a brief synopsis of the film before proceeding. A *Views and Film Index* Vitagraph advertisement included the following copy:

> Francesca receives letter from Lanciotto (a hunchback) asking for her hand in marriage — Falls in love with the brother Paolo who delivers the message — The marriage is consummated, and shortly afterward Lanciotto is called away to the wars, leaving his bride under protection of his brother — Paolo betrays his trust — Francesca is false to her vows — Bebbe [Pepe], the court jester, discovers the lovers and proceeds to camp and informs his master — Lanciotto kills the jester and returns to the palace, enters unexpectedly and finds the lovers in fond embrace — He kills his wife, then his brother, laughs insanely at his victims and stabs himself to death.[92]

The film consists of fifteen shots, thirteen in the long-shot tableau style typical of the period, with two insert close-ups of the locket.[93] The latter shots appear to be motivated by Lanciotto's glance, although they do not resemble the point-of-view structure of the classical Hollywood cinema. The action takes place against painted theatrical sets as well as exterior locations, both typical of the period, but the costuming and sets seem elaborate relative to those of other films of the period.

In both turn-of-the-century England and the United States a veritable Dante craze existed, at least among a restricted segment of society. As Henry Beers, author of *A History of English Romanticism in the Nineteenth Century*, put it:

VIEWS AND FILMS INDEX.

 VITAGRAPH

12 CENTS PER FOOT **FILMS** 12 CENTS PER FOOT

A COWBOY ELOPEMENT .... 365 Feet

Last Week { THE THIEVING HAND .... 325 "

SOLD AGAIN .... 250 "

THIS WEEK

FRANCESCA DA RIMINI

or, THE TWO BROTHERS

Copyright, 1907, by The Vitagraph Company of America

Francesca receives letter from Lanciotto (a hunchback) asking for her hand in marriage—Falls in love with the brother Paolo who delivers the message—The marriage is consummated, and shortly afterward Lanciotto is called away to the wars, leaving his bride under protection of his brother—Paolo betrays his trust—Francesca is false to her vows—Bebbe, the court jester, discovers the lovers and proceeds to camp and informs his master—Lanciotto kills the jester and returns to the palace, enters unexpectedly and finds the lovers in fond embrace—He kills his wife, then his brother, laughs insanely at his victims and stabs himself to death.

A Masterpiece in Motion Photography

LENGTH 990 FEET

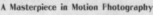

NOTE.—On and after February 6th 1908 deliveries of Vitagraph Films will be made on Thursday instead of Saturday.

Next Week **TWO BIG COMICS**

1908 Vitagraph advertisement in the *Views and Film Index*.

Since the middle of the century Dante study and Dante literature in English-speaking lands have waxed enormously. Dante societies have been founded in England and America. Almost every year sees another edition, a new commentary or a fresh translation in prose, in blank verse, in *terza rima*, or in some form of stanza. . . . Not that he will ever be popular, in Shakespeare's way; and yet it is far gone when the aesthete in a comic opera is described as a "Francesca da Rimini young man."[94]

The fact that the Oscar Wilde character in Gilbert and Sullivan's 1881 comic opera *Patience* describes himself as "a Francesca da Rimini, niminy, piminy, Je-ne-sais-quoi young man!" demonstrates that Dante was indeed well known within certain social formations. But it also seems intended to criticize Dante devotees as effete, silly, and affected.

In the United States, upper- and middle-class women seemed particularly enamoured of the Italian poet. The *Ladies' Home Journal* published William Dean Howells's article on the poet, and "enterprising publishers tried to exploit this Dante furore by issuing elegant Dante calendars."[95] In general, though, Dante emphemera seem to have been less widely available than Shakespearean and were never, as far as we know, distributed gratis. A set of Dante postcards, "A Visit to Hell with Dante—The Italian Poet," dating from around 1900, cost fifty cents for twenty-five "views," at least half-a-day's pay for wage earners such as elevator men, tailors, and grocery clerks.[96] But at the universities Dante societies and courses proliferated. A correspondent to *The Dial* noted that "the catalogues of many of our leading universities now offer special courses in Dante, and the leaven of this study is at work in our national life." Yet even this valorization of the Italian poet would not award him a cultural centrality equivalent to Shakespeare's. "It is possibly true . . . that 'there is no hope of Dante ever taking the place of a popular author with us, of becoming one of our intimates.' "[97]

Contemporary comments indicate that Francesca da Rimini may have been among the best known of Dante's characters. The nineteenth century produced numerous literary and dramatic versions of the story of Francesca. As early as 1867 *Wilkes Spirit of the Times: The American Gentleman's Magazine*, reviewing a French theatrical production of the tale, assumed a widespread reader acquaintance with the eponymous heroine. The Francesca story, said the magazine, boasts "of all of Dante's heroines the one most loved; of all of Dante's verses those most familiar to the world. If the English reader knows nothing else of the great Italian master, he is at least conversant with the story of Francesca."[98] Sixteen years later, in 1883, the *New York Times* traced the lineage of George H. Boker's dramatic version of the story. "The story of 'Francesca da Rimini' is one of the loveliest and most mournful episodes in poetic literature. It has been told by Boccaccio and Dante, and nobly told by Dante. Leigh Hunt's graceful account of this melancholy love tale is, of course, familiar to all readers."[99]

As the sources cited thus far might suggest, with Dante in general and Francesca da Rimini in particular, our intertextual evidence tended to be produced in and circulated by "voluntary" and commercially driven institutions, rather than by more pervasive and even state-mandated institutions. It thus stands in sharp contrast to intertexts related to such other cultural figures as Shakespeare and Washington. This pattern of restricted circulation makes it particularly difficult to assess the exposure of more marginalized social formations to Dante-related texts. Nonetheless, we do have some evidence that these populations might have known of the Italian poet and his works. In 1897 a correspondent to *The Dial* noted with amazement that in San Francisco there "is a settlement of Italian fishermen, whose condition is apparently without an aspiration other than to have a supply of the black bread they eat and sour wine they drink; yet *these people support a society for the study of Dante.* One wonders whether a similar organization could be found among English miners, for a knowledge of their great Shakespeare!"[100]

Our uplift organizations also included Dante in their cultural offerings, although not nearly as frequently as they did Shakespeare. The Bureau of Lectures sponsored several annual lectures on Dante during the first decade of the century. In the 1906–07 season, during which the bureau gave forty Shakespeare lectures, their offerings also included "Dante and His Friends" and "Dante's *Divine Comedy.*"[101] In 1909 there were two more lectures in English, "Dante, The Soul's Pilgrimage" and "Dante, Poet of Humanity," and two in Italian, "Dante's *Divine Comedy*" and "Dante Alghieri."[102] In 1899 and again in 1901 the People's Institute gave a course of six lectures on *The Divine Comedy.*[103]

The production and distribution of at least four Dante films in Italy— *L'Inferno, or Dante's Inferno* (Milano, 1909), *Francesca da Rimini* (Pathé, 1910), *Dante e Beatrice* (Ambrosio, 1913), and *Il Paradiso* (Psiche Films, 1911)[104] attests to Dante's popularity in his native land and makes it reasonable to assume that Italian immigrants were as familiar with Dante as Americans were with Shakespeare. The importing of at least two of these films into the United States and Vitagraph's remaking of the subject in 1910 suggest that Dante enjoyed a certain degree of popularity within this country as well. Nor was Dante's penetration into popular culture limited to the cinema. For example, George B. Bunnell, a nineteenth-century entrepeneur touted as the "legitimate successor to P. T. Barnum," featured a "Dante's Inferno" of "waxworks, mechanical contrivances and 'pictorial views' " as the principle attraction in his Bowery dime museum.[105] This carnivalesque encounter with the Italian poet apparently extended beyond dime museums to amusement parks. Even today the decaying Coney Island has a ride called "Dante's Inferno," while the 1935 film of the same name told the story of a park built around an elaborate reproduction of the circles of hell.

Thus, while their position in the social hierarchy may have precluded their gaining any distinction from a knowledge of Dante, the "lower orders" did not necessarily lack access to or familiarity with Dante texts. In fact, they may even have encountered texts specifically directed at social formations other than their own. For example, the heavily used reading room of the Educational Alliance offered patrons such journals as the *Atlantic Monthly*, *The Century Magazine*, *Harper's Magazine*, *Harper's Monthly*, the *Ladies' Home Journal*, the *Literary Digest*, *McClure's Magazine*, *Munsey's Magazine*, the *North American Review*, *The Outlook*, *Puck* (in German and English), the *Review of Reviews*, and *Scribner's Magazine*, many of which ran articles on the Italian poet.[106] Yet for the most part the Dante craze seems to have been limited to fairly restricted social formations, among which an engagement with Dante and the competence to proliferate readings served as a secondary marker of distinction.

Conditions of Production and Reception

With *Julius Caesar* there can be no question as to the precise texts on which the Vitagraph producers based their film. The case of *Francesca di Rimini* is somewhat more complex, however, since Dante's five lines gave rise to countless retellings, any one of which the Vitagraph producers could have drawn upon.[107] Looking at the multiple versions of the story in circulation during the first decade of the twentieth century, along with their sources, enables us to position Vitagraph among various cultural producers and permits speculation about probable patterns of reception.

In 1901 and 1902 four theatrical versions of Francesca, by George H. Boker, Gabriele d'Annunzio, Marion Crawford, and Stephen Phillips, were produced in London, Paris, and New York, all of which were reviewed in the United States.[108] Significant narrative differences among these plays lead us to believe that Vitagraph most specifically referenced Boker's *Francesca da Rimini*, originally written in 1855. As Boker said of his version, "Of course, you know the story, every one does; but you . . . do not know it as I have treated it."[109] Marked congruences between the Boker play and the Vitagraph film suggest that the Vitagraph producers were familiar with this particular version. These congruences may also have caused viewers to reference the Boker play, which may thus have formed an important component not only of the conditions of production but of the conditions of reception for the film.

Lawrence Barrett, one of the leading American actor-managers of the late nineteenth century, first staged Boker's play in November 1882, playing the role of Lanciotto, and revived the production several times over the next five years. As one early-twentieth-century sourcebook puts it, Boker's *Francesca da Rimini* was "a standard American play, which afforded to Lawrence Barrett a vehicle to popular favor as one of the foremost tragedians of the latter part of the nineteenth century."[110] Among the many congruences between this production of the play and the Vitagraph film we shall look at three particularly apparent similarities: set design, the narrative prominence of the jester, and the attitude toward Lanciotto.

An 1883 program for Barrett's production at the Star Theatre in New York City illustrates one probable influence of this version of the Boker play upon the Vitagraph film.[111] The program contains a series of seven detailed sketches, portraying key moments from each of the play's six acts. A remarkably close parallel to the film exists in terms of locations, set design, and composition, as well as the postures and positioning of the characters. While one would not, of course, wish to argue that Vitagraph consciously drew upon precisely this production, the correspondences may suggest a process of iconographic standardization. Presumably road show productions replicated elements of Barrett's mise-en-scène, helping to establish a tradition with which the Vitagraph producers were familiar.

The jester's prominence in the Boker play relative to his role in other versions again confirms the centrality of Boker's adaptation to the conditions of production. Whereas in many versions of the story the jester either does not appear or functions as a very minor character, the jester in the Boker version plays a role of great narrative consequence, both commenting on the action and bearing the tale of the lovers' infidelity to Lanciotto. The New York Times review of Barrett's 1885 production noted the jester's prominence. "Mr. Louis James as Pepe, the fool, is the incarnation of malice and vindictiveness in a fantastic guise. The pitilessness of the fool's tongue, his derisive attitude toward all things sacred, his evil eye and mocking laugh leave an impression upon the spectator scarcely less strong than that made by Lanciotto's sorrowful love and revenge."[112] The central role of the cinematic jester seems to have paralleled that of the theatrical jester.

The garden scene in play and film offers an explicit parallel. The cinematic jester spies on the lovers reading in the garden and then reenacts their tryst, using his staff as a prop. In gleeful and mocking fashion, he recapitulates their interactions, makes a cuckold sign, and finally turns and shakes his fist in the direction that Paolo and Francesca exited. Compare this with Pepe's actions in the play's garden scene.

> [PEPE steals from behind the bushes]
> PEPE: O, brother Lanciotto! — O, my stars! —
>   If this thing lasts, I simply shall go mad!
> [Laughs, and rolls on the ground]
>   O Lord! to think my lady puss
>   Had tricks like this and we ne'er know of it!

Other stage directions indicate that Pepe laughs and mimics Paolo.[113]

The Boker play grants the Lanciotto character a complexity and depth not readily apparent in the supporting characters, which the casting of the Barrett version reinforced. In contrast to some other authors, Boker presents Lanciotto not as an evil monster but as a complex character who, acutely aware of

Vitagraph production still from *Francesca di Rimini*. The jester spies on the lovers.

Illustration from 1883 program for Lawrence Barrett's *Francesca da Rimini*. The jester spies on the lovers.

Vitagraph production still from *Francesca di Rimini*. Lanciotto prepares to kill the jester.

Illustration from 1883 program for Lawrence Barrett's *Francesca da Rimini*. Lanciotto prepares to kill the jester.

his physical shortcomings, resists marriage with Francesca. Casting the company's actor-manager in one of the major roles suggests that the production would have employed an array of signifying practices to augment that character's narrative centrality. Although we have no promptbook to inform us of the production's deployment of these practices, reviews indicate that one signifying practice, Barrett's performance, did reinforce Boker's sympathetic depiction of Lanciotto. The *New York Times* said, "The first glimpse of Lanciotto reveals him as a man bearing a burden of secret sorrows; outwardly stern, his manner marked by insuavity. . . . Inwardly the hunchback keenly feels the degradation of his affliction."[114]

One could find other parallels between the Vitagraph film and the Barrett production. For example, the published Boker play ends equivocally with Lanciotto lamenting his fate, whereas the Barrett version leaves no ambiguity about Lanciotto's fate: he stabs himself and dies as in the film.[115] One could also look for resemblances between the film and other productions of the Boker play. For example, another theatrical luminary, Otis Skinner, who had played Paolo in Barrett's 1883 production, starred a few years later as Lanciotto. Again, the *Times* read Lanciotto sympathetically. "In Mr. Skinner's representation of the soul-racked cripple there is exhibited a strange mixture of savage desperation and womanly tenderness. Within that misshapen trunk there sprang despite the withering, blighting frost of malicious scorn a flower of sweetness. The soul rises above the cramping conditions of its ill-reared tenement."[116]

For all the above reasons—sets, the prominence of the jester, and the sympathetic approach to Lanciotto—we are inclined to identify the Boker/Barrett version of the Francesca tale as the Vitagraph producers' primary intertextual frame. This specification of one of the most proximate conditions of production not only suggests the cultural exposures and referents of the producer but illuminates the process by which Vitagraph sought to position itself among other cultural producers. The identification of these resemblances also permits us to speculate about readings of the film generated by that portion of the cinema audience that had previously been exposed to the Boker play. A viewer with such exposure might, for example, have been predisposed to sympathize with Lanciotto and to interpret the editing pattern of the insert locket shot and Lanciotto's collapse after the murders as permitting access to Lanciotto's subjectivity while constructing him as a sympathetic character. In this case, the determinate operations of the text work in concert with a particular intertextual frame to produce a particular reading. But does specifying the intertextual conditions of production enable us totally to specify the intertextual conditions of reception? In other words, would the film's viewers have deployed the same intertextual frame as the film's producers? Probably not, which requires us to adduce further evidence that encompasses a full spectrum of intertexts from the restricted to the popular.

New York Times reviews of the Crawford and d'Annunzio Francescas indicate that the Lanciotto of these plays conformed to a prevalent cultural stereotype of the evil hunchback. Of the Crawford Lanciotto the *Times* said, "Francesca's husband is a gnomelike monstrosity, who grovels at her feet in his amorous moods and is a fiend in his pursuit of revenge," and of the d'Annunzio Lanciotto, the "crippled hunchback last night was savagely virile and bestially cunning."[117] In these plays, both of which derived from Boccaccio's retelling, the character's evil nature is constructed not only from his physical appearance but from his actions. Far from resisting marriage to Francesca, for example, Lanciotto actively deceives her by having Paolo serve as his proxy until the wedding night. Even viewers who knew neither of these Dante-specific intertexts may nonetheless have encountered other texts featuring evil hunchbacks, the most famous of which was probably Shakespeare's *Richard III*. The oft-performed melodrama, *Under Two Flags*, also had a hunchbacked villain, Baroni. The hunchbacked Rigoletto, in an opera so popular that Biograph made a filmed version (*The Fool's Revenge*, 1909), mistakenly murders his own daughter in a vengeful frenzy. These intertextual references to hunchbacks may have interacted with some of the film's signifying practices, such as Lanciotto's obviously deformed appearance and his limp, resulting in a reading of the husband's revenge as a brutal and unjustified murder.

Other texts, however, portrayed hunchbacks in a favorable manner. In one of the most popular nineteenth-century melodramas, *The Two Orphans*, the hunchbacked Pierre Frochard, who is the one admirable member of a corrupt family, serves as the blind heroine's protector. Quasimodo, the hunchback of Notre Dame, also offers chivalric protection to a woman. In fact, physical deformation often coincided with noble character, as in the many folk and fairy-tale versions of the Beauty and the Beast legend first rendered in written form by the seventeenth-century Frenchman, Charles Perrault. As Jack Zipes suggests, the popularity of this tale may stem from the fact that, like Francesca, "younger women of bourgeois and aristocratic circles were constantly being forced into marriages of convenience with elderly men, who were not always physically appealing or likeable."[118] Viewers familiar with these or other favorable portrayals of unattractive men may have been inclined to sympathize with Lanciotto and to expect a happy ending. At the same time, some immigrants' firsthand experiences with arranged marriages may have inclined them to sympathize with the Vitagraph film's generally negative portrayal of the consequences.

The privilege accorded star-crossed lovers in texts ranging from "high art" to the popular, however, suggests an alternate reading that centers on Paolo and Francesca. A *New York Times* review of the 1883 Barrett production specifically referenced this intertextual frame.

The fate of Paglo [sic] and Francesca is like that of Launcelot and Guinevere, Heloise and Abelard, Romeo and Juliet—and popular interest in the world's cele-

brated and unfortunate lovers is as lasting as passion itself. A somewhat icono-
clastic history has made it tolerably clear to us that Francesca had been married
10 years when she sinned and died with her lover. . . . But the imagination of a
great poet has created them as they are really and permanently to us—two ardent
spirits sundered in the springtide of their youth, two beautiful and imperishable
ideals.[119]

The popularity of the story among a female readership suggests that members of certain social formations indeed foregrounded a reading of the tale that
privileged the tragic love of Paolo and Francesca. Women in fact produced a
good many romantic poems on the subject.[120] Julie K. Wetherill wrote "Francesca to Paolo" for the *Atlantic Monthly* in 1884:

> I know the spring makes merry far and wide,
>   And birds are building nests with songful cheer,
>   In yon green world, lovely and love-denied;
>   Lo! this is hell; but thou art with me here.[121]

The numerous paintings depicting the tale all center on Paolo and Francesca, who are shown embracing, either in life or in death, or floating through
eternity. Rossetti's *Paolo and Francesca*, for example, depicts the lovers clasped
in each other's arms in a medieval setting. In Cabanel's *The Death of Paolo and
Francesca* the dead Francesca lies on a couch, the dead Paolo on the floor
beside her, his arm round her shoulder. In the famous, and often referenced,
Dore illustration the shrouded couple floats past Virgil and Dante.
    A vast range of romantic literature may well have inflected readings of the
Vitagraph film even for those not familiar with Francesca-specific intertexts.
The heroes and heroines of countless period melodramas struggled through a
variety of vicissitudes before achieving union and happiness in the denoue-
ment, as did the characters in the immensely popular dime novels of Laura
Jean Libby.[122] Any and all of these romantic intertexts, whether Francesca-
specific or not directly related to that heroine, may have served to activate
certain of the Vitagraph film's signifiers so as to produce a reading that foregrounded the lovers. When Francesca shrinks in horror at her first sight of
Lanciotto and when Paolo collapses in empathetic despair, the film could be
seen as privileging the lovers. The film's placing of the couple in an elaborate
exterior garden setting and its focus on their interaction for three consecutive
shots would also suit a romantic reading.
    Other intertexts, however, may have encouraged a moralistic condemna-
tion of the illicit lovers and thus support for Lanciotto. Ouida (Louise de la
Ramée, author of *Under Two Flags* and other romantic novels) asserted that
Lanciotto was perfectly justified in killing the immoral pair. "We cannot but
absolve him. He did no wrong in the eyes of the church, nor would he in this
age be condemned for what he did by any tribunal."[123] In a lecture on Dante
given at the New York Public Library's Hamilton Grange branch as part of the

New York Department of Education's free public lecture series, Professor Christian Gauss of Princeton spoke of Francesca and Paolo as "those guilty of lust, blinded by passion, forever borne hither and thither by the wind in the starless sky."[124] A writer in the *New Catholic World*, while professing to understand Dante's compassion for "a doom so piteous," still asserted that "the law is a good law, and those who break it . . . confess in the tormented air that they deserve to suffer."[125] In fact, any adherent of the seventh commandment should not have condoned Paolo and Francesca's adulterous relationship.

Popular melodramas also had a high regard for this commandment and were rigidly puritanical in its application. Any melodramatic heroine unlucky enough to stray from the path of virtue into an adulterous relationship soon learned that the wages of sin are death. The most famous of these, the Lady Isobel in the perennial favorite *East Lynne*, left her husband for a philandering adventurer, returning by play's end to expire, repentant, in her spouse's arms. Those who frequented the melodrama may thus have viewed Francesca's death as her just deserts rather than as a piteous tragedy. Even less moralistically inclined popular venues reveled in recounting crimes of passion and love-triangle deaths, wherein, for instance, a wronged husband kills his wife and/or her lover. The *National Police Gazette*, the *National Enquirer* of its day, often found in saloons and barbershops, constantly ran stories of this type, typical of which were "Killed by Her Husband," "Shot Her through the Head," and "Brennan's Fatal Love"—all three in the May 28, 1892 issue. Devotees of this publication may have expected the Vitagraph film's narrative to resolve in the deaths of one or all of the principal characters, just as those familiar with the recent high society Thaw/White murderous love triangle may have expected Lanciotto to murder Paolo.

Some commentators on the tale of Francesca da Rimini suggested that infidelity, treachery, fratricide, and suicide were typical "Italian" behavior. The novelist Ouida took a particularly harsh view of Francesca, arguing that Dante "perhaps knew that Francesca had been of that temper (one to this day frequent amongst Italian women) to which it seems preferable that the beloved one should suffer in a common doom of misfortune rather than escape to be happy elsewhere." In addition to condemning Francesca, the author repeatedly advanced negative stereotypes of the Italian character. About the revelation of the lovers' liaison, she wrote that "the usual informer and eavesdropper, who is more general in Italy, the land of spies, than elsewhere, carried the tale of their intimacy to Lanciotto."[126] Edith Wharton also attributed the tragedy to Italian "racial traits," characterizing Lanciotto as "a stealthy, smiling assassin."[127] Period social surveys suggest that members of the "lower orders" shared Ouida and Wharton's antipathies. German and Irish immigrants called Italians "dagos" and believed that they were "spoiling the neighborhood" and given to cheating.[128] Newspaper coverage of the nefarious criminal organization, the Black Hand, undoubtedly reinforced negative ethnic stereotypes of Italians. The film's very title, *Francesa di Rimini*, may have been sufficient to activate these anti-Italian intertexts. A viewer deploying this intertextual frame would perhaps have derived satisfaction from having prejudices confirmed. Alternatively, such a viewer might have seen all the characters as equivalently immoral.[129]

For those unaware of Dante's high-culture status, Vitagraph's *Francesca di Rimini* may nonetheless have seemed remarkably consonant with very familiar texts, the popular melodrama of the "ten, twent', thirt'," "tank," or "blood and thunder" variety, all of which delighted their patrons with action-oriented plots structured around murders, suicides, seductions, duels, and general mayhem. In compressing the Boker play into a fifteen-minute silent version, the film necessarily highlighted the common elements that existed between the Francesca story and the myriad of melodramas. Since many film viewers had deserted the cheap melodrama for the nickelodeon, a large proportion of the audience had undoubtedly seen plays of this sort even if they lacked any exposure to Dante. Neither the Italian poet's high-culture associations nor the film's derivation from a source that few viewers had seen would have precluded the active making of meaning by the nickelodeon audience.

As we have seen, various related texts—different versions of the story, published receptions of these versions, and broader intertextual frames (hunchbacks, lovers)—may well have interacted with the film to produce a wide range of possible readings. The approach we have taken with *Francesca di Rimini* would thus permit us to continue to generate readings. But while the range of readings may be wide, it is not unlimited. In other words, this approach does not lead to the dread interpretive anarchy feared by those who place their faith in textual determinants. Our evidence permits us to speculate that viewers in turn-of-the-century America may have read the Vitagraph film as a story about star-crossed lovers or duplicitous Italians. But it does not permit us to speculate that they read it as a story about alien invaders from outer space. The various readings we have discussed, as well as other possible ones we could produce, are not randomly generated but rather historically grounded.

And while one could certainly debate the specific readings of *Francesca di Rimini* that we have extrapolated, the circulation of intertexts by various institutions of cultural reproduction does suggest to some extent which readings may have been produced by members of which social formations. For the most part, our intertextual evidence derives from venues that circulated among relatively circumscribed social formations, yet it also points to an extreme divergence in readings of the Francesca tale, so that one cannot identify a "dominant" reading even within this class fraction. Further, since Dante texts did not circulate widely in institutions of cultural reproduction, there was no overarching reading of Dante, no reduction of the text to key phrases and scenes familiar to members of all social formations, as there was with Shakespeare. Thus, while we can suggest historically grounded readings, we have no evidence that would allow us to indicate a socially prevalent or even preferred reading. Rather, the ability to proliferate diverse Dante-specific readings served to reinforce cultural distinction among those already favorably placed on the social/cultural hierarchy. Those not so fortunate could nonetheless have produced Dante-specific readings, had they somehow been exposed to the requisite texts, or more likely, in the case of the film, readings predicated upon more popular texts. In neither case, however, could they have appropriated these readings for purposes of social distinction. In a sense, then, individual interpretations are as meaningless in the case of Dante as in the case of Shakespeare. We have argued that the ability to indicate a nodding familiarity with the latter enabled participation in cultural consensus, whereas with the former the possession of the cultural capital required to produce "interpretations" reinforced the reader's or viewer's prior social distinction. Of course, identifying individual readings contributes to our understanding of the cultural positioning of these two figures and of the Vitagraph films, but individual interpretation is subsumed by the consensus/distinction appropriations of Shakespeare and Dante. In other words, although actual living subjects may well have produced totally idiosyncratic readings of the film, our method does not concern itself with these but rather looks at the probable readings produced by members of specific social formations.

Given Dante's fairly limited circulation, why would Vitagraph have made *Francesca di Rimini* at such an early date, before the company initiated its "quality film" strategy? And why would Vitagraph have remade the same subject two years later? Why did they not take the more popular approach to Dante evident in dime museums and make a *Dante's Inferno*, as did Milano Films in 1909? While we have not discovered an absolutely convincing explanation, several possibilities suggest themselves. The film may have reflected the cultural aspirations and preoccupations of Smith and Blackton or their desire to strengthen their company's position in the foreign market. Or it may have been designed as a last-ditch effort to regain the "respectable" audiences so recently lost with the change in exhibition venues. Or the story may have provided an excuse to depict adultery, fratricide, treachery, and suicide, all cloaked in the garb of ultrarespectability. Finally, Vitagraph may have perceived the film as a safe bet—acceptable to the medium's opponents but melodramatic enough for nickelodeon audiences.

Conclusion

This chapter has looked at the visions of literary culture endorsed and circulated by the film industry at a moment of cultural reconfiguration, detailing the means by which producers sought explicitly to emulate certain interpretations and certain modes of representation of the cultural figures or texts featured in their films. This examination in turn reveals how the film industry positioned itself vis-à-vis other producers of similar cultural commodities. In the case of Shakespeare, Vitagraph's *Julius Caesar* conformed in most regards to the "reduced" form that constituted the dominant Shakespearean mode of representation, with the significant exception of signifying practices that resembled the spectacular staging of the legitimate theatre. In the case of Dante, Vitagraph had no dominant mode of representation to emulate but positioned its *Francesca di Rimini* among competing cultural producers through the striking parallels with the Barrett productions of the Boker play. In both cases, the producers seem deliberately to have chosen signifying practices consistent with the cultural exposures of social formations whose members did not yet patronize the nickelodeons, in keeping with their rhetorical strategy of attracting more "respectable" audiences and "uplifting" their current patrons.

Our intertextual evidence concerning the conditions of production might thus seem to support the top-down social control framing of the quality films evident in period discourse. Our intertextual evidence concerning the conditions of reception, however, makes clear that such rhetoric conceals as much as it reveals. As we have argued above, Shakespeare's iconic status predated the Arnoldian appropriation and indeed made him the most suitable cultural figure for this purpose. Even though the majority of our evidence derives from well-established institutions of cultural reproduction, the residual traces of Shakespeare's indigenous popularity among marginalized social formations serve to challenge the blanket assertion of a top-down pattern. Despite our inability to identify motivations (assimilation, pleasure, what have you), members of marginalized social formations such as workers and immigrants would have come equipped with preexisting intertextual frames that would have influenced their individual readings of the films.

But we have also argued that Shakespeare's consensual function overarched individual readings. While it is true that members of all social formations simply had to demonstrate a nodding familiarity with the reduced form of Shakespeare that circulated most prevalently, it is also the case that engagement with this lowest common denominator—the "key phrase/key scene" Shakespeare—may have marked participation in but did not necessarily guarantee full incorporation into an emerging hegemonic order. Although this fairly weak symbolic assimilation, indicative of widespread familiarity with Shakespeare, may have provided some solace to progressives concerned with social betterment, it most probably fell short of the vision of a homogenous nation treasured by the more repressive types who admired the bard for his use of "crisp, sinewy Saxon."

Our discussion of Dante and *Francesca di Rimini* also challenges the rather crude top-down model of social control, revealing instead the taste hierarchies in operation. As we pointed out in the introduction, Pierre Bourdieu argues in *Distinction* that certain kinds of engagements with certain cultural commodities and figures, predicated on the possession of what he terms "cultural capital," distinguish the participating subjects from members of other social formations by providing them with symbolic power. The perceived aesthetic merit of cultural commodities, as well as the perceived ability to produce appropriate readings of these commodities, thus do not relate to the objective superiority of either the commodity or the consumer but are rather the product of the socially positioned subject's dialectical interaction with the culture producing the commodities. But the superior merit of both commodities and consumers becomes naturalized, thereby contributing to the maintenance of what we would term a hegemonic order. As Bourdieu says, "As perceptive dispositions tend to be adjusted to position [within classes and class fractions], agents, even the most disadvantaged ones, tend to perceive the world as natural and to accept it much more readily than one might imagine."[130]

With Vitagraph's *Francesca di Rimini*, we have demonstrated that those having no knowledge of Dante or of his high-culture status could have deployed familiar intertextual frames to produce meaning and may even have derived pleasure in the process. In our efforts to assert equivalency of narrative engagement across social formations, we have taken great pains to show the amazing range of readings that this one film might have produced, paralleling each Dante-specific reading—by definition "relevant" and "superior"—to a very similar reading derived from non-Dante texts. The contrast between readings of the film derived from knowledge of the Boker/Barrett production and readings derived from popular melodramas clearly illustrates how narrative comprehension predicated on the "correct" intertexts could be perceived as superior to that predicated on the "wrong" intertexts. A viewer who had seen the Boker/Barrett production may thus have produced a more "complex" and "subtle" reading of Lanciotto's character than one who deciphered the hunchback in terms of the rather broad brush strokes of the Manichean melodrama.

But while members of all social formations could have proliferated diverse readings depending on the intertexts to which they had been exposed, this ability served to reinforce cultural distinction only for those already favorably placed on the social/cultural hierarchy. In other words, while a white Anglo-Saxon university professor reading the original Dante and an immigrant laborer reading the *Police Gazette* may both have achieved a similar narrative comprehension of Francesca da Rimini as a story about a love triangle, only the former could have used this reading to his social/cultural advantage. Moreover, the more Dante-specific readings that the former produced would have been judged more nuanced and complex and hence better than the non-Dante specific readings produced by the latter. This judgment, however, would not have been grounded in any essential or inherent quality of the text but would rather have related to the existing cultural hierarchies that these "nuanced" and "complex" readings served to reproduce.

Historical Qualities:
Washington and Napoleon

> The great, immortal Washington
> Can nowadays be seen
> To cross a local Delaware
> With ice cakes painted green.
> Napoleon, too, is pictured
> On the field of Waterloo;
> The field looks quite familiar
> With its peaceful Flatbush hue.
>
> The fiery steed Napoleon rides
> Would not be known to-day
> As one that drew a Spring street car
> For years across Broadway.
> But moving-picture scenes are set
> In most peculiar ways
> To fit the public's latest fad—
> The moving-picture craze.[1]

THIS POEM appeared in the *New York American*, one of the city's two most popular working-class newspapers. Its presence there attests to the cultural pervasiveness of George Washington and Napoleon Bonaparte and the familiarity of potential nickelodeon viewers with these figures. During the period under consideration, American and European studios produced numerous films featuring these two characters.[2] In 1909 the Vitagraph Company released four films—*Washington under the British Flag, Washington under the American Flag, The Life Drama of Napoleon Bonaparte and the Empress Josephine of France,* and *Napoleon, The Man of Destiny*—that offered nickelodeon audiences abbreviated biographies of these "great" men. The historical films, by which we mean films focusing on specific historical characters rather than films merely set in earlier eras, formed part of the same quality film strategy as did *Julius Caesar* and *Francesca di Rimini*. But despite their strong resemblances to the literary films, they differed in several respects. Given their derivation from "real" past events, historicals entered into an expanded realm of intertextuality that consisted not only of representations of history but of historical artifacts such as costumes, furniture, and relics. By contrast, Shakespeare's *Julius Caesar* and Dante's *Divine Comedy*, although loosely based on historical characters and events, were seen as the originating *Ur*-texts. As a result, the primary intertextual referent was Shakespeare's or Dante's text, not the historical characters or events. Unlike literary films, though, historical films had no *Ur*-text to point to as the ultimate and authoritative source but derived instead from myriad and varied textual expressions associated with Washington and Napoleon.[3]

Historical texts were circulated by many of the same institutions of cultural reproduction as literary texts, such as schools, the advertising industry, and uplift organizations. Historical texts also circulated through such other venues as museums, patriotic organizations, and public celebrations. Although the surviving evidence permits us to document these circulation patterns, more ephemeral expressions would undoubtedly have inflected the conditions of reception for these films. The grounding of the historical films in lived experience, however distant, meant that oral history would have functioned as an important intertextual frame for some viewers, such as members of the Daughters of the American Revolution, for Washington, or European immigrants, for the emperor.[4] Although we have no way to determine the exposures of various social formations to oral history, we must at least acknowledge the importance of verbal transmission in structuring conditions of reception.

Finally, the claim of historical texts to be "true" representations of "actual" events connected the represented characters and events to current social conditions, lending to the historical films an explicitly political resonance that the literary films lacked. Historical figures were thus usually subject to more pointed partisan appropriations than the literary figures because specific groups could point to the actions and beliefs of these venerable figures as a model for present-day policies. Washington's central role in the revolutionary struggle and the formation of American "ideals" gave him a direct and tangible relevance to contemporary issues during a period of contested national identity. As Michael Wallace has suggested, this contention was closely related to the increased importance that certain social formations placed upon traditional values. "The Haymarket affair and the great strikes of the 1880s appear to have been the events that galvanized the bourgeoisie into reconsidering its disregard for tradition. . . . Class struggle was transmuted into defense of 'American values' against outside agitators."[5]

The late nineteenth and early twentieth centuries saw a resurgence of interest in the colonial past, as is evident in the activities of such interpretive communities as historians and historical preservation societies, as well as in museum exhibitions and the emergence of genealogical societies such as the Sons of the American Revolution and their higher-profile female counterpart, the Daughters of the American Revolution.[6] Those, such as the DAR, who exalted the noble American past as embodied in George Washington, implicitly contrasting him and it to the more ignoble present, often wished to repress those whom they perceived as threatening American values. By contrast, those who advocated incorporation rather than repression sought to encourage the broad acceptance of American values, of which Washington was a major exemplar. The competition among these interpretive communities for access to institutions of cultural reproduction resulted in the pervasive circulation of a somewhat "neutral" Washington in school lessons, public monuments, celebratory parades and pageants, and so on.

The late nineteenth century also saw a resurgence of interest in Napoleon so widespread among certain segments of American society that it was often labeled the "Napoleon fad." In 1894 *The Century Magazine* explained why its serialized biography of the emperor was particularly timely. "The interest in Napoleon has had a revival that is phenomenal in its extent and intensity—as evidenced in a flood of publications; in the preparation of works of art dealing with the period; in the demand for autographs, portraits, and relics of all kinds. Even the theatre has taken up the theme and still the craze increases."[7] In contrast to the focus on Washington, however, this intense interest did not usually extend beyond particular social formations, nor did Napoleon function as a particularly resonant symbol in contemporary political debates.

Before discussing the Vitagraph films, we will provide brief textual descriptions. (Trade press descriptions of all four reels can be found in the appendix.) The first of the Washington reels, *Washington under the British Flag*, consists of twenty shots. The first thirteen shots depict the young hero in the service of the British as a surveyor and an army officer, chronologically presenting a series of major battles and life events. The last seven shots, which show his courtship of and marriage to Martha Custis, maintain a greater narrative unity.

The second reel, *Washington under the American Flag*, consists of nineteen shots dealing with Washington's career from the beginning of the American Revolution to his retirement from the presidency. Washington does not appear in the opening two shots, the first of which shows Patrick Henry delivering his famous speech and the second of which shows the Battle of Bunker

Hill, including a trio of actors who resemble the well-known *Spirit of '76* painting. The next ten shots deal with battles and events of the Revolution. Again, these shots, such as those of Washington crossing the Delaware, the winter in Valley Forge, and the surrender at Yorktown, often resemble widely circulated images. The remaining shots chronicle his presidency and retirement.[8]

The first reel of the Napoleon films, *The Life Drama of Napoleon Bonaparte and the Empress Josephine of France*, depicts the imperial couple's romance, divorce, and tender parting. After a six-shot prologue introducing the characters—Napoleon, Josephine, Marie-Louise, Madame-Mère (Napoleon's mother), Talleyrand, and Napoleon's favorite generals—the film proper begins.[9] It opens and closes with "vision effects": in the first shot a fortune-teller shows Josephine her future as "more than a Queen," and in the ninth and final shot a bereft Josephine at Malmaison sees an image of her former husband rejecting her. The intervening shots recount Josephine's initial resistance and gradual acquiescence to Napoleon's desire for the divorce, as well as his pain at their parting.

The intertitle preceding the first shot of the second reel, *Napoleon, The Man of Destiny*, succinctly summarizes the film: "Napoleon goes to Malmaison after Waterloo and for the last time is in the room where Josephine died and has visions about his passion, triumph, survival and tragic end." The film repeatedly cuts from Napoleon to tableau shots of ceremonial events and battles, using what we shall call an integrated tableau structure to provide a synoptic overview of the emperor's career. This alternating structure grounds the otherwise discontinuous tableaux in Napoleon's subjectivity and creates an overarching "present tense" spatiotemporal continuity—Napoleon at Malmaison—for those who chose to read the film this way. A Vitagraph advertisement recounts the events: "Visions of Marengo—Napoleon, Emperor—Austerlitz—Jena—Friedland—Marriage with Marie Louise of Austria—Birth of the King of Rome, his education—Moscow—Abdication—Waterloo—St. Helena."[10] In the intervening shots, Napoleon's gestures convey his affective stance toward the past actions. The film ends with a shot of a bust of Napoleon surrounded by four French flags.

We will first discuss the intertextual derivations of the Vitagraph films in the context of the period's strategies for historical representation. We will then contrast the delimited visions of Washington's character and the resonant partisan appropriations made of him with the multiple visions of Napoleon's character and the fairly insignificant partisan appropriations made of him. In order to position Vitagraph's portrayals among those of other cultural producers, we will examine character representations in terms of both their appearance in a wide variety of texts and the patterns of their textual circulation. Finally, evidence concerning available readings, appropriations, and circulation will be used to suggest possible readings of the Vitagraph films.

Strategies for Historical Authenticity

Writing his memoirs late in life, Albert E. Smith, cofounder of the Vitagraph Company of America, reported witnessing a religious ceremony during his sojourn in South Africa in 1900. A tribal priest sprinkled powder into a fire and brought forth apparitions from a column of smoke shaped like the studio's monogram, a V.

> We sensed that something beyond the arms of the V was moving toward us. In the next instant it stepped through the smoke, seeming more to evolve from it—a figure of a person in the garb of some remote era. Other persons followed, handsomely and meticulously dressed. At first a few Greeks; then one we could not mistake, Julius Caesar himself, followed by Cleopatra and Napoleon Bonaparte."

Following the vision, said Smith, he and his companion compared notes. "We found that we had both seen the same characters. We also agreed the characters were those popularly illustrated in paintings and histories, otherwise we might not have been able to identify them."[11] This anecdote powerfully attests to Smith's reliance on intertextually extrapolated notions of historical character, impelling us to discuss at some length the strategies Vitagraph employed to ensure that its viewers would be able to identify the titular characters of its historical films. Through an extensive analysis of the conventions of historical representation in turn-of-the-century American popular culture, this discussion contributes a cinematic dimension to ongoing debates concerning the textual mediation of historical events.[12]

Given the time and money invested in its first two-reel production, the Napoleon films, Vitagraph orchestrated an unusually elaborate publicity campaign in the trade press, in which claims to historical authenticity featured prominently. The "accuracy" of these claims is attested to by a letter to a British trade journal, the *Kinematograph and Lantern Weekly*, in which the writer professes astonishment that the film could actually have been made in the United States.

> I am told the film was "made" in America, but this I cannot believe. The scenes, the characters, and the costumes make one think that genius, Mr. Blackton, when in Paris, must have arranged matters with the French Government, and that having obtained the actual costumes and the help of the leading French actors, he tenanted the empty rooms and repeated the important chapters of the world-known history.[13]

Much of Vitagraph's publicity for its historicals stressed the same commitment to historical authenticity, which consisted of correct period detail, accurate key events and images, and iconographic consistency, all intertextually derived. Similar strategies for historical representation appear in texts circulated by a wide range of institutions of cultural reproduction, from state-mandated ones such as schools to commercially dependent ones such as the theatre. Placing the Vitagraph films within this intertextual frame illustrates how the company sought to market its films as historical texts comparable to those of legitimate cultural producers.

Correct Period Detail

Mr. Blackton, for a time enamored of the Man of Destiny, had indeed traveled to France in the fall of 1908, ostensibly for the purpose of researching the film.[14]

> Among the places visited were the Palace of the Louvre, the Tuileries, the Grand Trianon, the Petite Trianon at Versailles, where Napoleon lived while married to Josephine; also, the chateau at Malmaison, Josephine's home after the divorce, and the palace at Fontainebleau. Careful sketches and photographs of the rooms, wherein the relics of Napoleon and Josephine are reverently preserved by the French government, were made. Every detail of furniture and decoration was noted and elaborate data relating to the customs and manners of Napoleon's time were secured. Not the least detail obtainable bearing upon the work in mind was left to the imagination.[15]

Judging by trade press reviews, which marvel at the "fidelity" and "historical accuracy" of the two reels, this invocation of correct period detail as a strategy for historical authenticity gave the film a certain cachet, setting it apart from ordinary releases. Yet this strategy relied on an accepted, although not necessarily authentic, sense of "correctness" or "verisimilitude" consonant with that of commercially driven institutions of cultural reproduction, as opposed to the antiquarian, artifactual accuracy of such interpretive communities as historians or museum curators. The actors were clothed not in "the actual costumes" referred to by the British correspondent but rather in "the entire wardrobe used by Miss Arthur and her company in *More than Queen*," a Broadway play, based upon Emile Bergerat's French original, mounted ten years previously. The furniture used in the films came not from the halls of Versailles but from "a loan exhibition of reproduction [sic] of Napoleonic furniture which were made in France expressly for the furniture department of the firm of Frederick Loeser & Co., of Brooklyn, NY." Vitagraph insisted that these reproductions were indistinguishable from the originals. "So exactly were the scenes and furniture reproduced that it was difficult to detect the least variation in detail from the photographs of the originals in France taken by Mr. Blackton."[16] Beyond attesting to the elasticity of the period's notions of correct period detail, the array of available referents implicitly suggests the variable levels of status associated with one-of-a-kind artifacts and mass-produced replicas. By proudly referencing the latter, Vitagraph positioned its film to align with the tastes of an emerging consumer culture.

Vitagraph touted its Washington reels as manifesting the same high standards of correct period detail as the Napoleon reels, a view echoed in the trade press. "Even in the minutest detail it is evident that the Vitagraph Company has spread itself to make this film historically accurate and pictorially perfect."[17] While the trade press generally received the Washington reels favorably, critics, perhaps having a stronger sense of verisimilitude for Washington than for Napoleon, did point to historical gaffes. The *New York Dramatic Mirror* said of the first reel:

> The Indian battles are fairly well represented, although the uniforms of the soldiers do not show the usage they should, and there are other discrepancies in detail that might have been avoided. The mansion where Washington marries Martha Custis is also too modern in appearance. The large panes of glass in the windows could have been corrected, it would appear, without much trouble. The interior scenes, however, are faithfully represented.[18]

The *Mirror* also noted an anachronism in the second reel: "the stars and stripes at Bunker Hill."[19] Clearly, a historical film could not hope to succeed critically unless the period details seemed correct.

Key Events

In keeping with the era's approach to "great man" history, Vitagraph structured its historical films around those events seen as central to the main characters' careers. In the case of Napoleon, Vitagraph bolstered its claims to authenticity by referencing a range of texts that derived from different authorized interpretive communities but favored personal and anecdotal material rather than academic histories: " 'The Memoirs of Napoleon,' by Madam Junot, a companion of Josephine; 'Personal Reminiscences of Napoleon,' by Constant, his valet; Ida Tarbel's [sic] 'Lives of Napoleon and Josephine' [sic], and works by Thiers, Bourrienne and other contemporaries of the Emperor."[20] These volumes provided Vitagraph with detailed chronicles of key events in the life of the emperor (dates of battles, marriages, births) and with well-known, if perhaps apocryphal, anecdotes.[21]

This strategy was consistent with that employed in period texts, some of which we suspect may have influenced the Vitagraph production. The critic for the *New York Daily Tribune* saw in *More than Queen*, a fictionalized account of Napoleon and Josephine's relationship, many of the key events known to him from other texts: "The old familiar pageants of the Napoleonic movement slowly succeed one another."[22] Another stage production, Lorimer Stoddard's *Napoleon*, commissioned by the eminent actor Richard Mansfield, epitomized the key-event approach. A program for the Mansfield production resembled the ad copy for *Napoleon, The Man of Destiny*:

Act 1—one half hour in the tent of Napoleon at Tilsit; Act II—return from Moscow, fall from power, treachery of his followers, incidents which are made to occur in the throne room at Fontainebleau; Act III—events at Elba; Act IV—right before Waterloo; Act V—Isle of St. Helena.[23]

Vitagraph's publicity for the Washington films did not reference well-known biographies, but the company's descriptions of the films, in the *Film Index* and the *Moving Picture World*, recall textbook recountings of important battles and dates. The *Film Index* said, "He set out at once from Philadelphia, arriving at Cambridge July 3, 1775, where he assumed command of the army. The Battle of Bunker Hill meanwhile had been fought, and thus proved to the British that their foe was more formidable than anticipated, their loss amounting to four times as many as that of the colonists."[24] Many popular histories and school textbooks would have presented Washington's career in the same key-event fashion as did these films.

Key Images

Vitagraph publicity for the Napoleon films also referenced a whole array of imagistic intertexts, containing what we term key images, that is, widely circulated visual renditions of events in Napoleon's life, reproduced so exactly that "anyone at all familiar with art will recognize them at once."[25] Many Americans would have been familiar with some of these "famous works of art," given their widespread circulation in the form of prints as well as book and magazine illustrations. For example, the critic for the *New York Daily Tribune* recognized in *More than Queen* a key image, calling the coronation scene "a skillful copy of James David's famous picture."[26]

The *Life Drama* references famous paintings throughout, and the crucial scene of the couple's emotional response to their separation may derive from at least three separate paintings by Chasselat, Didioni, and Pott. Famous paintings realized in *Napoleon, The Man of Destiny* include: Napoleon's crowning of Josephine, by David; the Battle of Friedland, by Meissonier; the marriage to Marie Louise, by Rouget; the presentation of the King of Rome to the people, based on Andrieu's medallion; the retreat from Moscow, by Meissonier; the farewell to the Old Guard, by Vernet; and Napoleon at Saint Helena, by Charlet. Some of the famous battle paintings realized in the film correspond in depiction but not in name to the cinematic battles. For example, the cinematic battle of Jena appears to be based on Gerard's *Battle of Austerlitz*.[27] Vitagraph employed the same strategy in the Washington films. Emmanuel Leutze's painting *Washington Crossing the Delaware* was well known, reproductions appearing in school textbooks and classrooms among numerous other venues.[28] About Vitagraph's *Washington under the American Flag* the *Film Index* commented, "The picture of the crossing of the Delaware is one of the triumphs of picture making and is realistic to the last detail."[29] The *Kinemato-*

graph and Lantern Weekly argued that this scene put the film into the same league as the Napoleon films. "The battle scenes are remarkably realistic, and that showing the crossing of the Delaware in a snowstorm will be generally voted equal to that showing the last stand of the Old Guard in 'Napoleon.' "[30]

Iconographic Consistency

While the inclusion of correct period detail, key events, and key images, all contributed to Vitagraph's construction of historical authenticity, the central characters also had to conform to society's conception of the appearance of the historical figures themselves. Clement Scott, the *New York Herald's* critic, discoursed at length about "How To Be A Stage Napoleon," comparing the performance of William Humphrey, the Napoleon of *More than Queen* (and of the Vitagraph films), to other stage portrayals of the emperor. Scott found many common denominators. "Last night we all saw the stage Napoleon, the strut, the curl on the forehead, the hand in the waistcoat, the hand behind the back, but where, oh! where, was the dear old conventional snuffbox?" Scott concluded that theatre audiences placed a high value on iconographic consistency. "To be a Napoleon who cannot look like a statue or a picture is not to be an actor."[31]

Vitagraph achieved iconographic consistency in the Napoleon reels by replicating an agreed-upon notion of Napoleon's appearance, drawn from hundreds of portraits of the emperor, and by casting Humphrey—who already had a reputation for "looking like" Napoleon and in fact seems to have made a career out of his resemblance to the emperor—in the lead role.

> Fortunately, he [Blackton] was able to secure the services of Mr. William Humphreys [sic], who carried the role of "Napoleon" in Julia Arthur's great dramatic production entitled "More Than a Queen" [sic]. In the play, Mr. Humphreys was credited with having given the best character study of Napoleon ever given on the American stage. In stature and personal appearance he bears a noticeable resemblance to the pictures of Napoleon with which the public are most familiar.[32]

Newspaper evidence in fact reveals that most theatrical critics, far from according Humphrey the status of the definitive Napoleon, had been fairly critical of his performance in *More than Queen*. Nonetheless, the actor did successfully replicate for Vitagraph the requisite identifying characteristics of the emperor, "needing only to whip the lock of hair down over his forehead and slip the hand inside the waistcoat to make the impersonation complete."[33] Iconographic consistency thus derived not only from correct period detail but from a narrow and conventional set of signifiers: the hand in jacket, the characteristic costume, the lock of hair.

No such reduced set of signifiers could guarantee iconographic consistency for Washington, since there was much period debate concerning precisely what the great man had actually looked like. For example, in an article in *The Booklovers' Magazine*, "What Did Washington Look Like? The Testimony of Contemporary Painters," William Curtis Taylor reported examining over four thousand engravings, paintings, and portraits of various kinds only to conclude that he could not determine what Washington looked like.[34] Surprisingly, although it was widely copied by other painters and reproduced on everything from dollar bills to insurance certificates, the Stuart portrait was not considered a good likeness. Nonetheless, it achieved iconic status as the primary representation of Washington.

With a theatrical or cinematic Washington, then, connotations of dignity seem to have substituted for specific denotative signifers such as a pose or a lock of hair. The *New York Dramatic Mirror* said about the second Washington reel, which starred a different and older actor than the first, "The character of Washington is much better done in this reel than the first one of the series. There is dignity and repose to the character, such as we like to attribute to the greatest figure in our history. We recognize in the part a well-known Broadway actor, Joseph Kilgore, who had previously appeared as Washington in *Captain Barrington*."[35] Kilgore had also received accolades for his dignity when he portrayed Washington on the stage. Commenting about what was essentially Kilgore's walk-on role in the play, the *New York Times* said, "The father of his country (played with commendable simplicity and dignity by Joseph Kilgore) appeared in the first act, heralded by such shoutings and orchestral salvos as are usually reserved for the star."[36]

Where a simple portrait or still pose of Napoleon may have been instantly recognizable to the majority of the nickelodeon audience, such was not the case with Washington. Additional cues—correctly furnished rooms, familiar settings such as Valley Forge, or familiar actions such as crossing the Delaware—would have been necessary to ensure audience recognition of Washington. Correct period detail, key events, and key images would all have served to compensate for Washington's somewhat weak iconographic presence. In addition, Washington's position in the center of the frame cues the viewer to his narrative centrality.

Even though Vitagraph simultaneously deployed the four strategies we have enumerated, they necessarily functioned somewhat differently when it came to the construction of fictionalized historical characters. Correct period detail contributed to a baseline "reality effect," such as that discussed by Roland Barthes, that encouraged readers or viewers to grant a text's claim to historical accuracy.[37] Correct period detail was thus a precondition for establishing a character's historicity but did not, in and of itself, define a historical character. Iconographic consistency, by contrast, was a crucial element in character definition and therefore varied considerably from character to character. As we have suggested, visual signs such as a pose and a lock of hair denoted Napoleon, while a dignified aura was necessary but not sufficient to connote Washington. Key events and key images functioned differently in the construction of fictionalized historical characters, and events were subject to an even greater interpretive latitude than images. They could be reduced to a name and date—Austerlitz, 1805—or expanded to a full length narrative, as in Gaumont's *The Battle of Austerlitz* (1909). As we will see, both the Washington and Napoleon films alternate between these strategies. Key images, by their very nature, presented only one moment. They were thus subject to less cinematic elaboration, even their "realization" in a film or play tending to freeze the flow of the narrative.

Visions of Washington

The above discussion of the strategies employed to convey historical authenticity usefully illuminates the intertextual frames within which the producers worked. But a fuller understanding of the conditions of production, as well as of the conditions of reception, requires going beyond producer discourse to examine Washington's and Napoleon's place in the larger culture. But let us begin by discussing how Vitagraph itself sought to position its films.

> The American flag over the box office, with a portrait of Washington in the center, is 18 by 10 feet, and this is flanked by smaller ones on the side, the lobby was a sea of red, white and blue, created by 200 incandescent colored lights. . . . A special song for the occasion, "Washington under the American Flag," . . . was sung by the boy wonder, S. Meenay, to enthusiastic audiences. . . . These special observances of patriotic holidays never fail to make friends for a house.[38]

Vitagraph's placement of Washington within a symbolic fabric of fervent nationalism—red, white, and blue, patriotic songs, flags—accords with trade press reviews and advertisements characterizing the films as emphatically patriotic. This emphasis on patriotism points to what may well have been the studio's primary motivation for producing the films. An industry pressured by the "respectable" components of society and by civic authorities stood to gain much by associating itself with such a powerful icon of nationhood as Washington. But the obvious benefits masked possible risks, inasmuch as the industry might have suffered untold damage from a film that failed to exhibit the proper reverential spirit or to meet people's expectations concerning Washington's character.

Although subject to broad changes over time, portrayals of Washington's character exhibited relative uniformity in the late nineteenth and early twentieth centuries. In 1906 Henry Van Dyke argued in *The Americanism of Washington* that contemporary politics would benefit from the application of the civic

The Senate Theatre in Chicago the morning after Washington's Birthday. Note the
announcement for *Washington under the American Flag*.

virtues embodied by the first president and his colleagues. At the outset of his
book, Van Dyke traced the changing nature of Washington's image from the
time of his death through to the turn of the century.

> First came the mist of mythology, in which we discerned the new St. George,
> serene, impeccable, moving through an orchard of ever blossoming cherry-trees,
> gracefully vanquishing dragons with a touch, and shedding fragrance and radi-
> ance around him. Out of the mythological mist we groped our way and found
> ourselves beneath the rolling clouds of oratory, above which the head of the hero
> was pinnacled in remote grandeur, like a sphinx posed upon a volcanic peak,
> isolated and mysterious. That altitudinous figure still dominates the cloudy land-
> scapes of the after-dinner orator; but the frigid, academic mind has turned away
> from it, and looking through the fog of criticism has descried another Washing-
> ton, not really an American, not amazingly a hero, but a very decent English
> country gentleman, honorable, courageous, good, shrewd, slow and above all
> immensely lucky.[39]

Pearson's Theatre in Somerville, Massachusetts, decorated for the Fourth of July.

Although the characterizations Van Dyke describes differed somewhat in terms of which aspects of Washington's life they foregrounded, they all shared the same positive affect toward their subject. In this case, then, seeming diversity actually masked conformity, the across-the-board agreement on Washington's "goodness" rendering all three versions essentially compatible.

Since all three characterizations figured in the period's visions of Washington, however, we shall briefly elaborate upon Van Dyke's typology. The Reverend Dr. Mason Weems, known as Parson Weems, contributed a great deal to the early mythification of Washington in his well-known biography for children, *The Life of Washington the Great: Enriched with a Number of Very Curious Anecdotes, Perfectly in Character, and Equally Honorable to Himself, and Exemplary to His Young Countrymen.*[40] Although by the latter part of the nineteenth century, Weems's sanctimonious and pious young Washington had been largely discredited, it was still being dispensed to young readers at the time that Vitagraph made the Washington films. Children's stories and plays followed Weems closely, repeating his famous cherry-tree anecdote and often including maxims from young George's copybook. The texts that portrayed Washington as hero tended to dwell on his military and political exploits. Speaking of the battles of Trenton and Princeton, Eugene Parsons said, "They were a revelation of Washington's military ability. They not only exhilarated the spirits of the colonists, but extorted praise and admiration from the foe."[41] Even Frederick the Great was reported to have admired Washington, sending him a portrait inscribed with the words "From the oldest general in Europe to the greatest general in the world."[42] Although the mythic and heroic characterizations of Washington still continued to circulate at the turn of the century, a countertrend was developing among historians and biographers who sought to give the great man more human qualities. In 1910 Frederick Trevor Hill, one of the revisionist biographers, contrasted the past century's treatment of Washington with the revisionism of the current century.

> Washington was exalted as a model of manners and morals—and portrayed as a prig; he was idealized as a hero—and rendered unreal; he was glorified as the father of his country—and denied all human fellowship with his kin; he was invested with every virtue—and divested of all virile character. . . . [Recently] there has been a notable effort to depict the man as he really was—a man with good red blood in his veins, good common sense in his head, good kindly feelings in his heart, and a good honest laugh. This humanizing of Washington has been the work of eminent editors, historians and collectors. . . . It is no longer true that Washington is "only a steel engraving."[43]

This humanization had two sides. Those who sought to depict Washington as "a man with good red blood in his veins" treated him as the first among equals, a man who answered his country's call under extraordinary circumstances but who would have preferred the quiet and undisturbed life of a country gentleman. These biographers portrayed Washington as an unpretentious man of the people, emphasizing anecdotes that revealed his simple lifestyle, his modesty, and his human foibles. While these biographies entailed a degree of psychologization, that is, an exploration of Washington's subjectivity, this was, with few exceptions, contained by the writers' reverential attitude. Others, however, portrayed Washington as a not-so-simple country gentleman with aristocratic pretensions, emphasizing his "court" etiquette, his exalted English antecedents, and the lavish costumes and surroundings he enjoyed. Typical of this approach was a children's play, *The Heir of Mount Vernon: A Colonial Play*. The front cover summarizes the little volume as "A Colonial Society Play . . . in which Washington's social life, sterling manhood, and courteous manners are portrayed." In a foreword the author explained how an actor should treat the role of Washington. "He is exceedingly graceful, gallant, and polite, bowing low to both ladies and elderly men." In fact, all of colonial society was portrayed as exceedingly well-mannered. "The rare charm of this little play lies in the quaint courtesy and reverence displayed between its characters. The ladies are demure, proper and sedate; always curtseying low to their elders and to gentlemen. The latter are deferential, gallant and polite, ever bowing low to the ladies and elderly men."[44] The elitist overtones of such a vision established Washington as prototypically Anglo-American in race and culture, in sharp contrast to the democratic qualities of the "man of the people" that the other humanizers portrayed. This "elitist human" vision of Washington would serve the needs of social distinction rather than consensus.

While Van Dyke's typology may be subject to dispute, it does trace the transformations of Washington's image over time, showing that readings of him as saint, hero, and human being were historically inscribed.[45] Moreover, each of these readings had specific implications with regard to the perception of historical causality. Washington as saint, embodying the manifest destiny of the American people, functioned in a far more mystified manner than Washington as red-blooded human, struggling for order in a politically contentious environment. Yet the period's appropriation of Washington for the purposes of patriotism to some extent overarched the disagreements about his "real" personality, since many interpretive communities simply conflated the first president with love of country and national identity. Chief Justice Melville Fuller, addressing the combined houses of Congress in celebration of the centennial of Washington's inauguration, spoke of how Washington overcame the partisan divisions of his own time, implying that the nation would do well to rally again behind this powerful symbol. "Between Jefferson and Hamilton there seemed to be a great gulf fixed, yet a common patriotism bridged it, and a common purpose enabled them for these critical years to act together. And this was rendered possible by the fact that the leadership of Washington afforded a common ground upon which every lover of a united country could stand."[46]

Just as Shakespeare's equation with respectability transcended particular readings of the plays, Washington's equation with patriotism transcended particular readings of his character. The ritualistic invocation of Washington on national holidays and his constant association with the red, white, and blue are symptomatic of the flattening of his historical specificity, and of American history more generally, in the service of patriotism. The connotative level of national pride and glory subsumed the denotative, factual level of battles, treaties, and elections. This overlay of patriotism was perhaps most apparent in the institution of cultural reproduction specifically charged with the transmission of historical information, the school system. At least one authorized interpretive community, however, the American Historical Association, contested the patriotic agenda of the schools. "The idea that the chief object in teaching history is to teach patriotism is so thoroughly ingrained . . . that it is extremely difficult to combat it. Yet it must be evident that the patriotism thus advocated is more or less a spurious one, a patriotism that would seek to present distorted ideas of the past with the idea of glorifying one country at the possible expense of truth."[47]

Coming when they did, Vitagraph's films offered a Washington who clearly accorded with the period's dominant representations, and Vitagraph wisely promoted the films by drawing upon Washington's conflation with nationhood at a time when national identity was in question. A review in the *Moving Picture World* made clear the connection of the Washington films to the ongoing cultural crisis. "No better films could be shown during the Independence Day season, and they cannot fail to inspire courage and patriotism wherever shown. In the large cities where many who see the motion pictures know very little of the history of this country, a picture of this character assumes an educational value quite apart from its entertaining features."[48] The "Photoplay Philosopher," most likely J. Stuart Blackton, took pride in the fact that historical films furthered the spirit of patriotism in the American public. "There is no doubt that the sentiment of patriotism has been greatly increased by Motion Pictures, and all our great heroes, like Washington and Lincoln, are better loved by the masses than ever before."[49]

Although love of country was almost universally considered an admirable sentiment, defining policies that might best serve the "national interest" remained the subject of fierce contestation. Moreover, while a wide range of interpretive communities shared in the overarching appropriation of Washington, they nonetheless gave very different meanings to the concept of patriotism. The seeming consensual appropriation thus masked contentious partisan appropriations, which further examination of the discourses of various interpretive communities reveals. Not surprisingly, Washington, the foremost symbol of patriotism, was appropriated by those in all positions on the political spectrum, ranging from jingoistic militarists to advocates of social reform, as part of the debate over the social and cultural crisis facing the country.

Justice Fuller, promulgating the image of the saintly Washington in his speech to Congress, took the opportunity to remind the legislators of the first president's policy on immigration. According to Fuller, Washington "discouraged immigration except of those who . . . could themselves, or their descendants get associated to our customs, measures and laws; in a word soon become our people."[50] In a similar vein, New York's influential Episcopalian bishop Henry C. Potter contrasted Washington's times, when "though not all of us sprung from one nationality, we were practically all one people," to the present "steadily deteriorating situation" brought on by importation of "the lowest orders of people from abroad."[51] Immigrants represented a problem not only because of their alien values but because the concentration of "foreigners" in urban centers might give rise to further labor unrest and destabilize the electoral balance of power.

While some accordingly invoked Washington to justify severe repression of the strikes, anarchy, riots, and insurrection plaguing the land, others painted him as an exemplar of democratic tolerance. Henry Van Dyke, more concerned about corruption at the top than disorder at the bottom, allied Washington with the progressive cause, portraying him as a simple man who willingly served the state without expectation of private gain. Van Dyke suggested the emulation of Washington as a remedy for "an age when the python of political corruption casts its 'rings' about the neck of proud cities and sovereign states, and throttles honesty to silence and liberty to death." All could participate in this battle against corruption, those "who claim our heritage in blood and spirit from Washington" as well as those "of other tribes and kindred who 'have found a fatherland upon this shore.' "[52] Far from seeking to enlist Washington on one side of an "us versus them" scenario, Van Dyke looked to him as a transcendent symbol of national harmony. For Van Dyke and other enlightened progressives, such as Charles Sprague Smith of the People's Institute, "patriotism" and "Americanization" still represented the cure for the nation's ills but entailed entirely different policies than those advocated by Bishop Potter and his ilk.

Such were some of the main partisan appropriations of Washington by members of specific interpretive communities in response to the nation's cultural and social crisis. Yet there was often a disjunction between the meanings produced by certain interpretive communities and those circulated by institutions of cultural reproduction, since, as we have suggested, the overarching conflation of Washington with patriotism and nationhood often subsumed other meanings. Consider, for example, the meanings given to one painting of

Washington crossing the Delaware. Emmanuel Leutze, a native German and American citizen, produced his *Washington Crossing the Delaware* partially as a response to recent events in his native land.[53] Washington and the American Revolution played an important symbolic role in the German Revolution of 1848. The so-called Forty-Eighters took the American Revolution as a model; the Frankfurt Parliament used the American Constitution as a guide; and the president of the Parliament was called "The Washington of His Country." Thus, for Leutze and many German immigrants, Washington was actually a symbol of revolution, although this radical potential was usually suppressed in the United States, as the commercial appropriation of Leutze's painting reveals.

A commercially driven institution of cultural reproduction, the advertising industry, commonly appropriated Washington, who appeared in everything from cigar advertisements to insurance company stationery, his familiar figure referencing the cultural consensus he embodied. Next to the Stuart portrait, the Leutze painting was the most common illustration in these commercial venues. A *New York Herald* article concerning the difficulties of filming historical subjects pointedly referenced this painting when discussing how to film Washington crossing the Delaware. About such a film, the article warned: "Any attempt to pack as much ice around the boat as appears in the pictures will give rise to the suspicion that it is an advertisement for the Ice Trust."[54] The author, who is referring to an attempt to control the price of ice in New York City at the end of the nineteenth century, does not exaggerate Washington's commercial potential.[55] At least one ice firm, the Washington Ice Company of Chicago, did indeed use the Leutze painting to advertise its product.[56]

Although the painting *Washington Crossing the Delaware* was produced by a member of an interpretive community that foregrounded Washington's radical potential, the text was variously appropriated by institutions of cultural reproduction for totally different purposes. Here, then, we have an example of an interpretive community failing to circulate its meaning through institutions of cultural reproduction. In fact, chromolithographs of the painting circulated primarily in institutions, such as schools, that suppressed its revolutionary meaning, reducing it to another iconic representation of the nobility of the "The Father of His Country."

The Leutze painting thus provides a sterling example of textual indeterminacy and of the occasional disjunction between interpretive communities and institutions of cultural reproduction as well as between various culturally derived portrayals and any "inherent" partisan meaning. Of course, the interaction of interpretive communities with the institutions of cultural reproduction through which their meanings circulated did not always result in the pronounced indeterminacy of advertising's use of *Washington Crossing the Delaware*. As we suggested at the outset, factors such as an institution's circulation patterns, its economic base, and the nature of its interface with the public

Vitagraph production still from *Washington under the American Flag* realizing Emmanuel Leutze's *Washington Crossing the Delaware* (1851).

Photograph of Vitagraph filming Washington crossing the Delaware.

empowered their attendant interpretive communities differently. As with Shakespeare, the most pervasive institutions of cultural reproduction, such as schools, circulated the most "reduced" Washington, while other institutions, such as the DAR, served as more direct conduits for the meanings produced by particular interpretive communities.

Washington Circulation

The rote invocation of the first president pervaded turn-of-the-century society to such an extent that even celebratory texts occasionally revealed a touch of cynicism. A children's play, *The Wrong George Washington*, begins with a group of children discussing their plans for Washington's Birthday. The children bemoan the fact that all the participants will do their customary, familiar turns: reciting poems, singing songs, performing pantomimes, and so on.

> LUCY: Jennie Rhodes is going to read "When Washington Crossed the Delaware." You remember it, don't you?
>
> JANE: Oh, yes, I've heard it.
>
> HARRIET: Heard it! I guess you have. She's been ferrying Washington back and forth across the Delaware every February since I can remember. . . . If I were you, I wouldn't print out the program. You'll have a bigger crowd if you just say an interesting program will be given.[57]

Like Shakespeare texts, Washington texts were culturally pervasive, mandated in school curricula, and often directed at immigrants and the working classes. And, like Shakespeare texts, while Washington texts functioned primarily to construct cultural consensus, the relative availability of textual expressions as diverse as original oil portraits, chromolithographs, and trade cards to some extent served to distinguish among social formations. Unlike Shakespeare texts, however, many Washington texts were incorporated into the civic process, not just in the form of public parades and monuments but in annual celebrations such as the Fourth of July and Washington's Birthday. As we shall demonstrate, the most widely circulating Washington texts, with the main exception of schoolbooks, were those that took the most "reduced" form, that is, referenced key images and key events, whereas more complex texts, such as books, circulated in more circumscribed venues.

Books featuring Washington tended to be primarily nonfictional and fell into two main categories: popular histories and biographies, and school textbooks. Of the histories and biographies published around the turn of the century, the two most important and widely circulated were Paul Leicester Ford's *The True George Washington* (1896) and Owen Wister's *The Seven Ages of Washington* (1907), both of which promulgated the revisionist "humanized" portrayal of Washington.[58] But other writers, concerned to highlight the great man's great antecedents, offset this humbling vision of Washington as all too human. Their books had titles like *An Examination of the English Ancestry of George Washington, The Pedigree and History of the Washington Family Derived from Odin*, and *Washington: The Most Distinctively American Character That Our Country Has Produced.*[59] Washington's humanity, for these writers, did not reduce him to the status of an ordinary man but rather apotheosized him as the bearer of national identity. As is apparent, then, books, the most complex of Washington texts, embodied the greatest diversity of viewpoints and often explicitly related to the partisan appropriations discussed above. For example, the book tracing Washington's derivation from Odin reflected the obsession with genealogical purity that emerged as a response to the supposed threat to American values caused by increased immigration.

The renewed interest in Washington in the last decades of the nineteenth century, coupled with the revisionist humanized portrayals, might lead us to expect a proliferation of Washington plays. We might also expect that such complex texts would lend themselves to partisan invocations. Our research, however, has uncovered surprisingly few plays that feature Washington as the central character. The preface to one of the rare exceptions, Martin F. Tupper's *Washington: A Drama in Five Acts*, explains why playwrights may have been reluctant to make Washington their protagonist. "Seeing there will be found due historical authority for most of the incidents, and a fair amount of truthful consistency pervading all the characters; everywhere, an indulgent auditor, who is conversant with Washington and his times, will detect touches of quotation from celebrated speeches, and allusions to famous anecdotes."[60] Unlike scholarly or semipopular historical investigations of George Washington, which were permitted to probe his personal life and even to suggest scandal, plays, by virtue of their very "incarnation" of the Father of His Country, trod on dangerous ground.

Playwrights thus had to treat Washington with nearly the same degree of reverence as Christ, foregrounding their fidelity to received history to avoid criticism. Given the implicit pressure to conform to the attitude exemplified by Tupper, the rare appearance of Washington plays, even on patriotic holidays, comes as no surprise. Producers seem to have preferred lively fictions set in the Revolutionary period, in which Washington made brief guest appearances, to plays in which Washington was the main protagonist. Even the Vitagraph producers seemed aware of the dangers inherent in bringing the Father of His Country to life.

Washington texts took visual as well as literary forms. Washington paintings, monuments, and commercial ephemera proliferated in the late nineteenth and early twentieth centuries, these "reduced" texts serving as one of the primary venues for the circulation of key images. In keeping with the reevaluation of the American past occurring during this period, the Metropolitan Opera House exhibited a collection of Washington portraits and relics in conjunction with New York City's 1889 celebration of the centennial of Washington's inauguration.[61] Those unable to attend this and other such exhibits would nonetheless have had access to a great many visual Washington texts. In this period, relatively inexpensive chromolithographs hung on the walls of many American homes and schools. Leutze's *Washington Crossing the Delaware* was widely reproduced in chromolithograph form, as was another image referenced in the Vitagraph Washington films, *The Spirit of '76*. This famous painting by Archibald M. Willard, painted for the centennial celebration in 1876, was produced as an inexpensive chromolithograph in time for the opening day of the Philadelphia Centennial Exposition.[62]

Washington commercial ephemera circulated at least as widely as did Shakespearean, much of it achieving the requisite iconographic consistency simply by reproducing the Stuart portrait, which served as the primary Washington icon on everything from currency to ceramic mugs.[63] For example, on a Reverente cigar box that shows a picture of George and Martha at home, the picture of Washington consists of the head from the Stuart portrait mounted on the body of a gentleman in colonial costume.[64] Other commercial ephemera used key events and key images, such as the scene from Valley Forge that appeared on a calendar for the Centennial Home Insurance Company.[65]

Washington texts also appeared in more public venues, since the Father of His Country was incorporated into the civic process to a much greater extent than Shakespeare or, as we will show, Napoleon. To take one example, New York City has a number of areas named after the first president, among them Washington Market, Washington Square, and Washington Heights. The city also has at least four prominently located Washington monuments, one on the steps of the Sub-Treasury building near Wall Street (1883), the Washington Square Arch commemorating the First Inaugural (1895), an equestrian statue in Union Square (1856), and another equestrian statue near the terminus of the Williamsburg Bridge in Brooklyn (1901).

Often reflecting the interests of particular interpretive communities, public spectacles, such as pageants and parades, disseminated the key events and key images found in visual and literary expressions to a wider audience. New York's 1889 Centennial Celebration of Washington's Inauguration included two huge parades, one military and one civilian, both organized by the Department of the Army. The military parade, held on the first day of the celebration, contained over forty thousand men, and the civilian, held on the second, had strong ethnic representation, particularly from Italians, Jews, Irishmen, and Germans. The "Star Division" of the second parade featured floats of "Washington and His Generals, Mounted," "Washington Crossing the Delaware on the Night of December 25, 1776," and "Washington at Valley Forge, Winter of 1777 and 1778." Such groups as the Hebrew Benevolent and Orphan Asylum and the Bartholdi Battalion, Grammar School No. 15, Brooklyn, acted as escorts. "Division A" included "Washington's Farewell to His Officers,"

"Washington Resigning His Commission at Annapolis, December, 1783," and "The Inauguration of Gen. Washington as First President of the United States of America," these floats escorted by the Knights of Temperance and the Second Battalion, Irish Volunteers, among others.[66]

Pageants were a national rage during the first decade of the twentieth century and were often pointedly assimilationist, involving ethnically diverse groups in community celebrations of American values in which Washington often figured prominently.[67] In 1909, for example, the city of Springfield, Massachusetts held a Fourth of July Pageant. Floats made by schoolchildren depicted key events, employing the same strategies for historical authenticity as the Vitagraph films. Two of the floats, those reproducing the signing of the Declaration of Independence and Washington crossing the Delaware, were said to "show careful study of costumes, persons and situations on the part of the actors and made real the stirring events of colonial and revolutionary times to the people who look on."[68] In addition to children, the Springfield pageant included black veterans, as well as Italians and Chinese.

The incorporation of various ethnicities into these celebrations pointed to a particular partisan appropriation of Washington in line with those interpretive communities that urged immigrants to assimilate into the national mainstream while maintaining their ethnic identities. But the very pervasiveness and familiarity of the celebrations' intertextual references would have created a sense of a common culture, while at the same time serving as reference points for subsequent Washington representations, reinforcing notions of correct period detail and iconographic consistency, and underscoring the key images and key events that constituted Washington's career.

While most residents of the United States would have been hard-pressed utterly to avoid the Father of Their Country, schoolchildren would have been exposed to him almost daily, quite apart from their regular history lessons. Children in the lower elementary school grades encountered history primarily through school celebrations of national holidays, which included activities ranging from the construction of paper hatchets and cherry trees to participation in plays, recitals, and drills.[69] The Stuart portrait, the Leutze painting, and *The Spirit of '76* hung in classrooms across the nation; school libraries contained many Washington biographies.[70] Schoolchildren's primary Washington exposures, however, would have been to the state-endorsed "reduced" texts that encouraged a sense of patriotism but not necessarily particular partisan appropriations.[71]

In addition to the systemized exposure of a certain age cohort to school curricula and the more random exposures of the general population to public monuments, parades, and ephemera, "the people below Fourteenth Street" may have had contact with Washington texts specifically designed for them by uplift organizations. Unlike the parades and pageants, which seem to some extent to have embraced ethnic diversity, the uplift organizations seem to have

served as a conduit for those interpretive communities advocating total assimilation of the immigrant. As one would expect, given that organization's
extreme assimilationist agenda, Washington had a fairly high profile at the
Educational Alliance. Among the alliance's young people's clubs were the
Washington Literary Society for boys and the Martha Washington Literary
Society for girls, while the Washington Travel Club afforded members the
opportunity for vicarious journeys of patriotic purpose. "Members of the . . .
club are very extensive travellers, in imagination mostly. Under the leadership
of Miss M. A. Hamm, they have travelled to the homes of the patriots and to
the village in England where George Washington's ancestors came from."[72]
The alliance's Social Committee "prepared celebrations upon various public
holidays such as Thanksgiving Day, Lincoln's Birthday, Washington's Birthday, Memorial Day and Independence Day. The exercises were of a patriotic
order, consisting of addresses and appropriate recitations and music."[73] The
Educational Alliance also sponsored lectures, such as that on the life of Washington delivered by Professor Guthrie and accompanied by slides of the principal scenes from the Revolution.[74] The Bureau of Lectures also regularly offered Washington lectures, in both English and other languages. In 1909
alone, for example, there were lectures in Italian on "Washington and Roosevelt" and "Washington and Garibaldi," as well as a Washington lecture in
Yiddish.[75] Lectures in English, which were repeated at different locations and
times, included "George Washington and His Times," "George Washington,"
and "Unfamiliar Things about George Washington."[76]

As with Shakespeare and Dante, information concerning the circulation
patterns of Washington texts enables us more fully to illuminate the conditions of production and reception for the Vitagraph films. Although Vitagraph
undoubtedly envisioned the Washington films as another step in the journey
toward respectability, putting the Father of His Country on film nonetheless
posed problems similar to those entailed in putting him on the stage. The
disjunctions and conjunctions between the meanings produced by interpretive communities and circulated by institutions of cultural reproduction provided the intertextual framework within which Vitagraph had to maneuver to
construct a widely acceptable Washington. And the various meanings in circulation provided the intertextual framework within which viewers would
make sense of the films.

The Washington Films

In 1909 an exhibitor wrote to the *Moving Picture World* complaining about his
patrons' impoverished intertextual frames. "How many of our young folks can
tell us the origin of the American flag, or recite the Declaration of Independence? They all know of Washington on account of the hatchet story."[77] The

exhibitor clearly had minimal expectations of his audience's knowledge of Washington, but, as we have seen, Washington texts in fact pervaded turn-of-the-century America. Most members of most social formations would thus have known more about the first president than the exhibitor suggests, if only through encounters with some of the visual texts we have discussed.

How, then, would Vitagraph's Washington films have accorded with the portrayals of Washington that were in contemporary circulation—mythic, heroic, and human? The exhibitor's identification of the supposedly most salient of Washington associations notwithstanding, the Vitagraph films surprisingly omit the cherry tree, together with other apocryphal anecdotes about Washington's youth. The films in fact omit the great man's boyhood entirely, beginning instead with Washington's adventures as a sixteen-year-old surveyor. The need for historical accuracy may have motivated Vitagraph to begin the films where it did, since the historical record does not provide a detailed chronicle of Washington's early life. Whatever the motivation, however, it is surprising that films probably intended in part as uplifting fare for children did not replicate the mythic vision of Washington promulgated in the elementary schools.

But the films do accord with the heroic status embodied in the key-event and key-image Washington texts that circulated most extensively in the period, Vitagraph's attempts to "realize" many of these images pointing to the company's desire to tap the intertextual frames of all possible viewers. The inclusion of key events and images most impressed the *New York Dramatic Mirror*, which spoke of "revolutionary scenes in which Washington is the central figure, including Valley Forge, crossing the Delaware, and at Yorktown and everywhere the scenes are faithful and complete."[78] Indeed, the majority of the scenes in the two reels concern either significant battles or pivotal political developments in which Washington played a central role.

Let us take as an example the Battle of Trenton scene, shots four to six of reel two. A title precedes shot four: "While the Hessians celebrate Christmas, Washington crosses the Delaware and gains a decisive victory at Trenton, December 25, 1776."[79] Washington does not appear in shot four, which is an interior view of the Hessians drinking and carousing. Shot five realizes Leutze's painting in painstaking detail, even down to a second boat in the background. This kind of realization of a key image serves to underscore Washington's heroic status, which shot six then elaborates in more narrativized fashion. After the Hessians raise a white flag, Washington enters riding a white horse, sword in hand. He dismounts and tenderly lifts the head of a wounded Hessian officer, who offers up his sword. Washington refuses the sword, the officer dies, and Washington and the American officers remove their hats in respect.

But if the films emphasized Washington's heroism while ignoring his mythic aspects, some of the scenes also reveal a consonance with texts that

Frame enlargement from *Washington under the American Flag*. Washington's triumphant progress to New York for his inauguration.

Currier and Ives's *Washington's Reception on the Bridge at Trenton* (1857).

portrayed Washington as human. This is surprising in light of the fairly limited circulation of the revisionist view of the first president. While some of the
period's best-selling books dealt more frankly with Washington's personal life
than had hitherto been the case, other media, such as the theatre, still shied
away from such potentially controversial material. Given early cinema's strong
reliance upon theatrical antecedents, as well as Vitagraph's desire to ally with
cultural arbiters, one would expect that Vitagraph would have maintained the
relatively safe key-event/key-image narrative structure throughout the films
rather than psychologizing the central character.

To psychologize a character entails providing access to that character's
interiority through the use of cinematic signifying practices that externalize
thoughts and emotions. The Vitagraph films rely on three techniques to psychologize Washington: a cut-in to emphasize character reaction, superimposition to give access to character subjectivity, and a multishot sequence that
privileges his emotional state. Shots fourteen through sixteen of reel two,
which deal with the inauguration, stand out with respect to the standard editing patterns of the 1909 cinema. Shot fourteen, a long shot that shows Washington and others standing on a flag-draped balcony above a crowd of spectators, realizes Felix Darley's well-known painting of Washington taking the
oath of office. Washington waves to the crowd as a man carrying a Bible enters
the frame. Shot fifteen then cuts in to a three-quarter view of Washington and
the other characters on the balcony. Washington takes the oath of office and
kisses the holy book. Shot sixteen returns to the setup of shot fourteen—the
Darley painting—as the men shake hands. What is unusual about the editing
pattern of these three shots is that the cut-in, which focuses closely on Washington, transgresses Darley's original composition, momentarily disrupting
the realization. It is as if, in the middle of a public event, the viewer is granted
a private moment with the president. This privileging of a moment of psychological intensity, and at the expense of a key image's realization, presages the
classical Hollywood cinema's treatment of character.

Shot nine of reel two also psychologizes Washington, this time through the
use of superimposed visions, a technique characteristic of the early cinema. In
this shot Washington, sitting alone in his headquarters, experiences two visions. In the first he sees a dying soldier whom he has just visited. In the
second he sees himself returning home to Mount Vernon, where he is greeted
by his wife, his two stepchildren, and the slaves. Washington, like all men at
war, is lonely and wants to go home, the vision implies. Both the access to
Washington's thoughts and the nature of those thoughts—compassion, loneli-
ness—humanized the central character, as the reviewer for the *Kinematograph
and Lantern Weekly* noted. "He is greatly affected by the death of a soldier
which he witnessed, and dozing later in his own room, re-enacts the scenes in
his dream—a good 'vision' effect also showing how his imagination turns to
his wife and children and the welcome they will give him."[80]

A minimum sense of emotional affect is of course implicit in any depiction of a human being. In the historical films, however, psychologization had to operate within the constraints of the four strategies for historical authenticity enumerated above. At one extreme, the depiction of key events through key images, necessarily accompanied by correct period detail and iconographic consistency, leaves little latitude for extended psychological development. The realization of the Leutze painting, for example, permits little more than the presentation of a noble and heroic Washington intent upon military affairs. At the other extreme, the use of correct period detail and iconographic consistency to identify a historical character but not a recorded historical incident permits tremendous license with regard to psychologization. For this reason, after Washington crosses the Delaware and defeats the Hessians, the film can show his compassion toward a fallen foe through a sequence of shots that do not necessarily conform rigidly to the historical record.

Shots fourteen through twenty of reel one, detailing Washington's courtship of and marriage to Martha Custis, provide the clearest example of this strategy. This portion of the film breaks with the key-event/key-image chronological narrative to dwell on the more personal aspects of Washington's life. Shot sixteen, for example, contains many of the period's standardized representations of romance. This interior shot shows a social gathering in an elaborately appointed colonial room. Martha plays the pianoforte and Washington leans over her, turning the pages. As George puts his hand on his heart, the host and hostess notice the couple's infatuation and quietly usher the other guests from the room. In the now empty room, George kisses Martha's hand and proposes. She accepts him and the couple embrace. The fact that practically a third of the reel concerns the couple's relationship attests to the relative importance of the humanized portrayal of Washington.

The *Moving Picture World* was quite taken with this depiction of Washington's courtship, despite its reservations about Vitagraph's showing Washington in the service of another nation.

> Probably patriotic Americans will care less for this picture than for that which follows it, wherein Washington is shown serving under the flag of that country which he made free. But patriotism apart, all unite in appreciating the almost idyllic beauty of the latter part of the film. . . . For it shows Colonel Washington in love. . . . We see him as the courtier, the love dalliant, and finally as the proud bridegroom leading his pretty wife to the altar. . . . Effective and stirring as were the early parts of this film, these must, we think, yield the palm for tenderness of beauty and sentiment to that which shows the gallant young Colonel in the role of lover and bridegroom. These scenes are very beautifully staged indeed, and well photographed, and we think they would linger in the mind of the average person longer than the impression of military exploits.[81]

Our circulation evidence confirms the centrality of the mythic and heroic portrayals of Washington in turn-of-the-century American culture. Our analysis of the Vitagraph reels, however, indicates that they do not conform to the dominant pattern. The films do use key events and key images to construct an heroic Washington, but they virtually ignore the mythic Washington. At the same time, they employ several techniques to humanize their central protagonist. What factors might explain why these films departed from the most pervasively circulated Washington texts?

The films' surprising construction of a humanized Washington might have stemmed from J. Stuart Blackton's reading of the best-selling revisionist historians. Blackton desired to appeal to those social formations, including his own, among whom these texts circulated while also ensuring that his films would be accessible to the majority of viewers by including key events and key images.[82] In this respect, Vitagraph's Washington reels resemble the company's *Julius Caesar*, which adopted a mode of representation—spectacular staging—familiar primarily to restricted social formations while maintaining congruence with the most widely circulating "reduced" Shakespearean texts. The need for humanization may also have been particularly pressing given the European market, where audiences would probably not have been satisfied with a purely mythic Washington. No matter what the reason for the inclusion of the humanized portrayal, however, the absence of the mythic portrayal suggests an alignment with the authorized interpretive community of historians rather than with the institution of cultural reproduction of the schools.

The films' psychologization of Washington may also reflect Vitagraph's desire to turn out a successful product, that is, a film that met contemporary standards of drama and human interest. Or it may simply attest to the producers' unconscious employment of contemporary intertextual frames. The key event/key image component of the films calls to mind an illustrated lecture, whereas the psychologized aspects of the films accord more closely with such period texts as historical novels and plays, themselves deriving from the legacy of dramatic and fictional conventions characteristic of Western narrative. While such speculations about motivation clearly threaten to embroil us in an infinite regress of causality, we must at least acknowledge the possible influence of an expanded realm of intertextuality.

The films, however, do little to ally themselves with particular partisan appropriations of Washington. Indeed, the films avoided contention to such an extent that they were expected to do well even in the British market. Given that the revolutionary shift from Washington's service under the British flag to his service under the American flag occurs between the reels, the films do not call attention to Washington's rebellion. In fact, Washington fights the French and the Hessians far more than he fights the British. Although a German immigrant familiar with Washington's radical potential might have chosen to read the films as supporting insurrection against established authority, nothing in the films themselves particularly encourages such a reading. Rather, the films avoid a great many issues that might have clearly connected them to a particular partisan appropriation: the omnipresent slaves are simply part of the background; the political strife in the new nation, such as the Whiskey Rebellion, is absent; and the Polish, German, and French aristocrats who aided in this rebellion do not appear. With appropriations as with readings: in the main, the films seem structured to coincide with the most pervasive of Washington texts and to avoid any contention.

Visions of Napoleon

A correspondent to *The Century Magazine* noted that one author's serialized life of Napoleon had elicited some disagreement among the readers. "Objections have been made to his conclusions, which is not strange when it is remembered that hardly two historians have heretofore agreed upon even the salient points of Napoleon's character."[83] This contention, manifest in the tremendous divergence of meanings produced by interpretive communities and circulated by institutions of cultural reproduction, may in fact have accounted for the continuing interest in the French emperor among certain social formations. As was not the case with Washington, Napoleon texts offered a multiplicity of contradictory portrayals, the *Moving Picture World* indicating as much in its review of the Vitagraph Napoleon reels.

> The Napoleonic legend will probably last for all time. There is an undying fascination about the character of the "little Corsican," who, by sheer force of will, got his heel on the neck of Europe 100 years ago. He was by turns a great military commander, statesman, ruler, legislator, and withal, a thoroughly immoral man. Indeed, his reputation in the latter regard, however much historians may whitewash it, will always be ineffaceably black.[84]

Not only was he commander, statesman, and so on, he was also, among many other portrayals, a romantic and tragic figure or a villain or the quintessential self-made man. Since all these portrayals figured in the conditions of production and reception, we must examine a representative range to discern both how Vitagraph positioned itself among other cultural producers and what meanings viewers may have produced.

The tragic-romantic portrayal, which focuses on his amorous entanglements, particularly with Josephine, seems to have been one of the most prevalent in the United States at the turn of the century. As J. Holland Rose complained

> The recent revival of the Napoleonic legend is mainly due to memoirs. The astonishing output of this kind of literature in recent years may be assigned partly to the insatiable craving of the many for romance in all its branches. . . . In vain did scholars point out the mistakes which so pleasingly diversified dull reality in most of these productions. The public liked the stories and hated the documentary evidence.[85]

Others argued that Napoleon's "dull reality" offered the reader more than most fiction. Sarah Knowles Bolton, author of *Famous Leaders among Men*, noted that Napoleon's life was "more interesting and pathetic than any novel. It will always remain one of the marvels of the world."[86] Not only was the story better than any novel but it provided, said the *Moving Picture World*, great material for a film. "The story of the man is so intensely human and dramatic that even a moving picture playwright can make use of it."[87]

Richard Sheffield Dement's play, *Napoleon and Josephine, A Tragedy*, typifies the romantic approach to the Man of Destiny. As Dement explained in his preface,

> The affection of Napoleon for Josephine is proverbial, and it is hardly necessary for me to do more than affirm that, perhaps, there is no recorded instance of higher or tenderer love between man and wife, and yet, love—the strongest passion of humanity, in which the soul reaches nearest to the Infinite—was made to yield to what would certainly have been a lower incentive, had he not believed that all heaven and earth stood in waiting for his action. [88]

These romantic recountings frequently portrayed Napoleon as emotionally vulnerable to a pathetic degree, despite his prowess on the battlefield, and often had Josephine caused the great general more anguish than all his enemies. Many writers and commentators noted that Josephine failed to respond to Napoleon's constant missives from the front, implying that she had non-epistolary preoccupations. These texts described the empress as a pleasure-seeking coquette, consistently unfaithful to her spouse.[89] Other writers, many of the female memorialists especially, presented the empress as the injured party, contrasting Josephine's fidelity and constancy with Napoleon's callous expediency. Still others saw them both as victims of an imperial tragedy beyond their control. Whatever the writer's attitude toward the main characters, however, the romantic-tragic portrayal to which many of the fictionalized expressions of the Napoleon cult conformed developed Josephine's character as fully as Napoleon's.

Negative portrayals of Napoleon's character tended to come from those who objected to the Napoleon "fad" and the cultish devotion it entailed to every aspect of the great man's life and career. These critics, often essayists and academics, asserted that Napoleon was not the brilliant, energetic, self-made man portrayed by his devotees but rather an opportunistic bully who used terror and intimidation to achieve his ends. Marc Debrit, writing in 1902, summarized "every wrong he had been so often reproached with, his egotism, his nepotism, his contempt for men and women, his jealousy of those whose military glory offended his own, his harshness towards the vanquished, his lack of scruples, . . . his preference for servile mediocrity, even for rascals such as Talleyrand and Fouche." Debrit further enumerated some of the many negative comments: "madman," "rash gambler," "irritable, haughty, contemning contradiction, going beyond all bounds in his wrath, insulting his most faithful servants," "ungrateful," "never satisfied."[90]

Some thus considered Napoleon a fearsome monster. Others, however, painted him as the epitome of the self-made man, a portrayal particularly evident in children's literature. "The Little Corsican" stressed the qualities of rugged individualism so prized in late-nineteenth-century America. "The primary object in creating this bond of sympathy with Napoleon is to arouse an enthusiasm for his energy, perseverance, and unconquerable will, without which the genius of the great general would have been useless."[91] Napoleon's youthful determination in the face of adversity is made to seem as admirable as Washington's youthful integrity, anecdotes about these qualities implying that both men were predestined for greatness.

Although the portrayals of Napoleon as romantic-tragic figure, villain, and self-made man seem to have been the most widespread during our period, many others also circulated. This proliferation of portrayals reveals a much higher degree of controversy over the "real" Napoleon than existed over the "real" Washington. The reverence and admiration accorded the Father of His Country ensured that the vast majority of utterances about him fell within strictly defined parameters. But while some revered and honored Napoleon, others reviled and despised him, so that almost any utterance about the French emperor was permissible. Yet we will argue that the plethora of portrayals are less important than, and in some ways even served as the necessary fuel for, a primary appropriation of the figure of Napoleon for purposes of social distinction.

Partisan appropriations may nonetheless have formed an important component of the conditions of reception for the Vitagraph films. For some, Napoleon was the strong man on the white horse whose imposition of strict martial control ended the Terror and the chaos of the French Revolution, as we saw in The Independent's proposed solution to the railroad strikes of 1877: "bullets and bayonets, canister and grape . . . constitute the one remedy and the one duty of the hour. . . . Napoleon was right when he said that the way to deal with the mob was to exterminate it."[92] In 1911 the Edison Kinetogram referenced Napoleon's iron fist in publicity for its Price of Victory, a film showing "the glories of the invincible Emperor who stepped into the gap that the Reign of Terror had left."[93] At the other end of the political spectrum, the New York Evening Call, a socialist newspaper, reminded its readers of Napoleon's anti-populist reputation. The paper used "Napoleon" as a term of opprobrium for New York City's Police Commissioner Theodore Bingham, referring to "Napoleon Bingham" and "Our Police Napoleon" in articles describing police abuses of power.[94] More generally, "Napoleon" served then, as it does to some degree now, to designate a tyrant or egomaniac or even an outstanding figure in a particular field, such as a "Napoleon of Finance."

There is some evidence to support the claim that the Napoleon fad was related in part to the rising militarism of the 1890s that culminated in the

Spanish-American War.[95] For some, however, far from offering a model of military glory, Napoleon provided the supreme example of the horrors of war, which allowed him to serve as a cautionary figure in jingoistic turn-of-the-century America. John Davis's article in *The Arena*, "Napoleon Bonaparte: A Sketch Written for a Purpose," debunked Napoleon's reputation for martial prowess in the hopes that Napoleon would come to be "considered in a less degree the model of 'all true glory' in military affairs. . . . If I have . . . aided ever so slightly in relieving the minds of my readers from that spirit of military hero-worship which is now being so industriously and powerfully nurtured by the plutocratic press of America . . . I have accomplished my purpose."[96]

Although partisan appropriations of Napoleon did exist, then, they were of minimal importance in comparison with the partisan appropriations made of Washington, since the latter was a far more resonant presence in turn-of-the-century America. But just as Washington's primary appropriation was for the purposes of building cultural consensus among diverse social formations, an appropriation similar to Shakespeare's, the appropriation of Napoleon served principally to distinguish among social formations, in a manner similar to Dante's—although obviously both historical figures contributed to the construction of a sense of "high culture." The strongest proof of the dissimilarity between Washington and Napoleon and the similarity between Napoleon and Dante comes from our circulation evidence. Washington texts not only pervaded all aspects of American society but occupied a prominent position in most institutions of cultural reproduction, ensuring that members of all social formations would have some degree of exposure to this figure. Both Napoleon and Dante texts, however, had a relatively limited circulation, remaining largely absent from the more pervasive institutions of cultural reproduction. Those who wished to participate in the Napoleon and Dante crazes thus had to make a special effort to acquire both artifacts and knowledge. Although institutions of cultural reproduction such as libraries and museums offered some degree of access, economic constraints would generally have prohibited members of many social formations from encountering certain kinds of Dante or Napoleon texts. In order to explore this social distinction further, though, we need to examine the circulation of Napoleon texts.

Napoleon Circulation

In 1894, reviewing a Napoleonically themed theatrical production, the *New York Times* commented on the raging Napoleon fad. "It happens just now that it is the fashion to read about him and to know, or pretend to know, all about his daily habits and personal peculiarities."[97] By the time Vitagraph produced its films the interest in Napoleon had somewhat abated, but the *Moving Picture World* still confidently expected these reels to resonate with a well-established intertextual frame. "Everybody with the smallest pretention to education is so familiar with the trouble of Napoleon and Josephine that we predict great popularity for this fine piece of moving picture work."[98] The number of foreign Napoleon films attests to the emperor's popularity in Europe. But among American studios only Vitagraph—which had to appeal to its large foreign market—and Edison made Napoleon films, leading us to question the emperor's American popularity during the first and second decades of the century. Examining the circulation patterns of Napoleon texts may help to explain why Vitagraph might have made these reels at a time when the Napoleon craze had already peaked among elites and what audiences might have made of them.

Book and magazine publishers enthusiastically fostered the Napoleon fad, turning out histories, historical novels, biographies, memoirs, and scores of articles on topics ranging from "Napoleon as a Book-Lover" to "Napoleon and America."[99] Between 1884 and 1893 twenty-eight books appeared on the subject of Napoleon. In 1894 seven more were published, in 1895 fourteen, and in 1896 another seven.[100] Public libraries acquired many of these publications, and, judging from the scattered evidence available, patrons avidly read them.[101] Members of all social formations would have had access to public libraries, but Napoleonic literature also found favor in more exalted circles. The Society for Literary Knowledge, a men's literary club that met at New York City's Harvard and Athletic Clubs and drew members from Park and Fifth Avenues, Scarsdale, and Boston's Beacon Hill, discussed "The Writings of Napoleon at St. Helena" in 1905 and, in 1911, "The Woman Napoleon Loved," by Tighe Hopkinson.[102]

Rather than simply enumerate and describe a wide range of Napoleonic publications, we shall use the differences between two important biographies by Ida Tarbell and William Sloane—both of which commenced serial publication in November 1894, the Tarbell continuing until April 1895 and the Sloane until October 1896—to position Vitagraph very precisely vis-à-vis other cultural producers. Vitagraph publicity references the Tarbell biography, and the Napoleon films bear a much stronger resemblance to Tarbell's vision of history than to Sloane's, since, as we will see, it made better sense for Vitagraph to emulate the former. Ida Tarbell, later to become famous as a muckraking journalist, hurriedly produced *A Short Life of Napoleon* as a series of articles to accompany *McClure's* reproductions of Gardiner G. Hubbard's collection of Napoleon engravings. *McClure's* commissioned the work to compete with *The Century Magazine's* biography, written by William Milligan Sloane, professor of history at Princeton. In contrast to *McClure's* rushed production, *The Century* had supported Sloane's years of research in French archives, among the Ashburnham papers at the Medici library in Florence, and in the English Record Office.[103] Not only did the fifteen-cent *McClure's* cost less than *The Century* but the Tarbell articles also appeared in a relatively inexpensive (fifty-cent) paperback edition in 1895. The Sloane did not come out until the following year, when it was issued as a four-volume set.[104]

The two authors' respective approaches to biography, Tarbell producing extended captions and Sloane a thoroughly researched history, are a function of the two journals' different conditions of production, which required choosing members of two quite different interpretive communities to author the respective Napoleon series. Measured by both qualitative and quantitative indices, *The Century Magazine* and *McClure's* seem to have had quite distinct perceptions of their target audiences and cultural function. Richard Watson Gilder, author of one of the Paolo and Francesca poems quoted in the previous chapter, served as *The Century's* long-term editor. Gilder's association with the antidemocratic wing of the Arnoldians and his status as arbiter of genteel culture were reflected in his journal, which mixed reactionary politics with high-culture aesthetics, printing articles such as "The Churches of Provence" (by one Mrs. Schuyler van Rensselaer) and "Old Dutch Masters" as well as letters from readers opposing women's suffrage and the influx of immigrants.[105] *McClure's*, a mass-market magazine founded by an Irish immigrant who had for a time worked with Gilder at *The Century*, strove to maintain a veneer of respectability while offering its readers gossip columns, celebrity profiles, and generalized muckraking.[106]

Sloane's and Tarbell's approaches to Napoleon were well suited to their respective publishers. Sloane claimed that he endeavored to show Napoleon "not merely as a man, a ruler, or a conqueror, but as a force in history."[107] Foregrounding his membership in an elite authorized interpretive community, the professor deliberately positioned his biography against the glut of Napoleona on the market, contrasting his objective treatment of the historical facts with the gossipy approach that characterized a great many other biographies. According to Sloane, memoirs—especially those penned by women—provided the scandalous fodder for biographies that pandered to the reader's prurient interests rather than analyzing the emperor's historical importance. "No one has suffered more at the hands of woman than Bonaparte. Mme. Junot and Mme. de Remusat forgot nothing which could place his rude passions in glaring contrast with their own chastity. . . . The buxom Mme. de Stael . . . turned against her antagonist the weapons of her spite, so ably wielded by her clever pen."[108] Undoubtedly aware of his competition in *McClure's*, Sloane implicitly compared his approach to Tarbell's.

> The "life" has not been put forth as a new series of memoirs, or as a collection of well-known anecdotes . . . but as a serious and scholarly historical study. . . . There is a type of mental flabbiness which would not be satisfied with anything short of a gossip's view of Napoleon, and to which the serious interest with which the world is now subjecting the ingredients of his reputation to a sort of quantitative analysis is nothing more than a mere "fad." The hunger for fiction . . . is in danger of becoming a sort of literary bulimia.[109]

Although Tarbell grounded her work in historical sources, she indeed relied heavily upon memoirs and anecdotes, presenting a much more "gossipy" view

of Napoleon than did Sloane, in keeping with *McClure's* emphasis on personalities. Her book used a key-event/key-image chronological narrative structure
laced with a heavy dose of psychologization of the central characters. In a
sense, the text was ancillary to the Napoleon engravings, the title page specifically foregrounding the images by declaring that the volume contained "250
illustrations from the Hon. Gardiner G. Hubbard's Collection of Napoleon
Engravings, Supplemented by Pictures from the Collections of Prince Victor
Napoleon, Prince Roland Bonaparte, Baron Larrey and Others."[110] Sloane, by
comparison, used fewer pictures and to different purpose, documenting his
account with portraits and maps but generally avoiding dramatic illustrations
of Napoleon's personal life.

The images in the Tarbell would themselves have been sufficient to provide
a synoptic presentation of Napoleon's life, but the text offered a psychological
elaboration on the visually depicted events. Tarbell frequently resorted to data
from memoirs and letters to describe Napoleon's emotional state. For example, she quoted a letter from Napoleon complaining about Josephine's failure
as a correspondent. "My life is a perpetual nightmare. A black presentiment
makes breathing difficult. I am no longer alive; I have lost more than life, more
than happiness, more than peace. . . . Write to me ten pages; that is the only
thing that can console me in the least."[111] Tarbell's omniscient third-person
narration also gives us access to the characters' thoughts and feelings. For
example, the book represented the emotional trauma of Napoleon's divorce
from Josephine as if it were attempting to position the reader with Napoleon.
Describing Napoleon's feelings after the incident, Tarbell used outward appearances to externalize inner emotions. "There is no doubt but that Napoleon
suffered deeply over the separation. . . . For a long time he sat silent and de-
pressed, his head on his hand. When he was summoned he rose, his face
distorted with pain, and went into the empress's apartment."[112] As our discussion of Vitagraph's films will show, the producers not only referred to the
Tarbell as a source but emulated its anecdotal, gossipy approach to history.

The illustrations in the Tarbell and Sloane are but two examples of the
outpouring of collections of Napoleonic imagery that the period's fascination
with Napoleon stimulated. Although the figure of Napoleon circulated primarily in the form of relatively expensive collectibles, his image occasionally
appeared in commercial venues.[113] As they did with Washington, manufacturers put Napoleon to work but in this case mainly in association with upscale
goods, connecting his figure with luxury consumables in venues ranging from
coffee cans to cigar advertisements. In addition to linking Napoleon with
"good taste," many commercial ephemera reinforced the key-image/key-event
approach to history. Examples include a souvenir "Napoleon Album" issued
by the Allen and Ginter Tobacco Company and a "Great Battles Series" of
cigarette cards issued by the American Tobacco Company.[114]

Although Napoleon's lack of incorporation into the civic process meant that the Man of Destiny appeared neither on public monuments nor in public celebrations such as pageants and parades, Napoleon was far more popular and prominent in theatrical circles than Washington, owing to the different positions of the two historical characters in turn-of-the-century American culture.[115] As we have noted, a theatrical incarnation of the revered Washington required delicate handling, whereas, in the United States at least, Napoleon did not enjoy the same venerable status. Moreover, the melodramatic aspects of his career provided excellent material for playwrights. Not surprisingly, Napoleonic plays reflected the range of disagreement over the emperor's character, some featuring him as hero and others as villain.

As with Dante texts, then, Napoleon texts seem to have circulated primarily among certain restricted social formations and in the less pervasive institutions of cultural reproduction. Unlike Dante texts, however, for which we have found comparatively little evidence of broader circulation, Napoleon texts, particularly in product form, did to some extent appear in venues (such as cigarette cards) that would have been accessible to immigrants and the working classes. Nonetheless, Napoleon texts were not systematically aimed at these populations, in contrast to Shakespeare and Washington texts, which constituted an important component of the offerings of schools and uplift organizations. Since most grade-school history focused primarily on the United States, Napoleon would not have appeared very often in the curriculum. The city of New York and the state of Pennsylvania, did, however, recommend Eugene Foa's *Boy Life of Napoleon* for inclusion in school libraries, although none of the other children's Napoleon books of the period are included on the recommended list.[116]

The People's Institute and the Bureau of Lectures occasionally sponsored talks on Napoleon, many of which were given in the context of lecture series on modern European history. In 1909 the Bureau of Lectures featured several talks on Napoleon, including one delivered by William J. Tilley at the YMCA Hall, Colored Men's branch. For the most part, these lectures appear to have been relatively unembellished, event-oriented histories rather than anecdotal biographies. For example, the eminent Columbia University historian James T. Shotwell gave two lectures for the People's Institute in 1909, "Napoleon—Austerlitz to Waterloo" and "Napoleon and the Foundation of Modern France."[117] "The people below Fourteenth Street," had they the interest, could also have gained access to Napoleonic texts through other means. Public libraries circulated many Napoleon volumes, the Educational Alliance library subscribed to both *The Century Magazine* and *McClure's*, and newspapers such as the *New York Evening Call* (and undoubtedly others) referred to Napoleon. As we have suggested, it is reasonable to assume that members of particular ethnic communities—Italians, Russians, Poles, and Germans, as well as the French—would have heard of Napoleon from their relatives, some of whom might have lived through the Napoleonic era.

Vitagraph production still from *The Life Drama of Napoleon Bonaparte and the Empress Josephine of France*. The courtship.

Although workers and immigrants may thus have encountered the character of Napoleon at least occasionally, they would have had relatively few opportunities to engage in the fully narrativized romantic-tragic portrayal most developed in literary and dramatic intertexts. More likely, they would have been exposed to Napoleon through commercial ephemera that presented the emperor as a relatively empty signifier of luxury or as a historical figure defined primarily by a series of battles. Those few intertexts aimed directly at these marginalized populations emanated from the same interpretive community that produced *The Century's* biography, that is, academic historians.

The Napoleon Films

Vitagraph's Washington films positioned themselves within a highly delimited range of similar portrayals of the Father of His Country, the differences among which were subsumed beneath the conflation of Washington with flag, nation, and patriotism, although the films aligned themselves more strongly with the

Vitagraph production still from *The Life Drama of Napoleon Bonaparte and the Empress Josephine of France*. Josephine reacts to news of the impending divorce.

heroic and human portrayals of Washington than with his more mythic aspects. By contrast, Vitagraph had available to it a wide range of highly divergent portrayals of Napoleon, all existing outside any overarching containment. And some of these divergent portrayals, such as the romantic-tragic depiction, themselves contained significant variations—pro-Josephine or pro-Napoleon, for example. Therefore, as with *Francesca di Rimini*, we can identify the particular intertexts, as well as the more general intertextual frame, that the Vitagraph producers drew upon. And, as with *Francesca*, adducing a wider range of intertexts permits us to speculate about intertextually extrapolated readings of the Napoleon films.

As we saw at the outset of this chapter, Vitagraph's producers facilitated our task of identifying relevant intertexts, since their publicity stated that they relied upon sources such as the Tarbell biography, various memoirs, and specific paintings. Moreover, anecdotal evidence from J. Stuart Blackton's life confirms not only the producer's proximity to particular texts but his participation in the Napoleon craze. Given what we know about Blackton's social ambitions, he would very likely have been aware of the social distinction to be gained through acquiring Napoleonic artifacts and knowledge. Even Black-ton's daughter, Marion Trimble, frames her father's obsession in terms of the family's establishment in "the ranks of the nouveau riche," Napoleon serving to nourish her father's "vanity" and her stepmother's "vaulting social ambi-tions." Trimble tells how her family collected Napoleona such as "priceless . . . miniatures," "costly" reproductions, and "beautifully bound volumes," trav-eled to France, where her father "brooded over Napoleon's Tomb," and even held Napoleon pageants at home, featuring William Humphrey, the star of the films.[118] In light of Vitagraph's identification of its sources, it seems that Black-ton belonged to that group whom William Sloane accused of exhibiting "a type of mental flabbiness which would not be satisfied with anything short of a gossip's view of Napoleon."

While such biographical material helps to illuminate conditions of produc-tion, an examination of formal homologies between the films and Vitagraph's acknowledged intertexts provides further insights. These formal components include, among others, narrative structure, the selection of incidents for inclu-sion, and strategies for character psychologization. As we have seen, Vitagraph claimed that its actors wore the costumes originally used in *More than Queen* and cast William Humphrey, who had appeared as Napoleon in the play, in the leading role. But the similarities of the Vitagraph films to *More than Queen* extend beyond costumes and casting, since both the play and the first reel, *The Life Drama of Napoleon Bonaparte and the Empress Josephine of France*, elaborate on the same episode in Napoleon's life. The *New York Dramatic Mirror* summa-rized the play's plot: "It is with the private rather than the public life of these famous personages that the play deals, its theme being the love of Napoleon and Josephine from its birth in 1795 to the divorce in 1809."[119] The play psychologized the characters by focusing upon the interaction between Napo-leon and Josephine, which points to one of the main contrasts between the figures of Washington and Napoleon. A few Washington texts, the Vitagraph films included, did psychologize the Father of His Country, but only within strict confines, whereas the latitude for Napoleonic psychologization was far greater, particularly, as we have suggested, in texts that constructed a roman-tic-tragic portrayal—novels, plays, and even the Tarbell biography. For these reasons, we shall look closely at the strategies for psychologization employed in the Vitagraph Napoleon films.

As its title suggests, *The Life Drama* focuses on a key dramatic moment in the lives of the imperial couple, treating it in a manner consistent with that of some contemporary films, with characters psychologized through visions, performance, editing, and camera movement. The film proper opens and closes with Josephine's visions. In the first shot of the story (as distinct from the six-shot prologue that introduces the characters) Josephine wanders in a garden on her island home. She meets a fortune-teller, who grants her a (superimposed) vision of herself in imperial garb upon a throne. The preceding intertitle states, "A fortune teller tells Josephine she will be more than a queen but she will lose this honor before her death." Some may dispute the subjective status of this vision, but there can be no debate about the subjectivity of the vision in the final shot of the film. The shot shows the divorced and dejected Josephine at Malmaison. A superimposed Napoleon fades in and then out as Josephine enters a room. She walks to a bust of her former husband, smiles, and kisses it. While Josephine plays the harp, the superimposed Napoleon reappears and waves a hand in rejection. Josephine reaches for the disappearing apparition and then staggers around the room, crying.

Despite the melodramatic connotations of staggering and sobbing, Vitagraph publicity and reviews claimed for the film a relatively subdued performance style that contributed to the emotional impact. The *Film Index* quoted Blackton as saying:

> We have gotten away from the old style of motion picture acting in this production, and have followed the most approved dramatic style. Formerly, when a motion picture actor wanted to indicate "impatience" he would pace the floor and tear his hair. The identical condition of mind is more impressively portrayed by comparative repose—an actor seated at a table nervously handling whatever may be within his reach will, by his attitude, convey the impression more certainly and convincingly. . . . The old method approximated that of the melodramatic actor. We hope to bring our future productions up to the standard of legitimate drama.[120]

The *New York Dramatic Mirror*'s reviewer, most probably Frank Woods, echoed Blackton's sentiment. "There is none of the hasty action which has marred so many previous Vitagraph subjects, but each character moves with natural feeling and effective restraint that distinguishes the high-class actor from the melodramatic."[121] In this period, many in the film industry, like Blackton and Woods, saw a new acting style, one based on natural feeling and restraint, as a more effective means of externalizing the thoughts and emotions of individuated characters than the "old method" employed by actors playing the stock characters of the melodramatic stage. Hence, it is not surprising that they tried to position the performances in terms of the new style, despite the actors' continued employment of the old.

Let us look more closely at how the first reel's signifying practices construct character psychologization, specifically those used in shots four through eight, which deal with the couple's divorce. The company's discourse about these shots refers to "a strongly pathetic scene," describes the "fifth scene" as "perhaps the most poignant," and says that "Napoleon and Josephine are both strongly moved and an affecting parting takes place."[122] In shot six Josephine enters Napoleon's bedroom, sees her husband, and starts backward; then the couple embraces, she kneeling before him. A cut-in to a closer shot privileges the emotional moment, as Josephine cries while Napoleon tries to comfort her, but then cries himself. In shot eight Josephine reels from the room, and the camera pans to follow Napoleon to his bed, where he kneels and cries again.

Napoleon, The Man of Destiny also addresses a pivotal moment in the emperor's career, although one less popularly narrativized than the imperial divorce. "The picture opens with Napoleon at Malmaison after the Battle of Waterloo. He visits the room where Josephine died, enters slowly, walks sadly around, looks at her portrait, then sits in a chair and falls asleep."[123] Although this description might imply an emotional crisis similar to that depicted in the first reel, the film actually consists of what we refer to as an integrated tableau structure. Key events in the emperor's career alternate with shots of a "present tense" Napoleon providing a gestural commentary on the past action, with the exception of one shot of the emperor at St. Helena that foreshadows the future.[124] Both the degree of psychologization and the strategies for its implementation differ from those of the first reel, in that, in a sense, the second reel consists entirely of a representation of the character's mental processes. Whereas the first reel externalizes the characters' thoughts and emotions primarily through performance, augmented by a cut-in at a particularly intense moment, the second reel does so through the integrated tableau form that literally shows the viewer what the character is thinking.[125]

The first shot of *Napoleon, The Man of Destiny* depicts Napoleon's tender feelings for the deceased Josephine through setting, props, and performance. He enters Josephine's bedroom at Malmaison, kneels by the bed, extends his hand to her portrait, and touches a bust of his late first wife. Here, as in the first film, the narrating agency permits access to Napoleon's thoughts and feelings through the character's gestures, which interpret the depicted historical events. But in *Napoleon, The Man of Destiny*, the narrating agency actually cedes narrative authority to the Napoleon character, as his memories motivate the flashbacks.

As we have seen, in terms of their overall romantic-tragic orientation (coupled with character psychologization) both Napoleon reels resemble the Tarbell biography more than the Sloane. Structurally, however, the first reel resembles *More than Queen*, inasmuch as it focuses on a particular aspect of the emperor's life rather than his entire career. But the parallels between the second reel and the Tarbell biography are striking. Key events structure the chronological narratives of both the biography and the second reel, both texts representing these events in key images: the Tarbell's reproductions of famous paintings and the film's realizations. Granted, the film's reliance upon key events and images also resembles the overall narrative organization of the Sloane or any other historical chronology. But the Tarbell, unlike the Sloane, attempts to provide access to the characters' subjectivity through devices characteristic of the historical novel—interior monologues, the use of emotionally descriptive adjectives, and authorial omniscience—while the film does so through the devices we have enumerated above.

Frame enlargement from *Napoleon, The Man of Destiny*. A realization of Jacques Louis David's *Coronation of Napoleon and Josephine*.

Jacques Louis David's *Coronation of Napoleon and Josephine* (1805–07).

Frame enlargement from *Napoleon, The Man of Destiny*. A realization of Horace Vernet's *Napoleon's Farewell to the Old Guard*.

Lithograph after Horace Vernet's *Napoleon's Farewell to the Old Guard*.

The intertextual homologies that we have identified as illuminating the conditions of production may have structured readings of the films to some extent but would not, of course, have precluded readings predicated on exposures to a wide array of other texts.[126] Napoleon texts may not have pervaded the culture to the same degree as Washington texts, but they did circulate widely enough to ensure that most members of most social formations would have been aware that Napoleon was a historical figure and probably would have encountered some visual representations of him as well. Hence, the vast majority of viewers would have made some connection, however tenuous, between the Vitagraph films and their prior knowledge of the emperor. Even those viewers lacking any exposure to Napoleon but familiar with the dramatic conventions of other films would have been able to relate to the first reel as a variation on tragic love stories. Given that the integrated tableau was fairly uncommon, the second reel would perhaps have been less accessible to viewers lacking Napoleonic exposure, but even they would probably have understood that the film was presenting "history" and might well have enjoyed the spectacular battle scenes and elaborate sets and costumes.

Viewers equipped with more detailed intertextual frames may, however, have produced a wider range of readings. Those acquainted with current trends in historiography may well have rejected the films' reduction of the complexities of historical causality to a great-man/great-event paradigm.[127] Yet even those who did ascribe to a great-man theory of history and thus to some extent equated history with biography could have produced very different readings of the Vitagraph films. Viewers who were familiar with the Sloane approach and accustomed to an event-oriented history may have preferred the second reel's synoptic overview of Napoleon's career to the pathetic rendering of Napoleon's love life presented in the first, whereas those enamored of the Tarbell and the various memoirs may have preferred what Sloane condemned as the "gossip's" approach to history. For instance, the *Moving Picture World* compared reel one favorably to those films that had "made the mistake of following too closely the written records of such [historical] characters."[128] Viewers most familiar with the Napoleon-as-villain portrayal may have seen the battle scenes as unmitigated carnage rather than enjoyable spectacle but have taken pleasure in Napoleon's comeuppance at the end. More didactically inclined viewers may have reveled in the opportunity to see history brought to life. Those who saw Napoleon as epitomizing the self-made man may have derived inspiration from, or learned the perils of, the aggressive pursuit of fame and glory. Consumers of luxury goods that referenced Napoleon in their packaging or advertising may even have welcomed the film as an excursion into the life-styles of the rich and famous.

Clearly, these and many other intertextually extrapolated readings are conceivable, but in fact the films themselves would have encouraged a delimited range of readings, as the *Moving Picture World*'s review of the first reel indicates. The reviewer referred to the emperor as "a thoroughly immoral man" whose "reputation . . . will always be ineffaceably black." But he also spoke of "Josephine's anguish" and "Napoleon's gloomy determination" and characterized some of the scenes as particularly "affecting."[129] This critic seems to have subscribed to the Napoleon-as-villain portrayal, but he nonetheless recognized that the Vitagraph films allied themselves with the romantic-tragic portrayal. Yet, as we have said, the significant variations within the romantictragic portrayal would themselves have inflected viewer response. On the one hand, the film's psychologization of and sympathetic affect toward both parties may have satisfied both pro-Napoleon and pro-Josephine viewers. On the other hand, those exposed primarily to the female memorialists, whom Sloane accused of portraying Josephine as the injured party and foregrounding Napoleon's "rude passions," may have felt that the films were unduly sympathetic toward the emperor.

Of course, given the circulations of intertexts discussed above, relatively few viewers may have been able to decipher the films through the intertextual frame of a Napoleon-specific romantic-tragic portrayal. We should, however, point to a curious anomaly earlier seen with Shakespeare. Although admittedly rare, we have found instances in which members of elite interpretive communities, such as the theatrical progressive Ben Greet with Shakespeare or Columbia professor James Shotwell with Napoleon, took interpretations and modes of representation normally the preserve of the dominant social formations and circulated them among workers and immigrants. Issues of social status and the ability to achieve cultural distinction aside, such evidence points to instances of parallel exposures at the very top and bottom of the social spectrum.

As we have said, the partisan appropriations of Napoleon were fairly insignificant in the United States. Nonetheless, viewers could have used the films to support their political positions. For example, those opposing America's aggressive imperial expansion might have pointed to Napoleon's dismal end as an object lesson for would-be conquerors. But the primary appropriation of Napoleon was for the purposes of social distinction. The film would have accommodated this appropriation perfectly, since the competence to produce various readings would have demonstrated the viewer's engagement with the fad and marked him or her as socially distinct—assuming he or she had the requisite social status. For those less fortunately positioned in the social hierarchy, Napoleon, unlike Shakespeare or even Washington, probably would not have been conducive to upward mobility. This is not to deny the possibility of an individual's involvement with Napoleon in the hope of gaining some social distinction, as may have been the case with Blackton. But the oral tradition of the immigrant whose ancestors had personally experienced the Napoleonic Wars would have counted for very little compared to the expensive artifacts or detailed familiarity with Napoleonic romances of a member of those social formations most actively involved in the Napoleon fad, since, as we argued with Francesca da Rimini, members of marginalized social formations would have had few opportunities to deploy their cultural capital.

In view of the relatively restricted circulation of Napoleon texts and their overarching appropriation for purposes of social distinction, why did Vitagraph make the Napoleon films? Given Napoleon's popularity among social formations whose members probably did not normally attend the nickelodeon, Vitagraph may have hoped to lure in new viewers or at least gain a certain measure of social cachet for the studio. As the laudatory reviews suggest, the Napoleon films may well have garnered Vitagraph a certain status within the industry. And they would certainly have performed well in the European export market so vital to Vitagraph's financial health. The films may also have been an extension of Blackton's social and cultural obsessions, allowing him to travel to France and to impress his friends. But Blackton was not engaging in sheer self-indulgence. The producers' personal and pecuniary motives notwithstanding, most viewers would have known enough about Napoleon to make the films of interest.

Conclusion

Washington's circulation through state-endorsed institutions of cultural reproduction resulted in familiarity with the character across all social formations. Indeed, given his centrality to the project of consolidating national identity at a time of perceived crisis, Washington circulated even more widely than Shakespeare, appearing in an array of public manifestations, from parades to statuary, and monuments. Although divergent portrayals—the mythic, the heroic, and the human—existed simultaneously, the circulation of a very "reduced" portrayal, Washington as iconic hero, facilitated this ubiquity and encouraged his widespread acceptance. Washington's reduced image connoted "patriotism," but a patriotism invoked at such an abstract level that it could be embraced by political factions pursuing antithetical goals.

It made perfect sense for Vitagraph to produce a Washington film, given that the diffused patriotism suggested by the character's reduced image might serve to improve the company's reputation among cultural arbiters. Yet while Vitagraph's films incorporated the key events and key images central to Washington's reduced form, they also referenced a humanized vision of Washington that had only a limited circulation within certain social formations. Viewers aware of current trends in historical scholarship would have seen a relatively familiar Washington in the humanized figure of the Vitagraph films, but the majority of nickelodeon patrons would probably have been more familiar with his reduced iconic form.

But the humanized portrayal, carefully presented, served to appeal to those social formations not yet regularly attending the nickelodeons while also entertaining current patrons. Vitagraph had to find a way to produce a *dramatic* rendering of the nation's most important and revered human symbol, a feat only very rarely attempted on the stage or in literature. Their solution was to ally themselves with one of the most influential interpretive communities, historians, in order to sanction what otherwise might have seemed irreverent—that is, the films' humanization rather than mythification of the title character. At the same time, the signifying practices the film employed to psychologize Washington by revealing his emotional states (the vision scene, the cut-in, and so forth) would have resonated with an audience by now accustomed to such conventions. Vitagraph thus sought to appease its current customers while not offending, and possibly even attracting, members of other social formations.

Viewers of the Vitagraph films no doubt enjoyed the dramatic elements, reading them through either Washington-specific intertexts or their knowledge of cinematic conventions, and would certainly have recognized the film's invocation of the diffused patriotism Washington connoted. Yet would viewing the film have served to incorporate audience members into a reworked hegemonic order, as the film industry implicitly claimed and those progressives supporting the new medium fervently hoped? Probably not, since we believe that the reduced form of Washington bore the same relationship to the hegemonic order as the reduced form of Shakespeare. In other words, familiarity and engagement with these cultural figures on this level entailed participation in, but not necessarily incorporation into, the hegemonic order.

Napoleon intertexts circulated in a far more restricted manner than did Washington intertexts, but, unconstrained by any overarching ideological utility, the character of Napoleon was subject to extremely wide-ranging interpretations and modes of representation. The resulting array of divergent expressions allows for a fairly specific determination of the producers' referents. With Washington, Vitagraph departed from very contained portrayals only by implicitly referencing the interpretive community of historians to justify their psychologization of the character. With Napoleon, however, Vitagraph deliberately rejected the historians' approach, since it would have unduly restricted the films' dramatic potential by limiting the incorporation of the romantic-tragic portrayal most prevalent in fictional Napoleonic intertexts. Vitagraph chose instead to rely on interpretations and modes of representation that emulated the theatre, as well as drawing on a popular history written by a nonhistorian who used fictional devices.

In terms of reception, however, we have demonstrated a wide range of possible readings grounded in a variety of intertexts, some of which circulated in restricted social formations and others of which circulated more widely, the Napoleon reels in this regard resembling *Francesca di Rimini*. This resemblance extends to the social uses made of these cultural characters. In both cases individual interpretations could contribute to viewers' social distinction provided they had the requisite cultural capital to produce acceptable interpretations and the requisite social standing to benefit from them. Hence, those such as European immigrants, who may have had the most direct and tangible knowledge of Napoleon, most probably derived little social status from it. In an era dominated by great-man history, the lived experiences of members of marginalized social formations would have counted for very little, even had one of these immigrants encountered members of social formations who participated in the Napoleon fad. Furthermore, the currency of this cultural capital would have been worthless among those contemporary marginalized social formations not participating in the fad. But as with Dante, the distinction function was not at odds with the project of cultural consensus, serving to underscore social hierarchies and thereby to maintain the hegemonic order.

Biblical Qualities:

Moses

ALMOST TWO YEARS after the release of the final reel of Vitagraph's five-reel *Life of Moses, Motography* reported that

> in Minneapolis there is a theatre, the Milo, that shows nothing but Biblical films. It shows all of them it can get, it shows them every night, and its patrons won't have anything else. . . . A majority of the patrons of the Milo are Jews, many of them Russian immigrants. . . . It is remarkable how proud the older ones are— how loyal to their race history. The very appearance of Moses on the canvas is the signal for wild applause that often continues for several minutes.[1]

Vitagraph's publicity for its Moses films, as well as other scattered evidence, would indicate that the Jews of Minneapolis were not alone in their "wild applause" and that the company's first biblical blockbuster succeeded admirably. But how could it have done otherwise? In comparison to such potentially vexed subjects as George Washington or subjects of such potentially limited appeal as Francesca da Rimini, or even to such controversial religious figures as Christ, Moses may initially have appeared not only widely familiar but wonderfully noncontroversial. But while the former is true, the latter is not. The incarnation on film of the Jewish liberator and lawgiver touched directly on one of the most divisive issues in contemporary religious circles. Putting Moses and the biblical events to which he was central "on the canvas" forced the Vitagraph producers to steer a course between liberal and fundamentalist theologians of both Jewish and Christian persuasion, who fervently espoused opposing positions on the "truth" of the Bible.

In this chapter we look first at the distinctive conditions of production for Vitagraph's *The Life of Moses*, exploring the company's probable motivations for making the films and the way Vitagraph diverged from the usual patterns of production, distribution, and exhibition in a conscious attempt to compete with producers of religious commodities. Next, we examine the period's theological disputes, showing how Vitagraph's promotional appeals sought to position their films with regard to contemporary religious discourses of the natural and the supernatural. Finally, in relation to partisan appropriations of Moses, we demonstrate that Vitagraph aimed at conformity with an overarching appropriation while trying to avoid the surprisingly numerous contentious appropriations of the period.

Although undoubtedly aware of the theological disputes, the Vitagraph producers probably chose Moses as the subject of their most prestigious and longest biblical production because they calculated that it would appeal to the broadest possible audience, while alienating as few viewers as possible, giving it the potential to generate profits as large as those of the filmed passion plays. As the *Film Index* pointed out, next to Christ, Moses was preeminent among biblical characters. "In the biblical history of the World, if we eliminate the divinity of Christ, there is no one personality which stands out so prominently as that of Moses, the liberator and lawgiver of his race."[2] Indeed, the New Testament mentions Moses more often than any other Old Testament figure.[3] Some period rhetoric even drew parallels between Moses and Christ. For example, Lydia Robinson offered a Christian perspective on the Jewish leader. "To him we stand in a very different relation from that in which we stand to Buddha or Mohammed. . . . Moses and Jesus are in our minds inseparably connected. In Moses we see a direct predecessor of Jesus,—the point of departure of the great religious movement which has found its historical conclusion and spiritual perfection in Jesus."[4]

But a Moses film, unlike a Christ film, would appeal to Jews as well as Christians. Then, as now, all practicing Jews, regardless of ethnic, class, or religious differences, accorded Moses and the Pentateuch a central position in their cultural identity. Every synagogue, whether Reform or Orthodox, had an ark containing the Torah scrolls, the Hebrew texts of Genesis, Exodus, Leviticus, Numbers, and Deuteronomy. A portion of the Pentateuch, usually translated from the Hebrew into the congregation's vernacular, was read each Sabbath and served as the text for homiletic exegesis. "Even in theologically liberal congregations which take for granted that the scroll contains a variety of materials from different times and sources, the reader will recite, 'This is the Torah that Moses placed before the people of Israel to fulfill the word of God.' "[5]

In its publicity Vitagraph stressed that the films would appeal to members of all sects. "One of the most important features about this Life of Moses series that we cannot impress too strongly upon you is the fact that the pictures are non-sectarian. They are proving as popular with Hebrews as with Christians."[6] The *New York Dramatic Mirror* reported that "upward of one hundred letters have been received by the company commending the series, and many of these have come from Jewish people, who are much gratified at the broad spirit and fine dignity with which the great Biblical subject is being treated."[7] As we will see, however, despite this broad appeal, sharply contrasting visions of Moses and biblical interpretations complicated Vitagraph's representation of the Jewish leader.

Vitagraph's *The Life of Moses*

The Vitagraph films adhere in the main to the life of Moses as presented in the Pentateuch. For those readers without benefit of religious indoctrination, we reproduce Vitagraph's fairly pithy summary of the five reels.

> The first reel of the series deals with the condition of the Jews in Egypt prior to the birth of Moses when they were under the most abject slavery. The picture opens upon a scene illustrating the cruelty of the taskmasters. Then follows the dictating and promulgating of the decree that all males of the Jews shall be killed, the carrying out of that decree and the terror of the Mother of Moses when she learns of the danger to her child. She hides the child in the bulrushes; it is discovered by Pharaoh's daughter and adopted by her.
>
> In the second reel Moses appears as a young man. He has been deeply touched with the hardships of his people and subsequently kills one of the taskmasters for cruelty to the workmen. For this act he is compelled to flee the country, escaping to the land of Midian, where he becomes a shepherd and takes a wife. The Lord appears to him in a Burning Bush and commands him to return to Egypt and free the Hebrews from bondage.
>
> The third picture brings Moses before Pharaoh demanding the freedom of his people. Pharaoh's refusal is followed by the Ten Plagues, the Passover and the death of the First Born, depicted with startling realism. After this Israel is led out of the house of bondage by Moses and guided on their way by a "pillar of cloud by day and a pillar of fire by night." The incident of crossing the Red Sea on dry land and the destruction of the hosts of Pharaoh which attempt to follow them is shown in this picture.
>
> The Wandering of the Children of Israel in the Wilderness for forty years is the subject of the fourth reel, in which the notable incidents are the Falling of the Manna from Heaven, Moses Smiting the Rock from which water sprang to quench the thirsty multitudes. Moses Sitting in Judgment Over the People. The battle

between the hosts of Israel and of Amalak when the hands of Moses were held up until the enemy was defeated.

The fifth and last reel deals with the incidents of the Ten Commandments given to Moses by the Lord on Mount Sinai; the Golden Calf; the Tabernacle and the Ark of the Covenant; Moses taking leave of his people and the grand finale when he views the Promised Land which he is forbidden to enter from the heights of Mount Pisgah and then death.[8]

To this description of the narrative, we should add that the deployment of visual signifiers in *Moses* bears a stronger resemblance to that of the pre-1907 cinema than to that of the transitional period when the series was produced. Indeed, the films seem somewhat retrograde even in comparison to the other quality films that we have discussed. One of the primary indices of this is the almost total lack of psychologization of the central protagonist, the Moses films having no equivalents to psychologizing signifiers such as the motivated inserts of the locket in *Francesca di Rimini* or the vision scenes in the Napoleon and Washington reels. The tendency of quality films to be formally retrograde seems related to the degree of constraint imposed by the relevant institutions of cultural reproduction and interpretive communities, and to the pervasiveness of the circulation of related intertexts. *The Life of Moses*, in this regard, resembles cinematic passion plays (and even Kalem's 1912 *From the Manger to the Cross*), which at a relatively late date still deployed the signifying practices associated with the early cinema and avoided psychologization of the central character.[9]

Distinctive Production Practices for *The Life of Moses*

In April 1910, during the Lenten season, the Plumb Opera House showed all five reels of the Vitagraph Company's *Life of Moses*. The house manager advertised the show with a "corking good" poster touting the "Superb, Spectacular Production of the 'Life of Moses.' " A single sentence provided a succinct narrative synopsis of the entire production: "The sublime story of the Young Hebrew, who put aside the Diadem of mighty Egypt, and became an outcast with a price on his head that he might deliver his people. Told in Five Thrilling Scenes." The poster elaborated upon these scenes: (1) Moses and Pharaoh's Daughter; (2) 40 Years in the Wilderness; (3) The Seven Plagues of Egypt; (4) The Crossing of the Red Sea; (5) In Sight of the Promised Land. Hailing the films as a "Monumental Biblical Epigraph," the poster claimed that $50,000 had been expended on the "Production of the Greatest Scriptural Narrative ever told. 5000 Feet of Film. Reverent and dignified portrayal of the Wonderful Story of Moses revealed by the Greatest Triumph of Photographic and Mechanical Art ever achieved. 1½ Hours of Biblical Narative [sic]." For thrill-

The Plumb Opera House poster for *The Life of Moses*.

seeking viewers, the poster promised in bold type, "The Miracle of the Red Sea. A $10,000 Water Scene." "Pictorial vocal solos" would accompany the films. What's more, all this could be had for a mere five cents for children and ten cents for adults.[10]

The Plumb Opera House's advertising indicates the anomalous position of *The Life of Moses* in contemporary production, distribution, and exhibition practices. In this period, self-contained one-reelers constituted the majority of releases; the two-reel historicals discussed in the previous chapter were unusual. *Moses* not only ran for five reels but was occasionally shown in its entirety in venues, such as the Plumb Opera House, outside the usual distribution networks. In a period when exhibitors were just beginning to experiment with advertising and exploitation, *Moses* received relatively intensive advance publicity. If the poster was accurate, each reel of *Moses* cost significantly more than the average one-reeler of the time—in fact, more than ten times the amount.

Vitagraph had, in fact, made several biblicals prior to the Moses films: *Salome, or the Dance of the Seven Veils*, in August 1908; *Saul and David*, in February 1909; and *Judgment of Solomon* and *Jephtha's Daughter: A Biblical Tragedy*, in May 1909. But these films rivaled *Moses* neither in length (three of the four were split-reelers) nor in publicity, *Salome* alone being accorded an illustrated trade paper advertisement. The Moses series, Vitagraph's longest production until March 1914, was thus an early example of multiple-reel release and exhibition as well as the most prominently publicized of the company's quality films—Vitagraph's first biblical blockbuster. The anomalies in the production, distribution, and exhibition of the films appear, moreover, to reflect Vitagraph's desire to ally itself with Sunday school teachers and clerics and to mollify the industry's opponents. In 1909 a great deal of the pressure against the moving pictures stemmed from religious authorities who feared that the medium would have deleterious effects upon their constituencies. As *Motography* said in 1911,

> All sects and denominations were sufferers from the inroads of these amusements a year or so ago. Jewish, Catholic and Protestant felt the pull of the scenes and sensations that were being shown to the picture patrons. The educational and amusement value of the pictures has been known for a long time, and many of the city institutions, church institutions and homes have been using them for years; but the idea of coming out into the open and using the films as a means of routing Satan is still so new that in some quarters it cannot be entertained. The fact that the picture show is on the outside, is undignified and sometimes immoral, has helped to keep it from being used by many militant churches and earnest ministers.[11]

While *Moses*, like the other quality films, helped to better the cultural status of the new medium, the biblicals were particularly designed to deal with the industry's most vociferous opponents, the clergy, and to counter their most potent weapon, Sunday closings. The Sabbath debates that rendered the clergy a vital constituency for the film industry help to explain why Vitagraph treated the biblicals somewhat differently from the literaries and historicals. *Moses* constituted Vitagraph's major attempt to make religious subjects that, by placating clergymen, would aid the unfettered operation of the nickelodeons.

The 1907 New York City debate over Sunday closings would have made a film company headquartered there keenly aware of the need for biblical films. Section 1481 of the Charter of the City of Greater New York forbade the Sunday operation of "public exhibitions," which were defined as "any interlude, tragedy, comedy, opera, ballet, play, farce, minstrelsy or dancing, or any other entertainment of the stage."[12] When a Supreme Court justice unexpectedly handed down a ruling requiring strict compliance with this section, politicians representing the city's ethnic communities—which had no tradition of

Blue Sundays—supported amending the charter to allow at least "sacred or educational, vocal or instrumental concerts, lectures, addresses, recitations and singing so long as they don't disturb the public peace." This amendment took the form of the Doull Ordinance, passed by the Board of Aldermen over the objections of many of the city's Protestant clergy.

On Sunday, December 22, after the passing of the Doull ordinance, the *New York Times* reported that theatres had made arrangements for moving pictures of an educational or religious nature such as views of the Panama Canal and a passion play.[13] On December 23 the *Times* reported that on the previous day:

> Most of the moving picture shows and penny arcades were closed by iron fences, designed to keep the public from trespassing upon their front spaces. Here and there crafty managers of ten cent theatres which thrive on vitagraph views had put away their signs telling about the lifelike representation of "a hot time with Satan" and had raked together a ragged soloist, a 'violeen' player, a 'sacred' and 'educational' monologist, and did a roaring trade at five cents a head.[14]

Sabbatarians pressured the film industry in all locations, these pressures forming an important component of the conditions of production for the biblical films. The *Film Index*, typifying the many trade press references to the issue, reported a Sabbath debate in Detroit.

> During the past three weeks the moving picture shows in Detroit have furnished a talking point from the pulpits of local churches, the clergy arguing that the Sunday performances at the nickelodeons proved too enlivening entertainment to the 'children' present. As a result of this there has been a considerable demand for suitable religious subjects and on Sundays the film exchanges present a church-like aspect, the conversation of the exhibitors bearing largely upon biblical films.[15]

A publicity article for *The Life of Moses* in the *Film Index*, which, one should remember, was jointly owned by Pathé and Vitagraph, claimed that Vitagraph's biblicals indeed met market demand. "The widespread interest and enthusiasm created by the Vitagraph's religious subjects is somewhat responsible for the public demand which has led to the increase of Vitagraph releases to three reels per week. These subjects are especially suitable for Sunday exhibitions and particular attention has been given to them for that very reason."[16]

Another clear economic incentive also factored into the production of biblicals. Films suitable for Sunday school could not only allay the fears for the moral welfare of children that figured prominently in the clergy's attack on the film industry but could also potentially expand exhibition venues, since the biblicals would directly compete with other media, such as lantern slides, chromolithographs, and stereographs, that were commonly used for religious purposes. The trade press often gave a platform to sympathetic clergy, urging church use of moving pictures. In 1908 the *Views and Films Index* ran an article entitled "Moving Picture Sermons?" which included testimonials from ministers across the country. The Reverend Archer, of the Jefferson Avenue Presbyterian Church in Evansville, Indiana—who had already adopted the illustrated sermon and illustrated hymn—said, "It is as essential to appeal to the eye as well as to the ear of the congregation. The stereopticon has been used for years by ministers, teachers, missionaries, lecturers, and with a great degree of success. Why not the moving picture sermon and the illustrated hymn?" Secretary Mogge of the YMCA commented, "I believe that the moderate use of the stereopticon and of moving pictures for illustrated songs and sermons in the church will prove helpful in attracting, interesting and instructing larger audiences. . . . If modern conditions are handicapping the church in reaching the masses it is worthwhile to try any legitimate method to gain their attention."[17]

Whether by happenstance or planning, the release dates for *Moses* seem to reflect one possible strategy for encouraging Sunday school film use. The first reel was released at the end of 1909, just as Sunday school students across the nation completed their study of Moses in the international lesson plan, a uniform method of Sunday school instruction adopted by most of the evangelical Protestant sects. The seven-year cycle of lessons worked through the Old and New Testaments so that all students everywhere studied the same texts simultaneously, with teachers framing the material suitably for different age levels. The lesson plans, which often reflected their authors' positions in the debate over biblical "truth," drew out each text's moral implications as well as using quotations from authoritative sources, in conjunction with illustrations, to ground the text historically. Even those not attending could still have kept pace with the lessons through commentaries published in various popular magazines such as the *Ladies' Home Journal* and *The Outlook*. In 1908 the *Morning Telegraph* suggested that films be used to illustrate the lesson plan. "What of the Sunday schools of the next year or two in which the lesson—the Bible episode—of "Joseph and His Brethren" or "The Departure of the Holy Family For Egypt" or "Moses in the Bulrushes" [can be] shown as a little historical play on the screen?"[18] The Reverend Madison C. Peters, Vitagraph's clerical consultant, would certainly have been aware of the material covered in the lesson plans and may well have suggested Moses for this reason.

In fact, the employment of the Reverend Madison C. Peters as a special consultant—variously credited as the producer, writer, and director[19]—gives the clearest indication of the connection between the desire to placate the clergy and the distinctive production practices of *Moses*. Peters, a clerical free agent of sorts, was ordained in the Ministry of the Reformed Church but became a Presbyterian and then a Baptist, before abandoning institutional affiliations entirely in order to devote himself to more ecumenical activities. Dubbing himself "The People's Preacher" in an attempt to reach the urban masses, Peters gave up the ministry in favor of delivering popular-priced lectures to large audiences and holding services in theatres and public halls. He also wrote syndicated newspaper articles and books, among which were *Justice to the Jew* (1899), *The Jew as Patriot* (1902), *The Birds of the Bible* (1901), and *Sermons That Won the Masses* (1908).

Peters was perhaps the most prominent of those clergymen championing the motion picture and indeed had already exploited the visual potential of the stereopticon and films in his public lectures, many of which dealt with his travels to the Holy Land. As early as 1898 he had endorsed the Eden Musee's projection of the *Passion Play of Oberammergau*. This, together with his advocacy of the Jews and his high public profile, made him the obvious choice for Vitagraph. Before the release of the first reel, Vitagraph went so far as to assert that Peters's "enthusiastic personal attention to these films is significant of the marked change in the attitude of the clergy toward motion pictures."[20]

Prior to Peters's Vitagraph stint, the *Views and Films Index* reported that

> among the latest acquisitions of the moving picture field is Reverend Madison C. Peters, the brilliant preacher, author and orator of New York whose fame is widespread. He has embarked upon the lecture branch of the picture tide and is making a big success of it. . . . Dr. Peters gives his lectures at popular prices. He is giving the masses what they have been unable to reach heretofore. He preaches in the Belasco Theatre, New York, every Sunday morning and in the evening describes his "Tours of the World," illustrated with moving pictures.[21]

Although Vitagraph had consulted written authorities for its Napoleon films, with *Moses* the producers clearly felt the need for the authoritative presence of a member of a religious interpretive community. Peters's familiarity with the Holy Land, coupled with his knowledge of and belief in the literalness of the Bible, ensured the authenticity of *Moses*, while his lack of affiliation with any particular sect guaranteed his interdenominational appeal.

But Peters's employment also related to the pressing need for reverential treatment of biblical subjects that stemmed partially from previous divisiveness over the issue of theatrical passion plays. Although the Oberammergau passion play had been staged for centuries, many in the United States found such theatrical productions profoundly offensive, believing that no actor should portray Christ's suffering. By contrast, cinematic passion plays had found broad acceptance, although Vitagraph managed to sidestep the heart of the controversy by filming an Old Testament subject. (In fact, Vitagraph produced only one film dealing with the New Testament, *The Illumination* [1913], in which Christ was shown only as offscreen light.) As early as 1887 John Fraser defended a theatrical representation of Moses in a critique of the play *Moses and Pharaoh*. " 'Moses' appeals to that large class of moral church going and pulpit filling citizens, who have been educated to believe little good of the stage and its productions. . . . Even those who shudder at the idea of a 'Passion Play' portraying the earthly career and sufferings of our Savior need have no feeling of aversion to a reverent and serious dramatic treatment of the life of

Madison C. Peters "directing" *The Life of Moses.*

the great Hebrew law maker."[22] But even for those still inclined to object to cinematic representations of biblical characters, the presence of Peters would ensure such reverential treatment that Vitagraph could claim: "The Life of Moses, as staged by careful hands, is not apt to contain many pictures that can offend even the most fastidious."[23]

Peters, said Vitagraph's publicity, had even insisted upon a pious attitude on the part of the crew as a precondition of his employment. "I consented to make 'The Life of Moses' only on the condition that the work be thoroughly done; that those taking part in the picture reverently approach the subject and that no expense be spared in the artistic production. . . . Those taking part in the making of the picture could be seen through the weeks in the study of the Bible in order that they might, in spirit, enter into what I had outlined in my manuscript story."[24] Peters in effect became Vitagraph's guarantor of reverence, enabling the company to deflect any criticism by pointing to the higher authority that the Reverend Doctor represented.

The involvement of someone like Peters represented a marked departure from the period's standard production practices. Given the film exchanges' ceaseless demand for product, Vitagraph and other studios usually had neither the time nor the money for outside consultants. Most films were shot in a few days on a fairly limited budget with minimal opportunity for retakes.

But the *Moses* publicity indicates that this film diverged from other productions with regard to its budget. The Plumb Opera House poster spoke of a $50,000 expenditure for the full five reels in a period when the Biograph production budget averaged $500 to $600 per reel.[25] Vitagraph also professed to have reshot the entire second reel since it had not initially met the high standards set by the first reel. The company's "earnestness to make this series the acme of excellence may be shown by the fact that a complete negative of the second of the series was discarded after the first print was seen on the screen. The expense attached to this alone would bankrupt many a smaller concern."[26]

Vitagraph dubbed the Moses reels "special releases" and recommended that exhibitors make advance preparations for booking and exhibiting the films.[27] In conjunction with these special releases, the *Vitagraph Bulletin* mounted an intensive publicity campaign, exceeding that for any of the other quality films, and suggested a range of promotional strategies to exhibitors. The *Bulletin* urged exhibitors to drape the house with company-provided color posters and to plant stories in the local newspapers.

> Beginning with the release of the second reel of The Life of Moses . . . we will issue our own lithograph posters in three colors, for each reel released. These posters will be artistic one-sheet pictorial productions (28 × 42), giving more comprehensive ideas of the subjects than the previous posters and as the designs of the lithographs will differ from the prevailing posters they will add variety and distinction to your poster display.[28]

The reader will note that even the posters for *Moses* differed in format from those for regular releases. The company pulled out all the stops for the fifth reel, providing an unusually elaborate four-color poster to facilitate the exhibition of the five reels as a complete show. The poster was "designed so that it can be used in advertising either the last reel separately or the full series of five reels. This will be welcome intelligence to those who contemplate giving complete exhibitions of the entire series as a single entertainment."[29]

Vitagraph also prepared for exhibitors a "series of articles for the newspaper press, the publication of which you can readily secure in your local papers, either for exhibitions in your own house or for special exhibitions in churches or for religious societies."[30] Vitagraph later told exhibitors that the results of this strategy had exceeded even their own expectations. "The press matter sent out for use in your local papers in connection with the famous Moses series . . . has been productive of such good results that we have determined to send you from time to time other press matter for use in the same way regarding Vitagraph features."[31] Although we do not know how much success local exhibitors enjoyed in placing these stories, the congruences of articles in the various trade journals and the *Vitagraph Bulletin* suggests that the trade press apparently ran practically unaltered versions of these planted stories.[32]

The elaborate posters may have been designed to impress the new patrons that the company hoped the Moses reels would attract. The *Bulletin* urged exhibitors to use the Moses reels to reach out to opinion leaders and to more affluent and educated viewers, arguing that exhibitors would benefit not only themselves but the whole industry by screening these films. "There are other ways to make profit from The Life of Moses series. . . . Besides adding to your cash receipts you would thereby add immensely to your reputation and to the reputation of the motion picture business."[33] Vitagraph clearly intended *The Life of Moses* to persuade those who might lead a community's opposition to the moving pictures that the medium had the potential for good. "This great 'Moses' series is one of the strongest arguments you can present to newspaper editors of the elevating and educational character of present-day motion pictures. Invite the newspapermen especially to visit your theatre and view the Moses series, and invite also all clergymen, educators and cultivated people generally."[34] Not only would *Moses* placate community leaders, it might also be expected to bring in women of a different class than those already patronizing the nickelodeons. "There is not an exhibitor or film exchange who has not been put to [task] for the lack of films of a religious character which would appeal to mixed audiences and the commendable enterprise of the Vitagraph Company in supplying this want will no doubt meet with due appreciation."[35] Vitagraph's self-congratulation took up a good deal of *Bulletin* copy while the Moses films were in release, with the following perhaps articulating most clearly how Vitagraph intended the films to intervene in the ongoing debate about the medium.

> Have you ever stopped to think about how much substantial good our "Moses" series and similar films have done for the general reputation of moving pictures? You have realized in the past the prejudice that has existed in certain uninformed circles against moving pictures as an institution and how difficult it has been to break that prejudice down. It is films like the "Life of Moses" series that have taken the ground right out from under the feet of the "Knockers," and we feel just a little bit proud of our efforts in this connection.[36]

But as we pointed out in chapter 2, Vitagraph's protestations of altruism did not preclude appeals to baser financial interests. Filmed passion plays had made money, as the *Vitagraph Bulletin* reminded its customers. "There has been no similar opportunity since the Passion Play, and you cannot fail to recall the vast amount of money that was made from Passion Play exhibitions. The same thing can be done with The Life of Moses. Book a route of churches and halls in towns surrounding your own and give this idea a try. . . . Depend upon it, there is money in this proposition and the first ones out will gather the cream."[37] The passion plays may have made a great deal of their money during the Lenten season, traditionally a bad time for the entertainment business. Vitagraph accordingly offered the Moses reels to exhibitors who wished to emulate the passion play strategy and profit even during the pre-Easter doldrums. "Do you realize what it means to you, Mr. Exhibitor, to have the five reels of The Life of Moses for exhibition during Lent? Lent is the period to which every amusement man looks forward for reduced attendance. . . . Moving picture houses suffer. . . . You can make The Life of Moses your life saver if you will."[38]

Vitagraph had released all five reels of *Moses* prior to the 1910 Lenten season. By persuading exhibitors to screen the Moses reels in their entirety, the studio managed to give its prestige production a second life. The *Film Index*, not surprisingly, joined in Vitagraph's publicity campaign. "The Vitagraph Company is expecting great results from this series, so there are numerous ways in which it can be used by exhibitors to their advantage especially during Lent. In large houses the entire five reels may be run in one day, preferably Sunday, or they can be run in successive days, one each day."[39] This advance publicity was presumably intended to convince the film exchanges to purchase sufficient copies of each reel upon initial release to meet the subsequent Lenten demand.

Moses enabled the film industry to transform the Lenten doldrums into a profitable season while simultaneously enhancing the industry's reputation by holding religious celebrations of sorts at the local nickelodeon. But Vitagraph's use of the Moses series in persuading Sunday schools to incorporate biblical films into their religious instruction promised to provide longer-term financial benefits not only for itself but for other studios as well. The trade press seems to have been cognizant of this financial incentive, for it printed numerous statements from Peters and other ministers concerning the pressing need of the Sunday schools for more stimulating pedagogical methods. Said Peters:

> It is safe to say that churches looking for a unique entertainment will be looking this way; while I venture the prophecy that the Sunday schools of the future will be using the motion picture to set forth the story of the Bible. The present method of teaching is a failure, and the children do not want to go because they are not interested. . . . But the motion picture setting forth religious truth will keep the Sunday schools crowded all year round.[40]

An official textbook of the International Sunday School Association, *The Pupil and the Teacher*, lends credence to the industry's claims.

> Schools and colleges are just awakening to the possibilities of moving pictures as an educational instrument. The Sunday school, too, would do well to bring before its pupils now and then moving pictures of the Passion Play, of scenes in the Holy Land of today, . . . and the like. The spread of moving picture shows which has in the past few years spread over the country is but an indication of the interest which pupils are bound to feel in pictures which actually bring life before them.[41]

But in bringing Moses to cinematic life in order to meet the "needs" of the churches and Sunday schools, Vitagraph faced conflicting visions of the liberator and lawgiver.

Discourses of the Natural and Supernatural in Vitagraph's *Moses*

Even though adherents of all Judeo-Christian religions might have been expected to respond more or less favorably to a cinematic depiction of Moses, such a film had, either by omission or commission, to take a stand on the intense debates currently raging about the "truth" of the Bible. Since the conditions of production and reception for the biblical films were structured by the competing paradigms of two coalitions of loosely allied interpretive communities struggling to disseminate their opposing views on the matter of biblical truth, a brief discussion of these doctrinal issues will help more fully to illuminate the broad parameters within which the Vitagraph Company positioned the *The Life of Moses*. Yet these doctrinal issues must themselves be understood in light of religion's character as an institution of cultural reproduction, particularly with regard to the distinctive role of interpretive communities.

Biblical interpretation, ultimately predicated on faith, differed fundamentally from both literary and historical interpretation, the former thriving on difference and the latter relying finally on an appeal to empiricism. W. T. Harris, United States commissioner of education, pointed to this difference as the basis for the separation of religious and secular education: "The principle of religious instruction is authority; that of secular instruction is demonstration and verification."[42] All institutions of cultural reproduction circulated delimited meanings produced by interpretive communities, but, by its very nature, religion required the most strictly controlled meanings in order to ensure its continuation. Religious interpretive communities, unlike those concerned with literature and history, produced meanings predicated on faith and reified into doctrine, producing a cohesion among believers, but one that could tolerate only limited dissent. In some institutions of cultural reproduction, such as higher education, dissent, within certain limits, helped to maintain the institution, since academia is in part defined by debate. Dissent in religion, however, threatened the very existence of institutions defined by strict adherence to doctrine. Matters of biblical interpretation therefore had far more profound and tangible implications for its institution of cultural reproduction than did literary or historical interpretations for theirs.

The last third of the nineteenth century saw profound transformations of American religious belief, many centering on the Bible and relating to advances in literary criticism and recent scientific discoveries, coupled with a general predisposition to accept some degree of historical relativity.[43] Drawing on work initiated by German theologians, academics at the more prestigious American seminaries began to pursue the higher criticism of the Bible, a method of literary analysis that sought to answer questions of authorship and textual genealogy and to historicize the meaning of the scriptures. Proponents of the higher criticism thus substituted human agency, with all its contradictions and inaccuracies, both geographical and historical, for the divine inspiration previously accepted as the wellspring of the Bible. Darwinism, and scientific advances generally, compounded the challenge of the higher criticism to the Bible's veracity. In response, fundamentalist theologians steadfastly maintained that the Bible manifested God's word and propounded the doctrine of biblical inerrancy on matters both secular and sacred.

These debates occurred mainly among theologians at institutions of higher education and in fact resulted from the academization of biblical study. Nonetheless, they filtered down to the lay public through popular religious journals such as *The Independent* and *The Outlook*.[44] Widely publicized judicial disputes about the Bible's presence in the public schools also touched upon issues of biblical veracity.[45] While we do know that the general population was to some extent aware of these debates, we cannot, as we did with Shakespeare or Napoleon, suggest those specific social formations most involved, since a position on the matter of biblical truth did not necessarily correlate with income, education, or even social status.

Inasmuch as Vitagraph dared to present a cinematic incarnation of Moses, the debate about biblical truth became a critical component of the conditions of production. In fact, any Old Testament character whom the studio chose would have necessitated careful positioning with regard to this debate, although, as we will show, Moses was potentially the most contentious. Obviously, a New Testament character would have required the same degree of sensitivity. A portrayal of Jesus Christ, for example, would have activated debates not only among Christians but among Jews concerned that the depictions of Christ's suffering had anti-Semitic overtones.

Moses' alleged authorship of the Pentateuch became one of the defining issues between the two loosely allied cross-denominational coalitions contesting biblical truth. The fundamentalists, who asserted that Moses had transcribed the first five books of the Old Testament at God's behest, insisted upon the inerrancy of the Pentateuch. Those who ascribed the Pentateuch to human agency, however, saw the Bible as more metaphorical in nature and questioned whether Moses had performed the miracles ascribed to him or had even actually existed.

In our period, all Jewish sects considered Moses the linchpin of their faith, but their belief in his reality as a historical figure and in his authorship of the Pentateuch differed. Reform Jews embraced the new scientism wholeheartedly. "We hold that the modern discoveries of scientific researches in the domains of nature and history are not antagonistic to the doctrines of Judaism, the Bible reflecting the primitive ideas of its own age, and at times clothing its conception of Divine Providence and justice, dealing with man in miraculous narratives."[46] Reform elements, among whom may have been many of the assimilated, uptown, German Jews who funded the Educational Alliance, would thus have considered Moses a metaphoric symbol and would not have thought of the Pentateuch as literal truth stemming from his pen. Ahad Ha-Am, a Hebrew essayist and early-twentieth-century proponent of cultural Zionism, saw Moses as "a creation of the Jewish people, a heroic figure created in their own image."[47] By contrast, Orthodox Jews held as a matter of doctrine that the whole text of the Torah had been revealed to Moses on Mount Sinai and hence accepted it literally.[48] "Jewish Orthodoxy has . . . always staunchly upheld the theory of verbal inspiration in its extremest form—at least so far as the Pentateuch is concerned. 'Higher Criticism' of the Pentateuch is flatly rejected and is considered a major heresy."[49]

Catholics experienced similar contention, although divisions were ulti-mately contained because of the hierarchical nature of the church. The Euro-pean Catholic movement of modernism sought "to incorporate modern his-torical criticism, evolutionary philosophy, and literary exegesis into theology and Scripture Studies."[50] In 1907, however, Pope Pius X issued an encyclical condemning modernism that resulted in a crackdown on liberalizing forces in the United States, whereupon theological innovations that had been appear-ing in the Catholic press ceased.[51] In 1910 an oath against modernism was instituted for all candidates for the priesthood and all those teaching in the seminaries.[52]

Moses again served to crystallize some of the debates. In 1910 Henry Poels, professor of scripture at the Catholic University of America, was dismissed for questioning Mosaic authorship.[53] Yet the *Catholic Encyclopedia* of 1911 pre-sented a somewhat equivocal view of Moses' historicity. "To deny . . . or to doubt . . . the historic personality of Moses, is to undermine and render unin-telligible the subsequent history of the Israelites. . . . Taken singly, these pop-ular tales [of Moses] are purely imaginative, yet, considered in their cumula-tive force, they vouch for the reality of a grand and illustrious personage. . . . The Bible furnishes the chief authentic account of this luminous life."[54]

The dispute over biblical truth proved most divisive among Protestant de-nominations, where the higher criticism flourished in the seminaries, to the extent that even those supporting biblical inerrancy used arcane literary analy-sis to make their case. In response to the increasing academization of this interpretive community, alternative interpretive communities sprang up among laymen, such as the Moody Bible Institute, established in 1889 by the evangelist Dwight Moody. The members of these self-appointed interpretive communities, who wished to preserve Bible study as the domain of the aver-age man, contested the hierarchization concomitant with academization. The vast majority of these popular preachers also tended to be of fundamentalist disposition and so insisted on Mosaic authorship. The conservative cleric I. M. Haldeman said in his guide to Bible study, "And he who will sit down and study his writing will understand what the Son of God meant when he said: 'Moses wrote of me; if ye believe not his writings, how shall ye believe my words?' "[55] For these fundamentalist Christians, then, questioning Mosiac authorship threatened to undermine the very foundations of their faith.

As might be expected, many in the seminaries did indeed question Mosaic authorship. Feelings ran so high over this issue that Charles A. Briggs, a professor of theology at the Union Theological Seminary, left the Presbyterians after being charged with heresy for asserting that the Pentateuch had been written by multiple authors. The politically conservative Episcopalian bishop Henry C. Potter, whose anti-immigrant sentiments were quoted in the previous chapter but who was also a member of the Anglican "broad church" movement that wanted to accept the higher criticism and other liberal theological trends, then ordained Briggs as an Episcopalian priest.[56] Potter's action attests to the complexities surrounding issues of biblical interpretation and contemporary politics.

Vitagraph's claim that *The Life of Moses* corresponded "closely to the conception which has been inculcated in the minds of people who have attended church and Sunday school" suggests the constituencies to which they hoped the film would appeal.[57] Yet the competing biblical discourses of reason and faith circulating within religious institutions potentially complicated Vitagraph's representation of the Jewish leader. As we have noted, Vitagraph's advertising foregrounded the Reverend Madison C. Peters's contributions to the production. "With his vast knowledge of the Holy Land of biblical times as well as today Dr. Peters is splendidly qualified to prepare a series of films that shall be accurate in history and setting, replete with dramatic action and reverent in spirit."[58] The phrases "accurate in history and setting" and "replete with dramatic action" point to the two main strands that Vitagraph drew from contemporary religious discourse to sell its *Moses* to clergymen and laymen alike, its promotion emphasizing the films' attention to natural history as well as to spectacular miracles. We will term these two strands the discourse of the natural and the discourse of the supernatural. Paradoxically, though, both those who questioned the Bible's veracity and those who insisted on its inerrancy agreed on the selective use of archaeological, botanical, and geographical evidence to establish the historical background of the biblical texts. But whereas the former used such data to argue for the irrationality of literal interpretations, the latter used them to bolster faith.

In the mid-nineteenth century, mainstream religions reached an accommodation that made the natural sciences (loosely defined) the handmaidens of faith. The full title of an 1857 Bible illustrates this accommodation perfectly: *The Pictorial Bible: Being the Old and New Testaments According to the Authorized*

Vitagraph advertisement for the second reel of *The Life of Moses*.

Version; Illustrated With More Than One Thousand Engravings, Representing the Historical Events, After the Most Celebrated Pictures; The Landscape Scenes, From Original Drawings, or Authentic Engravings; and the Subjects of Natural History, of Costume, and of Antiquities, from the Best Sources.[59] This Bible's illustrations for Exodus include Lossing's *Plague of Thunder and Hail*, which gains greater authority from being accompanied by a botanically correct illustration of the flax (*Linum usitatissimum*) that the plague smote. The chapter also contains numerous images drawn from natural history and archaeology, including Egyptian jewelry, Egyptian asses, and a detail of a leprous hand.

This discourse of the natural did not pose a serious threat to faith until the 1880s. In fact, scientific evidence of the kind deployed by the *Pictorial Bible* was so accepted as to be incorporated into the international Sunday school lesson plans. Together with his wife, the Reverend Francis Peloubet, a proponent of biblical inerrancy and Mosaic authorship, wrote a widely adopted commentary on the lesson plan that is replete with historical, geographical, botanical, and archaeological information.[60] The Peloubets asserted that all these data confirmed rather than challenged the Bible's veracity. "As to the accuracy of the book [the Pentateuch], which is the main point with which Christians are concerned, it has been strikingly confirmed by excavations and explorations in Egypt, Chaldea, and the desert, while nothing in the important and constant archaeological discoveries of recent years tends to discredit it."[61] Exodus 16:13–15 provided the Peloubets with an opportunity to deploy the discourse of the natural. The verses read:

> And it came to pass that at even, that the quails came up, and covered the camp; and in the morning the dew lay round about the camp. And when the dew that lay was gone up, behold, upon the face of the wilderness there lay a small round thing, as small as the hoar frost on the ground. And when the Children of Israel saw it, they said one to another, it is manna.

The Peloubets invoked no less than four different authorities on the migratory habits of the quail to demonstrate the Bible's plausibility, even including an illustration of *Coturnix vulgaris*, the common quail.[62] The appearance of the manna was not, unfortunately, susceptible to similar scientific explanation, there being no such naturally occurring substance, but the Peloubets used the discourse of the natural to lend credence to the miraculous phenomenon. If the miracle of the quails was borne out by scientific proof, then why not accept the miracle of the manna as well?

In addition to the international lesson plan, Sunday school students learned the discourse of the natural from numerous other teaching aids, many of which placed a heavy emphasis on the visual, thus providing a primary source of imagistic intertexts. For example, in 1869 the Methodist Sunday School Union opened a biblical museum at Columbus, Ohio, which housed a collection of diagrams, photographs, relics, curios, models, and so forth. The museum, one of many in existence during the second half of the century, was designed to "furnish pictorial and model representations of Bible topography, manners, and customs, and thus render more comprehensible the facts and allusions of the Divine Word."[63] Sunday school teachers commonly used such visual representations of the buildings, landscapes, and flora and fauna of the Holy Land as instructional aids. The fundamentalist Reverend J. L. Hurlbut, writer of popular guides to the Bible and the Holy Land, produced the *Manual of Biblical Geography*, which included colored diagrams of the Jerusalem temple, along with maps, plans, review charts, and engravings of points of interest in the Holy Land.[64] Sunday school teachers incorporated visual aids into their lessons to such an extent that specialized publishers supplied the market. Fred Pattee, in his *Elements of Religious Pedagogy*, recommended various sources from which illustrations could be obtained. "The Perry Picture Company, of Malden, Massachusetts, and the W. A. Wilde Publishing Company of Boston, furnish excellent copies of standard pictures at one cent each. The Globe Bible Publishing Company, of Philadelphia, furnishes photographs of the Holy Land at ten cents each, and Underwood and Underwood, of New York, are headquarters for stereopticon views."[65]

Even those media viewed with suspicion by many fundamentalists, namely, theatre and film, could be employed in the visual representation of the discourse of the natural. Both American and foreign studios produced actualities of the Holy Land, in 1903 alone the Edison Company releasing *Tourists Taking Water from the River Jordan*, *A Jewish Dance at Jerusalem*, *Herd of Sheep on the Road to Jerusalem*, and *Jerusalem's Busiest Street Showing Mount Zion*. The occasional theatrical production tried to recreate the splendor of the biblical past. *Moses; Or, The Bondage in Egypt: A Biblical and Historical Spectacle*, a pageant written by members of the Order of Cincinnatus (descendants of members of George Washington's staff), ran in Cincinnati during August 1890. The pageant's program calls attention to the scientific and archaeological bases of the production. "It remained for modern scientists to find the lost key by which this wealth of history should be unlocked. The ever-encroaching sand has yielded up its treasures to the indefatigable efforts of the explorers, and today Egyptologists are reading the hieroglyphics as easily as we read the alphabet, and are slowly but surely revealing the marvelous deeds of a marvelous nation, confirming many traditions and supplementing much that was utterly unknown."[66] A six-page foldout panorama of the set of Memphis, the Royal City, is captioned: "Beginning at the left: the Temple of Isis; the Pyramid of Dahshur; the Apium (house of the Apis or Sacred Bull); the White Castle (a fortress); in the distance the Necropolis (burial place); the Step Pyramid; Serapeum (tomb of the Sacred Bull); pyramid of Busiris."[67]

The *Film Index* reviewed *Moses* in terms that make explicit Vitagraph's placement of the film within the discourse of the natural that dominated mainstream Protestant circles. "Notable Series of Biblical Pictures Produced under the Direction of Rev. Madison C. Peters, D.D., Eminent New York Divine—A Remarkable Historical, Educational and Scenic Creation Marked by

Correct and Elaborate Costuming and Revealing Profound Study and Research of Tradition."[68] The rest of the trade press, often echoing Vitagraph's publicity, repeatedly commented on how well the films conformed to the notions of historical authenticity generally accepted in the churches and Sunday schools. Reviewing the second reel, the *Moving Picture World* remarked, "The staging is a marvelously accurate reproduction of Egyptian scenery and costuming and undoubtedly presents one of the best of modern conceptions of life and customs in the ancient world. For this reason, perhaps, it should be accorded special praise, since anything that can add to the information, or increase our knowledge of that age, deserves commendation."[69] The phrase "the best of modern conceptions" was undoubtedly intended to indicate Vitagraph's reliance upon the latest archaeological data. The *Film Index* likewise noted Vitagraph's dependence on authoritative sources. "From the array of talent that has been drawn upon it is evident that the Vitagraph producers have procured the most complete and authentic data available."[70]

The *Index*'s reference to "talent" probably alluded to the Reverend Dr. Peters, who was foregrounded in both Vitagraph advertising and in trade press reviews as the source of the film's historical authenticity. The company's promotion exploited Peters's reputation as an expert on matters of biblical geography, customs, and manners, in this fashion further linking *Moses* to the discourse of the natural. According to Vitagraph, the films were "staged under the direction of one who has travelled in the Holy Land and Egypt, and who has been given free hand to make the series perfect in detail."[71] *The Nickelodeon* also commended the authenticity of *Moses*, indirectly ascribing it to Peters. "We have become accustomed to minor anachronisms and property faults in moving pictures; but this one has none of them. The careful attention to costuming and staging is carried to such an extreme of minor detail as to show beyond question that it pays to employ a specialist."[72]

Perhaps in order to achieve consonance with the vision of the Holy Land inculcated in the Sunday schools, Vitagraph supplemented Peters's expertise by referencing familiar paintings, following the same strategy employed with the historicals. The *Vitagraph Bulletin* said, "Among the many great artists whose works have been consulted in preparing the appropriate scenic background for this great Biblical are the following: Tissot, Gérôme, Gustav-Dore, Edwin Austin Abbey, Briton Reviere, Sir Lawrence Alma-Tadema, R. A. Joseph Israel and Benjamin Constant."[73] Conformance to the scenic backgrounds depicted by these artists would ensure that, even if the films were not precisely consistent with the latest archaeological findings, they at least adhered to popular conceptions.

Vitagraph's publicity claimed that the company had taken great pains to provide a visual representation of the discourse of the natural. Six months in advance of the first reel's release, the *Film Index* reported that Vitagraph's "scenic staff has been increased to permit the proper handling of the heavy and

Vitagraph production still for *The Life of Moses*.

unusual scenery required and the property room also has put on an additional force."[74] Although we have no other evidence that the films were actually in preproduction at this early date, the publicity plant indicates an unusual commitment to publicizing the films' intended accuracy. The *New York Dramatic Mirror* commented on the results. "In the matter of distance and perspective this reel is a remarkable triumph of scenic art. Only the expert can discover the difference between the studio and outdoor scenes, a number of which represent views that would have been ruined if the complete sense of vast distance had not been properly conveyed. The result is that an atmosphere is given to the picture that aids wonderfully in adequately presenting the theme."[75]

The discourse of the natural foregrounded in Vitagraph's promotion appealed to all comers insofar as it conformed to church and Sunday school usage. Further insistence on science (on Darwin's theories, for example) would, however, have proved dangerous insofar as it threatened the discourse of the supernatural. Belief in the literalness of biblical accounts of miracles was one of the chief distinctions between the liberal and fundamentalist theologians. According to W. T. Harris, United States commissioner of education, the latter hewed to the traditional vision of the Lord's powers given in the Old Testament.

> God in the Old Testament was seen not so much as a Providence creating and nurturing individuality into freedom and responsibility through nature, as a God manifesting his independence of the world and of its laws by interference for occasional reasons with the order of nature. Hence, too, death, and its causes through pestilence, famine, floods, storms, conflagrations, accidents by sea and land have been dwelt upon in the past by religious teachers with more emphasis as revelations of divine power than the far deeper revelation of the divine in nature as creative and nurturing power.[76]

Lyman Abbott, a Congregationalist theologian of such liberal propensities as to accept Darwinism—he had authored *The Evolution of Christianity* (1892) and *Theology of an Evolutionist* (1897)—came perilously close to debunking miraculous divine intervention in the popular Christian journal, *The Outlook*, which he edited. The journal ran his series of commentaries on the international Sunday school lesson plan, including his discussion of the parting of the Red Sea, which explained the supernatural in terms of natural causes, arguing that the wind changed the pattern of the water's flow over marshy soil and that quicksand trapped the Egyptian army. For Abbott, though, departing from the literal truth of the Bible did not have to undermine belief in a divine providence. "Was there, then, no miracle? That depends on the answer to the question, What is a miracle? There was no violation of the laws of nature, but there was such a use of the forces of nature as accomplished the divine purpose."[77]

Whereas liberal theologians such as Abbott willingly accepted scientific explanations of biblical phenomena, resorting to supernatural explanations only in the last instance, the fundamentalists insisted that God directly intervened in the natural order precisely as the Bible described. In other words, the liberals believed that God worked through nature and the fundamentalists that God reconfigured nature. Abbott's discussion of "What is a miracle?" illustrates this distinction.

> After the battle of Long Island, while Washington's army lay encamped on Brooklyn Heights, a fog settled over the city, which served as a veil under the concealment of which Washington's army escaped [from the British]. . . . The Hebrew writer would have said that God sent a cloud between the advancing and retreating armies; and the Hebrew writer would have told the truth. . . . The difference between Hebrew and American history is not that there is less of a God in the world now as then, but that there was more vision of God in the Hebrew historians than there is, say, in the American journalist.[78]

In a conflict between the Bible and the natural order, the liberals gave precedence to the latter and the fundamentalists to the former. Thus, while both liberal and fundamentalist theologians shared the discourse of the natural, although to different ends, the latter also firmly believed in miraculous disruptions of the natural, thereby putting their faith in the discourse of the supernatural as well. Disregarding this discourse, insisted the fundamentalists, was tantamount to dismissing the Bible entirely. The conservatively disposed D. R. Dungan, author of *Moses, The Man of God*, typified the fundamentalists in insisting on strict adherence to the Bible's accounts of Moses' life and miraculous deeds. "We have neither time nor disposition to stop for any modern criticism which denies his existence or work, or even changes the account of his life in any matter of importance. Ninety nine percent of all competent criticism accepts the account of the life and work of this great man substantially as given in the Bible." Having listed every book of the Bible that contains references to the lawgiver, Dungan later declared, "Hence, to change the form of faith on this subject is to change nearly the whole Bible."[79]

Vitagraph's conformity to the discourse of the natural would have appealed to theological liberals and fundamentalists alike. But in order not to alienate the latter, the studio avoided, both in the film and in its promotional materials, scientific explanations that challenged the discourse of the supernatural, taking the Hebrew writer's rather than the American journalist's approach and again conforming to church and Sunday school usage. Just as Sunday school students learned to deploy the discourse of the natural in support of biblical authority, they were also taught to believe in the discourse of the supernatural, the lessons often taking visual form.

Pedagogical authorities advised Sunday school teachers to expose their charges to as many of the masterpieces of Western religious art as possible. Pattee explained that "the child should be shown always the best. He should be brought up with copies of the great masters. In this way there will be cultivated in him not only a taste for the best in art, but also a knowledge of Biblical things and a reverence for the old Bible stories such as nothing else could bring."[80] Obviously, the great masterpieces preceded the religious disputes of the century's end and would thus have reinforced belief in the discourse of the supernatural. Each week of the Peloubets' commentary on the international Sunday school lesson plan suggested pictures for discussion. For the Moses lessons they recommended Raphael's *The Israelites Passing through the Red Sea*, Rosselli's *Moses and the Israelites after the Passage of the Red Sea*, Michaelangelo's *Moses: The Lord Gives Manna to the People of Israel*, and Raphael's *Moses Striking the Rock*. The great masterpieces were often supplemented with cheaply printed Bible cards illustrating Mosaic miracles.[81] Nor was the visual representation of biblical phenomena confined to still images, for theatrical presentations also staged Mosaic miracles. For example, pages one through six of the twenty-five page script for *Moses the Liberator in Biblical Drama* focus primarily on the miracle of the burning bush and other of God's manifestations. The rest of the play deals with the ten plagues and the parting of the Red Sea, ending with the drowning of the Egyptian army.[82]

But film obviously had a major advantage over both painting and the theatre with regard to the reenactment of miracles, since the early cinema had quickly developed a battery of special effects techniques, often showcased in a genre known as the "trick film." In fact, pre-1907 films foregrounded spectacle over narrative to such an extent that some film scholars have dubbed this period the "cinema of attractions."[83] While reproductions, stereographs, and even illustrated lectures could rival film's capacity to engage in the discourse of the natural, no other medium could hope to engage in the discourse of the supernatural through faithful recreations of biblical miracles. As *The Nickelodeon* remarked about biblical films, "From the point of view of popular interest, the only fault of the Bible is that it is not sufficiently illustrated. The people like pictures, even of the kind that do not move, although the indications are that they like the moving kind a good deal better."[84]

Again, the Reverend Madison C. Peters, a believer in God's intervention in the natural order, provided Vitagraph's link to the discourse of the supernatural. In 1901 Peters had expressed his faith in the literalness of the Bible. "I believe in the inspiration of the Bible from lid to lid—not in spots only. I use the word inspiration in its literal meaning—God inspired—God breathed."[85] Ten years later, after he had served as Vitagraph's consultant, his faith remained constant. Speaking of the appearance of Moses and Elijah to Christ, Peters said, "Moses and Elijah were not creations of excited imagination, but actually present and surely visible, and their presence there was intended to teach that centuries after their death, those heroes of Israel were alive, active and interested in the same great subjects as when on earth."[86]

While Peters presumably insisted on the inclusion of literally represented miracles, the solemnity conferred by his presence also ensured that the films would not descend to the level of mere razzle-dazzle showmanship. The *Moving Picture World* commented that Vitagraph's careful presentation of the miraculous made the films suitable both for the new venues to which the studio aspired and for more general audiences. "While the main dramatic features of the Biblical narrative have been seized upon, there is nothing 'stagey'—nothing out of keeping with the character of the subject or that unfits it for exhibition in Sunday school or church gatherings. Yet it is handled with a fine dramatic spirit that will win the approval of any audience."[87]

Vitagraph asserted that its presentation through trick photography of the most cinematically compatible miracles of the Moses saga offered the fundamentally inclined the opportunity to view "the reproduction of things heard of but never before seen since their actual occurrence."[88] The Vitagraph films indeed incorporated as many miraculous events as possible, the plagues of Egypt providing a splendid opportunity for the employment of cinematic special effects. *Variety* commented about these miracles, "The latest release deals with a series of miracles in which trick photography serves an effective purpose."[89] The films depict the six most "cinematic" of the ten plagues, including a stop-motion transformation of a rod into a snake, water changed into blood by virtue of tinted stock, hail and painted lightning, and the Angel of Death walking through walls with the aid of double exposure.

Vitagraph's promotion emphasized the Red Sea miracle most heavily. The *Film Index* ran a special article about the *Moses* production, going on at length about the difficulty of cinematically representing the parting of the Red Sea. "The fourth reel of 'Moses' . . . displays remarkable ingenuity in portraying the performance of the miracles. One of the most wonderful and at the same time difficult effects to reproduce was the dividing of the Red Sea which was accomplished only after much experimenting and study." As the article explained, the studio took great pains to recreate the supernatural event.

> Those who were not in it cannot realize what it means to perform the marvelous feat of drowning the Egyptians in the Red Sea. . . . A dozen ways were tried to do it—mechanical, scenic and otherwise, until it was decided nothing but a real sea of water would suffice and get it across to the audience. . . . It was not pleasant to be called upon in the middle of January to take a cold bath in the deep 'Red Sea' and yet it was tried time and time again before it was successfully accomplished.[90]

Vitagraph seems to have deployed the entire battery of special effects at its disposal in its eagerness to achieve what we have termed the discourse of the supernatural.[91] Nowhere, however, does their promotional material suggest that they considered representing a more naturalistic explanation of the miracles along the lines sketched out by Lyman Abbott. To have done so would have challenged biblical inerrancy and alienated the fundamentalists. In fact, the *Vitagraph Bulletin* insisted on direct divine intervention. "Coming to the Red Sea, which bars their progress, Moses lifts up his hands and the waters of the sea are divided by a strong east wind."[92] Through the magic of double exposure the film shows the Israelites walking through the Red Sea, walls of water looming up on either side of them, just as described in the Bible.

Whereas Vitagaph's foregrounding of historical accuracy, a diluted form of the discourse of the natural, would have made the films acceptable to a wide cross-section of Jews and Christians, the foregrounding of the discourse of the supernatural may have raised objections among those inclined to a metaphorical view of the Bible. For example, Reform Jews might have felt that stressing the dramatic elements of Moses' biography obscured the moral and theological lessons of the Pentateuch. As we have mentioned, Ahad Ha-Am, the popular Jewish essayist of the period, saw Moses as metaphorical rather than a real person.[93] Henry Leipziger, of the Bureau of Lectures, who was influential in Jewish educational circles, asserted that parents and educators should not reduce Moses to a series of children's stories by emphasizing his miraculous performances.

> Children under 12 years of age cannot grasp [the deep meaning of the Moses story], and if it is told them too early they will only belittle it and be prevented from forming the pure conception of the character of the liberator and prophet

which ought to exist in their minds. A mere miracle worker will take the place of the prophet and legislator and this is actually the case with most people who have read the Biblical stories too young. The sublime character and vision of Moses is commonly not appreciated for that very reason.[94]

The well-known pundit Elbert Hubbard's stance on Mosaic miracles exemplified the very undermining of faith that the fundamentalists feared would result from questioning biblical inerrancy. Hubbard, an advocate of various brands of naturalistic monism and thus more consistent in his use of the discourse of the natural than Abbott and more insistent on the metaphorical than Leipziger, argued that Moses had indeed been a great man and a great teacher but that claims regarding his supernatural deeds simply reflected ignorance and superstition. Speaking of the ten plagues, Hubbard asserted,

> The plagues that befell the Egyptians were the natural ones to which Egypt was liable—drought, flood, flies, lice, frogs, disease. The Israelites very naturally declared that these things were sent as a punishment by the Israelitish god. I remember a farmer, in my childhood days, who was accounted by his neighbors as an infidel. He was struck by lightning and instantly killed . . . [and] our preacher explained at length that this man's death was a 'judgment.' Afterward when our church was struck by lightning, it was regarded as an accident. Ignorant and superstitious people always attribute special things to special causes.[95]

Vitagraph thus had to conform to the discourses of both the natural and the supernatural to placate clergymen and open up new venues. At the same time, it could not risk alienating those operating the film exchanges and the nickelodeons with too much piety. Perhaps in an attempt to mute the sanctimonious nature of much of its promotion, Vitagraph itself revealed the production circumstances behind the films' miracles, essentially subverting the illusion by providing natural explanations. While the *Vitagraph Bulletin* maintained a consistently reverent attitude, the company's other outlet, the *Film Index*, published two articles, "Dodging Snakes" and "Troubles of the M.P. Actor," devoted to behind-the-scenes anecdotes.[96] The first article relates the difficulties encountered in filming Moses' first miracle, the turning of the rod into a snake. Apparently, the sandal-shod extras objected to an overfriendly serpent, and one can, in fact, see some rather nervous shifting of feet in the final shot. In the latter article, the *Film Index* reprinted a story from the *New York Sun* about an extra who had appeared in *Moses*. The extra, jocularly dubbing the man who hired him "Moses," reported on working conditions.

> Moses said the pay would be a $1.50 per, and he made good alright while we was travelling through the desert. We earned the money alright too, for the wilderness was down at Brighton Beach, and that's a mighty cold place for bare legged Israelites in January. We had to roll up our trousers so they wouldn't show under the costumes, and the sandals they gave us in place of our shoes and the stage paint tan we put on our legs weren't much protection.

The extra then related how Vitagraph had produced manna from heaven.

> We had a chance to warm up a bit scrambling around that manna scene. When that came along a chap handed each of us Israelites a handful of breakfast food and then climbed up on a roof with some boxes of the chaff and showered it down until the ground was covered. We Israelites do some of our best acting in that scene when we paw at the stuff like starving Cubans and pretend to gather it up and eat it while really munching down the handful we had all the time. It was a dry diet and suggested beer.[97]

More typically, however, Vitagraph attempted to position its *Moses* by drawing on the most prevalent intertextual frames, tailoring the films to appeal to important constituencies while ignoring more marginal elements. The studio's attempt to placate the fundamentalist forces through special effects–enhanced miracles ignored, for example, Leipziger's fears that such an approach would obscure Moses' moral messages. Both Vitagraph's widely publicized effort to ground the imagery of the films in careful archaeological research and its employment of Peters indicate a wish to use historical and scientific evidence to buttress rather than question biblical authority. Nonetheless, the liberals, had they seen the films, might not have been offended, provided they were willing to consider a literal interpretation of the Bible simply a faithful literary adaptation.

Appropriations of Moses

Although our discussion to this point has focused primarily on Vitagraph's production patterns and its attempts to appeal to a specific yet divided constituency, the general reverence accorded Moses in turn-of-the-century American culture would itself have provided a strong incentive for the production of the Moses films. But this reverence also posed potential hazards. Given the centrality of Judeo-Christian morality in this period, as exemplified in the constant invocation of God and the Ten Commandments, Moses—often conflated with a transcendent moral order—was subject to an appropriation even more overarching than was Washington, who was conflated merely with the nation-state. The Rabbi Isaac M. Wise, the founder of the American Jewish reform movement, spoke of Moses as the supreme embodiment of Western values. Moses was "the man who has given law and religion to the civilized world; whose standard of right and justice is fast becoming the world's beacon light . . . whose doctrines of religion, of God, human dignity, freedom and righteousness conquer the masses."[98]

In a period of social upheaval, the figure of a lawgiver must have been a powerfully attractive symbol of stability to those fearing the dissolution of the social fabric, particularly since, in the United States, civil law is ultimately predicated upon Mosaic law. The statue of Moses on the appellate court building in New York City (erected in 1900) stands as testimony to one of the cornerstones of Anglo-American law. But Moses and the value system he epitomized would have resonated not only with Anglo-Americans but with most members of most social formations. Whereas an immense cultural distance would have existed between a Russian Jewish immigrant and Dante, or an Italian immigrant and Shakespeare, or an immigrant of any nationality and Washington, most newcomers to the United States would already have been deeply imbued with a Judeo-Christian morality, which is most strongly expressed in the Ten Commandments. This shared value system would have been reinforced in the new country both through the immigrants' own religious institutions, whether churches or synagogues, and through any exposure to the legal system.

The moral appropriation of Moses most prevalent at the turn of the century may have overarched even the inter- and intradenominational strife concerning the factual versus the metaphorical nature of the Bible. Moses' pervasiveness, which assured his widespread familiarity throughout all social formations, coupled with the legal system's indebtedness to Judeo-Christian morality, ironically rendered the Hebrew lawgiver a more powerful figure of assimilation to American values than George Washington himself. In theory, then, incorporation into the social structure through an appeal to immigrants' preexisting religious beliefs would not require the mobilization of nationalist rhetoric. Given the chauvinistic zeitgeist of the period, however, Moses was often connected to the political project of the nation-state.

Rhetoric dating back to the foundation of the Republic had identified the United States as the Promised Land and the new Jerusalem. In 1857 Rabbi Wise prepared a prayer book, *Minhag America* ("The American Rite"), that omitted references to a Messiah and a return to a homeland on the grounds that America was Zion and "Washington our Jerusalem."[99] Orators often spoke of Moses as the proponent of a nascent freedom and democracy that would come to fruition in the United States. Said Henry Leipziger, "from the land of despotism comes the truth of freedom—from the land of caste comes the forerunner of democracy—from the land where the many toil in order that the few may enjoy comes the prophet of humanity."[100] Rabbi Wise expressed the same sentiments in more explicitly American terms. "Standing before Moses you face the first declaration of independence, the first proclamation of liberty, the first and eternal blast from the trumpet of freedom."[101] Similarly, parallels were drawn between the liberator of the Israelites and the liberator of the American people. James Hamilton, for example, compared Moses to Washington. "As the Tell or Washington of early Eastern story, he would have claims on our admiration; as the first assertor of national independence; as the leader of the first war of religious emancipation; as the liberator of his people; as the divinely commissioned conductor of Exodus."[102]

References to Moses and the Promised Land were used to frame the establishment of the Republic as well as to point to its privileged position among contemporary nations. Madison Peters, in *The Jews Who Stood by Washington*, discussed Moses' centrality in the formation of American political doctrine. "The earliest constitutions of several New England colonies were framed upon the model of the Mosaic Code as a guide and preachers, who were the progressives and radicals of their day, constantly drew their civil creed from the history of those times and held up the old Hebrew commonwealth as a model for our government."[103] By the turn of the century, the United States represented the Promised Land to the "huddled masses yearning to breathe free" and unfortunate enough to live in foreign climes. Frances S. Kempster, chair of the Daughters of the American Revolution's National Committee to Prevent Desecration of the Flag, said, "This is a fair land of ours. In truth, almost a land flowing with milk and honey. We are told on every hand that we are at this moment *too* prosperous. The poor foreigner over the seas hears, from his brother in America, such tales of opportunity, independence and affluence, that compared with his own meager life, America is to him as the land of Canaan to the wandering Israelites."[104] But a Promised Land that permitted anarchic contestation for the milk and honey would not serve ends of those in power. Hence, a moral appropriation of Moses that ensured order, stability, and the maintenance of the status quo remained dominant, the rhetoric of the Promised Land serving to disguise the unequal distribution of resources.

Moses' special relationship with truth, justice, and the American way would thus have constituted another powerful incentive for Vitagraph's choice of biblical character for a five-reel film. Although Vitagraph's publicity did not explicitly activate this overarching appropriation, they may well have expected potential viewers to do so. A surprising assortment of political factions had, however, appropriated Moses for specifically partisan purposes. Consequently, there were other, somewhat narrower, appropriations that Vitagraph may well have wished to avoid activating.

Moses' association with a higher authority and the American way made him especially useful to those defending American values against the array of perceived threats discussed in chapter 1. The Peloubets' commentaries on the international lesson plan provide a good example of this appropriation. Seen in the context of attempts to regulate the Sabbath—and especially the leisure activities of the working class, who had to toil for the other six days of the week—the Peloubets' recommendations for keeping Sunday holy seem oppressive. The Peloubets told students how they could obey the seventh commandment to "Remember the Sabbath Day": "(1) By planning ahead for Sunday, 'remembering' it through the week, getting our work out of the way. (2) By entering upon the day in the spirit of worship, with Bible reading and prayer. (3) By giving God always the benefit of the doubt when we hesitate concerning Sunday work. (4) By carefully refraining from making needless work on Sunday. (5) By setting an unmistakable example."[105] The Peloubets also derived a strong temperance lesson from the tale of Aaron's sons, Nadab and Abihu, who ignored the Lord's admonition: "Do not drink wine nor strong drink, thou, nor thy sons with thee, when ye go into the tabernacle of the congregation, lest ye die." The two young men drank and died a fiery death. On the strength of this incident, the Peloubets launched into standard temperance rhetoric about the unemployability of imbibers, related statistics about the evil influence of the saloons, and recommended reading sensational tracts such as "Who Killed Joe's Baby?"[106] As with the observance of the Sabbath, temperance was intended to curb the leisure activities of the underclasses, and the international lesson plans accordingly included temperance lessons every quarter.[107]

The Reverend Charles Parkhurst, the New York City antivice crusader, invoked Moses in his 1894 campaign against the Tammany machine. He recited the Ten Commandments at a political rally and was taken aback by the response. "One of the most thrilling experiences which I have had in this entire campaign was the enthusiastic applause which greeted . . . the Ten Commandments. The idea of a big New York audience giving three cheers for the Decalogue, is—I don't know what it is—there is no word that will quite cover the situation."[108] Parkhurst advocated a theocracy as the solution to the city's ills. Speaking to his fellow ministers, he said, "If your ministry is being rendered in this city . . . [it] is as justly subject to the mastery of your inspired and imperial words as were the people of Israel amenable to the holy dictatorship of a Moses." Clearly, only the clergy could provide the moral leadership that the urban masses so desperately needed.

> Ninety percent of the material of social and civic questions being ethical, what reason is there why pulpit prophets should not marshall the army of event? They used to do so, why shouldn't they now? If there is any Moses who can climb onto the top of Sinai and commune with God and behold with an unabashed eye the realities that compose the tissue of all history, why should he not lead the waiting host when he gets back to the foot of the mountain? Why leave it to dirty Aaron, who meantime has been stripping the people and building golden calves?[109]

Some, then, invoked Moses to justify the status quo. At the same time, progressives and radicals foregrounded aspects of the Pentateuch that were usually suppressed. Richard T. Ely, professor of political economy and director of the School of Economics, Political Science, and History at the University of Wisconsin, was one of the first to formulate the doctrine of the Social Gospel, which advocated the involvement of Christians in contemporary problems. In his influential book, *Social Aspects of Christianity and Other Essays*, Ely asserted that Moses should set an example for the modern church. "Moses founded a commonwealth which, for generations, continued free, happy, prosperous, knowing neither pauperism nor excessive wealth; and Moses, viewed merely as a statesman, probably never stood so high in the estimation of scholars as he does to-day. Yet the Church passes over the Mosaic economic legislation as of no consequence, or as of no binding force."[110]

The Mosaic economic legislation that Ely referred to had formed the corner-stone of the political campaigns of the radical socialist Henry George. Pointing to the principles of the fair distribution of resources propounded in the Penta-teuch, George called for a reform of the tax system that would tax land alone. Referencing Leviticus 25:13 and 23 as well as Numbers 33:54, George argued that Moses "not only provided for the fair division of the land among the people, and for making it fallow and common every seventh year, but by the institution of the jubilee he provided for a redistribution of the land every fifty years and made monopoly impossible." Yet George realized that many who believed that "the Mosiac institutions were literally dictated by the Almighty, would nonetheless denounce this scheme of land ownership as 'irreligious and 'communistic.' " More generally, George attacked the most prevalent use of the Ten Commandments in turn-of-the-century American society. "It is not the protection of property, but the protection of humanity, that is the aim of the Mosaic code."[111] So contentious were George's policies that Father Edward McGlynn, a Catholic priest engaged in political activity among New York City's immigrants, was excommunicated for supporting George's 1886 bid for the mayoralty.[112]

Just as the strict application of the Mosaic code would fundamentally have subverted property ownership, it would also have subverted that other tenet of entrepreneurial capitalism, interest. As Ely pointed out, usury, which in biblical times simply meant the charging of interest, was forbidden to the Israelites.[113] Edward H. Rogers, another advocate of the Social Gospel, wrote *"Like Unto Me"; or, The Resemblance Between Moses and Christ: A Workingman's Views of the Relation of the Church to the People*, which also attacked usury. He argued that Christ accorded with Moses in abhorring moneylending. More generally, Rogers argued that the Protestant church allied itself with the status quo by suppressing the more radical aspects of both Christ and Moses. Rogers attempted "to show that the conception of Christ, which is held in the Protes-tant Churches, is partial in its nature, and is therefore inadequate, inasmuch as it omits or fails to give due weight to certain strongly marked peculiarities of Moses which were equally prominent in Christ."[114]

Elbert Hubbard, who believed that Moses had been a great man but not a miracle worker, lamented the fact that his contemporaries could more readily accept the ten plagues than they could those aspects of the Mosaic code in-commensurate with industrial capitalism. "The laws of Moses still influence the world, but not even the orthodox Jews follow him literally. We bring our reason to bear upon the precepts of Moses, and those that are not for us we gently pass over." Hubbard explained how most managed to ignore the Moses-mandated land redistribution. "We explain that in this instance the inspired writer lapsed and merely mirrored the ignorance of his time. Or else we fall back upon the undoubted fact that various writers and translators have tam-pered with the original text."[115]

Critics of the social order, particularly those allied with the labor movement, drew parallels between the tyranny of the Pharaoh and the tyranny of capitalism. A Portland railroad worker drew a lesson about labor and management from the Pullman strike and boycott. "Were Moses now living, and the Almighty should send him to a General Manager's office to protest against corporation robberies, he would be forthwith arrested and thrown into jail, and if Moses should appeal to the Supreme Court, the infamous proceedings would be sustained and declared constitutional; and therefore, the way I look at it, the corporation slaves of the United States are in a worse case than were the slaves of Pharaoh."[116] J. A. Crawford, Illinois district president of the United Mine Workers, talking about biblical precedents to unionization, made Moses and Aaron sound like shop stewards. "The third attempt at organizing labor was made by the authority of Jehovah, instituted and carried to a successful termination by 'The Walking Delegates,' Moses and Aaron, for the purpose of redeeming Israel from Egyptian taskmasters."[117]

Depending upon their intertextual exposures and social determinants, viewers of *The Life of Moses* could thus have applied a variety of interpretive frameworks, ranging from the overarching moral appropriation to the right- or left-leaning partisan appropriations. *Moses*, however, does nothing to encourage the more politically extreme appropriations, eliding those aspects of the Pentateuch seized on by reactionaries and radicals. The films avoid partisan controversy primarily through omission, for example, by not showing Moses mandating land redistribution, or by not showing the deaths of Aaron's sons. In an age when religion was often employed to uphold the social order, however, Vitagraph may well have expected the films to resonate most strongly with the prevalent moral appropriation, not only in the clerical constituencies to which the company hoped to appeal but more broadly among both repressive and progressive reformers concerned with the problem of cheap amusements.

Conclusion

We opened this chapter with a description of the warm reception with which the Orthodox Jews of Minnesota's Milo Theatre greeted Vitagraph's cinematic rendition of their "racial" hero. Although we have no direct evidence about how the films were received in New York, *The Life of Moses* may well have elicited the same enthusiastic response in lower East Side nickelodeons. The denizens of this area even had the opportunity to see the films in an "educational" setting, since the Educational Alliance showed the Moses reels accompanied by a lecture and musical selections.[118] Although the Reform Jews who funded the alliance may well have objected to Vitagraph's literal rendition of Moses' miracles, they seem to have tolerated the films, perhaps, as we have suggested, because they considered them literary adaptations and thus subject to the same interpretive latitude they granted the Bible.

The little available evidence indicates that Protestants, too, responded favorably to *Moses*. In February 1910 Charles Sprague Smith of the People's Institute arranged a "special program of educational motion pictures" for "clergymen and church workers" in order to "demonstrate the possibilities of pictures for social entertainment and instruction, and to acquaint church workers with the truly excellent qualities of motion pictures and the wide range of subjects included by the manufacturers." Smith told the audience that, "the gathering . . . was the first of a series of similar demonstrations that would be given at the various churches of the city." The vast majority of the films were actualities, with such titles as *From Egg to Spit* (Pathé) and *Fishing Industry at Gloucester* (Edison), the only exceptions being *Pippa Passes* (Biograph, 1909) and the fourth reel of *Moses*.[119] Clearly, Smith intended to appeal to his audience's Victorian didactic instincts by presenting a program that strongly resembled those shown during the prenickelodeon era by high-class vaudeville houses and traveling exhibitors such as Lyman Howe, rather than the mix of comedy and melodrama presented at contemporary moving picture shows.

Although direct evidence of the reception of *Moses* remains scanty, Vitagraph seems to have succeeded in placating the Protestant establishment—from which came both the industry's most vociferous opponents and ardent supporters—while at the same time appealing to a wider audience that included both Orthodox and Reform Jews. As we have suggested, this was no easy task, since the seemingly ideal subject of Moses was, in fact, quite contentious both in terms of his representation and his potential appropriation. With regard to representation, Vitagraph engaged in the unifying discourse of the natural, guaranteeing conformance with both sides of the debate over biblical truth and thereby achieving wide acceptability. When forced to take a stand on the discourse of the natural versus the supernatural, as in the representation of the miraculous, the company wisely opted to side with the fundamentalists who spearheaded the attacks against the industry. With regard to appropriations, Vitagraph offered nothing to encourage the more extreme partisan appropriations. In all probability, they simply expected the films to be interpreted within the framework of the overarching image of Moses as lawgiver.

The Life of Moses offers perhaps the clearest example of the dangers to be avoided and benefits to be gained by appropriating a revered cultural figure for presentation in the low cultural venue of the nickelodeon. Through its strategy of carefully positioning itself with regard to other cultural producers, evident in the studio's employment of the Reverend Peters and the care it took to accommodate what we have termed the discourses of the natural and supernatural, Vitagraph placated its most vociferous opponents. Although the particularly vexed nature of religion—as an institution of cultural reproduction that brooked little dissent—potentially rendered any cinematic incarnation of Moses more offensive than that of a literary or historical figure, such an endeavor also offered the opportunity to garner more praise. A carefully mounted film would appeal not only to those preachers damning the new medium but also to a much broader spectrum of the population, given the absolute centrality of Moses in a Judeo-Christian culture.

IN 1912 the Vitagraph Company staged a motion picture exhibition for President Taft and several members of his cabinet. *Vitagraph Life Portrayals* reported that "for the first time in the history of the United States moving pictures were exhibited in the White House. The Senatorial room was transformed into an exhibition parlor and the Vitagraph Company of America gave an exhibition lasting thirty five minutes. . . . The pictures shown were *The Battle Hymn of the Republic* and *The Signing of the Bill for the Admission of the Territory of Arizona as One of the States of the Union*." When President Lincoln appeared in *The Battle Hymn of the Republic*, President Taft was "visibly and deeply impressed."[1]

The Battle Hymn of the Republic, a Vitagraph historical, recounts the writing of the famous song by a divinely inspired Mrs. Julia Ward Howe. The film consists largely of a series of discontinuous tableau shots grounded in the sleeping Mrs. Howe's subjectivity. Following the intertitle "He is sifting out the hearts of men before His judgment seat" comes a shot featuring a procession of famous historical personalities. Familiar costumes and gestures suggest the characters of Cardinal Richelieu, Napoleon, Nero, George Washington, and Dante, all of whom walk toward the camera and then offscreen as if approaching the judgment seat. Inasmuch as it incorporates characters related to Vitagraph's literary, historical, and biblical subjects, *The Battle Hymn* might be termed a compilation quality film.

In a few short years, film had been transformed from a cheap amusement despised and feared by many "respectable" Americans to a form of entertainment appropriate for the most respectable American of all, a transformation signaled by the screening of a quality film at the White House. Should we then conclude that the alliance of quality films with the counterattraction strategy and the uplifting rhetoric of the assimilationists played a central role in the repositioning of the film industry in American culture? As we argued in chapter 2, no single factor determined this repositioning. Yet the quality films, although they represented but a fraction of the industry's output, constitute the clearest instance of the film industry's deliberate attempt to upgrade perceptions of the medium among key authorized interpretive communities and institutions of cultural reproduction. This effort did not fully succeed until late in the teens—coincident, curiously enough, with a decrease in the number of quality film productions.

The unusual clarity of the struggle of dominant social formations to contain the period's perceived cultural crisis through top-down control motivated our focus on the sociocultural function and status of the quality films and our rejection of some of the more traditional methods of film studies. We have not engaged in "connoisseurship," that is, evaluation of film as an aesthetic object. Nor have we interpreted the films either through presentist, textually extrapolated schemata or through an exclusive reliance on industry discourse. Rather, we have chosen to offer a detailed consideration of the industry's alliance with respectable culture by looking at the operations of interpretive communities, institutions of cultural reproduction, texts, and readers or viewers within the realms of literature, history, and religion. Authorized interpretive communities generated interpretations and modes of representation of cultural texts and figures circulated by institutions of cultural reproduction often specific to one of these three realms. Consequently, the patterns of exposure, readings, and social appropriations for literary, historical, and religious texts differed significantly from one another. Sensitivity to these differences has led to a more precise understanding of how discursive alliances, adherence to endorsed interpretations, and the emulation of certain modes of representation positioned the Vitagraph producers among other cultural producers, and of how viewers' probable intertextual exposures may have inflected reception of the quality films.

In the production of the five quality films discussed in this volume, Vitagraph paid great attention to the discourses of various authorized interpretive communities and institutions of cultural reproduction, hoping to placate particularly influential factions. With Shakespeare, Vitagraph emulated the spectacular staging of the Broadway theatre while simultaneously adhering to the reduced key phrase/key scene form most common in Shakespearean ephemera. With Washington, Vitagraph drew on the authority of historians for their humanized portrait while again relying on the key image/key event approach to present the heroic Washington familiar from statuary, parades, and chromolithographs. With Moses, Vitagraph incorporated elements of both the discourse of the natural and the supernatural.

The textual polysemy inherent in such wide-ranging referents seems to have been calculated to appeal not only to the "better classes" whom the industry wished to attract but to current patrons as well. The industry's own rhetoric of "dual address" reinforces this conclusion and speaks to the bourgeoisification debate current among scholars of the early American cinema. Many scholars of early film assert that the industry during this period attempted to attract a middle-class audience by upgrading cinematic subject matter and signifying practices to accord with those of more respectable media. The discursive framing that positioned the quality films among diverse authorized interpretive communities and institutions of cultural reproduction would lead one to conclude that while bourgeoisification certainly aimed at the inclusion of new viewers, it did not entail the exclusion of current viewers, as the industry sought to create a mass audience.

Yet the industry does not seem to have assumed that the quality films would elicit a uniform response across social formations. In fact, in associating its quality figures with the period's notion of "high culture," industry discourse implicitly suggested a disjunction between the position of these films in the cultural hierarchy and the cultural exposures of its current patrons. Although Vitagraph's publicity insisted that all viewers would enjoy the quality films, it also implied that certain viewers lacked the requisite intertextual frames to produce "correct" readings, that is, "informed" and "nuanced" interpretations congruent with the producers' references. Our presentist assumptions about cultural exposures would tend to confirm the industry's judgment, leading us to wonder what marginalized audiences might have made of *Julius Caesar* or *Napoleon, The Man of Destiny.*

But our evidence concerning viewers' probable intertextual exposures permits us to examine the space between the intertextual frames referenced by the producers of the quality films and the intertextual frames that actually inflected the conditions of reception for these films. Contra expectations, we have shown that the attribute "high" is to some extent misleading, in that such cultural figures as Shakespeare and Napoleon were part of most people's everyday experience. Members of all social formations would thus have had intertextual frames for making sense of the quality films, even though some would have been more widespread than others and some would have been more culturally sanctioned than others. Our demonstration of the multiple ways to make sense of these films obviously challenges notions of intrinsic textual meaning. More importantly, though, it attests to the social function of textual engagements—that the reasons for perceiving some engagements as superior to others are always wholly external to the text. Patterns of textual circulation and the rhetoric of institutions of cultural reproduction suggest, moreover, that textual engagements, no matter what their form, were perceived as incorporating subjects into the hegemonic order, either through the acknowledgment of consensual values or through the reinforcement of cultural hierarchies.

During the period, the array of "acceptable" engagements, that is, those encouraged by the authorized interpretive communities with which the film industry wished to ally itself, were often associated with "uplift" and "assimilation." Hence, the industry's discourse clothed all the quality films in the garb of "uplift" and "assimilation," rather than distinguishing among literaries, historicals, and biblicals—even though, as we have shown, these terms took on different meanings and signaled different relations to the hegemonic order within the three realms of literature, history, and religion. Engagement with Shakespeare, thought the assimilationists, would expose the reader to the taste, discrimination, and gentility characteristic of the "best that has been thought and said," an exposure that emphasized the putative humanizing potential of the hegemonic order while masking the brute realities of the dehumanization it perpetrated. In the case of Washington, "uplift" meant endorsing the hegemonic order in the specifically nationalist terms of patriotism and Americanization. For Moses, "uplift" entailed an acknowledgment of the moral underpinnings of the hegemonic order in terms that transcended nation, extending to Judeo-Christian society as a whole.

Although the realms of literature, history, and religion bolstered the hegemonic order in distinctive ways, a surprisingly minimal level of textual engagement was deemed sufficient for this purpose. Indeed, the rhetoric of educators, cultural critics, librarians, and other representatives of institutions of cultural reproduction implied that textual encounters could fully incorporate subjects into the hegemonic order. We have shown, however, that these encounters may have elicited little more than simple recognition of the cultural figure or text and nodding obeisance to the hegemonic order connoted. This is not surprising given the incredibly reduced forms in which many of these cultural figures and texts circulated in the most pervasive institutions of cultural reproduction—schools, civic festivals, advertising, and so forth—all of which produced intertexts that figured so centrally in Vitagraph's conditions of production. In other words, such textual encounters may well have fallen far short of eliciting full acceptance of the agenda of dominant social formations. Moreover, even the passing recognition of these cultural figures and texts may not have been activated by exposure to endorsed intertexts but rather have arisen from encounters with nonendorsed intertexts or, as in the case of Shakespeare, from what might be termed indigenous exposures within the communities of marginalized social formations.

Paradoxically, engagements with cultural texts or figures that permitted a very wide range of interpretations and modes of representation also served to reinforce the hegemonic order. As we have seen with Francesca da Rimini and Napoleon, the diversity among circulated intertexts, which arose from the lack of an explicitly consensual function, encouraged an equally broad spectrum of textual engagements, some endorsed, many not. And while the competence to produce any particular endorsed engagement would have served the immediate goal of helping to mark the reader's position in the social hierarchy, it also served to legitimize the social order as a whole, naturalizing and sustaining the unequal distribution of economic and political power.

This volume has of necessity focused on the conditions of production and reception for the quality films as they related to the hegemonic order, given that the process of historical filtration tends to privilege evidence emanating from authorized interpretive communities or well-established institutions of cultural reproduction. Should we then consider the hegemonic order totalizing and assume that the reciprocal functions of consensus and distinction fully account for the interface between the quality films and the larger, historical social context? The weight of our empirical evidence might support such a conclusion. For each of our cultural texts or figures, however, we have uncovered a few provocative data that suggest potential textual engagements outside the hegemonic processes of consensus and distinction.

Arising from intertexts neither produced by authorized interpretive communities nor circulated by dominant institutions of cultural reproduction, these inherently marginalized engagements—Moses as socialist land reformer, for example—nonetheless constitute the sole remaining traces of an ongoing contestation of dominant interpretations and modes of representation. These alternative textual engagements may even attest to the presence of countervailing hegemonies, that is, opposing views of how the world might work, that are more than purely reactive to the existing order. And we have at least demonstrated that mainstream cultural products can be selectively appropriated for very different ends than those imagined by their producers. If the atomized nature of the evidence admittedly forces speculation, the alternative is a silent acceptance of the voices of dominant social formations.

Speculation, however, should not necessarily be recommended as a methodological approach to the complexities of historical reception and cultural transformation. Our fundamental principle has been Marx's injunction to work from the concrete to the abstract, which has encouraged us to avoid engaging in abstract theorizing and imposing a totalizing model upon the complexities of history. While this book reveals the interplay of historical, social, economic, and cultural forces at a particularly vexed moment for both the film industry and American culture, the very historical specificity of our analysis precludes the adducing of an easily generalizable model for future scholarly endeavors. Rather, we can only urge full consideration of texts, intertexts, and contexts, carried out with sensitivity to the interplay of historical forces and discourses, coupled with an overall awareness of contradiction, complexity, and overdetermination, all of which can lead to a productive dialectical interaction between theoretical assumptions and empirical evidence.

APPENDIX

Vitagraph's Description of
the Washington and Napoleon Films

Washington under the British Flag and *Washington
under the American Flag*
(From "Vitagraph High Art Films: The Career of Washington in Film Form,"
Kinematograph and Lantern Weekly, August. 19, 1909, pp. 719, 721)

SCENE ONE of WASHINGTON UNDER THE BRITISH FLAG reveals the future President on a surveying expedition. Pretty scenes of woodland suitably tinted are introduced. The small party are attacked by Indians and Washington's abilities as a soldier are thus early displayed in putting them to flight.

Later, on his appointment of Agent-General in the British Forces, Washington is dispatched on a mission to the Indians to protest against attempts by the French to seize certain lands. He is well received, smokes the pipe of peace with the chief, and successfully carries out his mission.

War now breaking out with the French, Washington is placed in charge of Fort Necessity. Outnumbered, he surrenders after a stout resistance, but is allowed to march out with military honours—a very effective scene.

Washington next joins the Staff of General Braddock, in charge of the troops in the Colony. Braddock, disregarding the advice of Washington to send out some scouts, is ambushed and loses many men. Braddock himself is mortally wounded.

Washington, now Commander-in-Chief, sets out to capture Fort Duquesne. The French commander withdraws his troops during the night, and Washington arrives to find the Fort in flames. Very effective scenes show the firing of the Fort by the French, their retreat with their Indian allies, and the arrival of the British forces, and the hoisting of the British flag on the ruins.

This section of the film closes with some daintily presented scenes, showing Washington's courtship and marriage. A pretty garden is the scene of his first meeting with Martha Custis. Later, in the drawing room of the house, he is seen leaning over her as she sits at the piano. His men outside the house are seen impatiently waiting for their chief, looking impatiently at the windows of the drawing room through which the guests can be seen engaged in a dance (another good effect).

THE WEDDING appropriately concludes this section of the film. The ceremony is shown in church, and the bride and bridegroom drive away amid the cheers of their friends gathered on the verandah.

WASHINGTON UNDER THE AMERICAN FLAG begins with a finely staged scene— one of the best of the subjects—showing the Virginia Legislature on the occasion when Patrick Henry's famous speech which lighted the first spark of the Revolution was delivered. The acting here is superb, both on the part of the orator and on that of his audience, who are worked up to a passion of excitement. Shortly hostilities commence in earnest and the next scene shows—

BUNKER'S HILL—The view is taken from within the American fortifications— beyond can be seen the sea and the British ships of war. Three drummers—an old grey-haired man and two mere boys—parade in the trenches. The English troops attack the position, the Americans resist bravely but are forced to give way, and then the flag is pulled down and the Union Jack run up in its place.

Defeat is soon succeeded by victory, and to Washington falls the honour of defeating the British at Trenton. To engage the Hessians, under Raff, it was necessary to cross the Delaware in a blinding snowstorm. A wonderfully presented scene shows the boats forcing their way between the ice hummocks— the snow swirling around them and danger from the presence of the ice always threatening. On the other side the Hessians are completely surprised and forced to surrender.

IN CAMP AT VALLEY FORGE shows the "darkest hour" of the campaign. Washington halted here for some time to develop new plans, train his troops, etc., and all the news is of defeat and loss. He is greatly afected by the death of a soldier which he witnessed, and dozing later in his own room, re-enacts the scenes in his dreams—a good "vision" effect also showing how his imagination turns to his wife and children and the welcome they will give him.

THE SIEGE OF YORKTOWN marks the turn of the tide. The English troops are forced to march out and their officers to deliver their swords to Washington, which he returns to them.

ON THE WAY TO INAUGURATION shows his triumphal progress to the capital, welcomed at every town by children who strew roses in his path.

THE FIRST INAUGURATION shows the hero taking the oath on the platform erected at New York, before a large assembly, which cheers him madly.

HOME AT MOUNT VERNON shows the declining years of the great national hero. He is seen instructing servants in his garden, receiving guests with old world courtesy, and with his wife by his side, holding an informal reception on the steps of the house.

The *New York Dramatic Mirror*'s review indicates that both the *Kinematograph and Lantern Weekly*'s description and the surviving print of *Washington under the American Flag* do not include what may have been the final shot of the original release print. "The film ends with a symbolical picture which should have been omitted, as it does not measure up to the rest. In it there is a scene-painted make-shift representing a statue of Washington that is a shock to the eye after the excellent scenes that have preceded it" (*NYDM*, July 17, 1909, p. 17).

The Life Drama of Napoleon Bonaparte and the Empress Josephine of France and *Napoleon, The Man of Destiny*
(From "Vitagraph Co. of America," *Film Index*, April 10, 1909, p. 8)

THE LIFE DRAMA OF NAPOLEON BONAPARTE AND THE EMPRESS JOSEPHINE OF FRANCE

Scene 1.—The Prophecy.—Josephine, while walking in the gardens on the island of Martinique is told that "she will be more than a Queen and yet outlive her dignity."

Scene 2.—Napoleon Meets Josephine At Madame Tallien's Salon And Falls In Love With Her.—Josephine with other ladies are seated about as Napoleon enters and is introduced. It is a case of love at first sight. As Napoleon makes ardent love to Josephine, the others thoughtfully withdraw.

Scene 3.—Napoleon's Departure To Take Command Of The Army Of Italy Three Days After His Marriage To Josephine.—Napoleon bids good-bye to Josephine, mounts his horse and rides away, his staff and the troops following.

Scene 4.—Napoleon Having Been Crowned Emperor Of France, Longs For A Son To Perpetuate His Name And Contemplates Divorce From Josephine.—Napoleon enters the throne room, walks restlessly up and down and at last calls his valet whom he directs to summon Josephine. She enters with her attendants. Napoleon dismisses the ladies, tells Josephine that he must have a son. She, having expected this, is resigned and turns away in a swoon.

Scene 5.—The Public Proclamation of Divorce Between Napoleon And Josephine In The Grand Salon Of The Tuilleries.—The members of Napoleon's family, the Imperial Council of State are assembled as Josephine enters, signs the paper and leaves the room.

Scene 6.—The Parting Of Napoleon And Josephine After The Divorce.—In his bed-chamber, Napoleon is discovered in great grief. His valet is endeavoring to calm him. The door opens and Josephine enters. After a pathetic farewell, she staggers from the room.

Scene 7.—Josephine At Malmaison After The Divorce—Memories Of Napoleon.—Josephine seated on a chair, sees a vision of Napoleon. She crosses to the mantel, caresses the bust, sits down and plays the harp. As the vision vanishes, she stretches out her arms in despair and falls to the ground.

NAPOLEON, THE MAN OF DESTINY

The picture opens with Napoleon at Malmaison after the battle of Waterloo. He visits the room where Josephine died, enters slowly, walks sadly around, looks at her portrait, then sits in a chair and falls asleep. In successive visions he sees:

Marengo—The Austrians' charge. Napoleon with his generals pass. The "wall of granite" is impregnable.

Napoleon, Emperor.—The Coronation scene. Court assembled in Noter [sic] Dame. The Pope blesses Napoleon. He places the crown on his own head then crowns Josephine.

Austerlitz.—Picturing Napoleon and his staff in the center. The Austrian generals approaching and surrendering their swords in token of defeat.

Jena.—Napoleon mounted on his famous white charger in the thick of battle.

Friedland.—The charge of the Cuirasseurs. Napoleon watching the battle through a telescope.

Marriage with Marie Louise of Austria.—Ceremony being performed by an Archbishop in the grand gallery of the Louvre. Napoleon's mother, brothers and relations in attendance.

Birth of King of Rome.—The court assembled in an ante-chamber as Napoleon enters carrying the infant.

Education of the King of Rome.—Napoleon's son playing with his soldiers, the Cardinals, Bishops, Generals, and Soldiers watching.

Moscow.—The retreat with the dead and wounded in the blinding snow. The city of Moscow burning in the distance.

Abdication.—Farewell to Old Guard. Napoleon embraces the general and kisses the flag as the soldiers weep.

Waterloo.—The dying soldiers cheering their leader. Napoleon on his horse seeing defeat. Marshall Soult leads the general's horse away.

St. Helena.—The exiled emperor standing on a rock meditating, looking sadly out to sea.

Notes

THE FOLLOWING abbreviations are used throughout the notes:

CSS   Charles Sprague Smith Papers
CU   Cooper Union Library
HLP   Henry Leipziger Papers
MPW   *Moving Picture World*
NYDM   *New York Dramatic Mirror*
NYPLPA   New York Public Library for the Performing Arts at Lincoln Center
PIR   People's Institute Records
RBMD/NYPL Rare Books and Manuscripts Division, New York Public Library
VB   *Vitagraph Bulletin*

Please note that the bibliographic information for several of the trade press journals is of necessity somewhat inconsistent, given that these publications tended to change format from time to time. In all instances, we have tried to provide the most complete documentation available.

Introduction

1. Albert E. Smith, *Two Reels and a Crank* (Garden City, N.Y.: Doubleday, 1952), p. 218.

2. Ibid., p. 263.

3. The exact release dates for these films are: *Francesca di Rimini, or The Two Brothers*, February 8, 1908; *Julius Caesar*, December 1, 1908; *The Life Drama of Napoleon Bonaparte and the Empress Josephine of France*, April 6, 1909; *Napoleon, The Man of Destiny*, April 10, 1909; *Washington under the British Flag*, June 29, 1909; *Washington under the American Flag*, July 3, 1909; *The Life of Moses: I, The Persecution of the Children of Israel by the Egyptians*, December 12, 1909; *II, Forty Years in the Land of Midian*, January 4, 1910; *III, Plagues of Egypt and the Deliverance of the Hebrews*, January 25, 1910; *IV, The Victory of Israel*, February 12, 1910; *V, The Promised Land*, February 19, 1910 (Paolo Cherchi-Usai, *Vitagraph Company of America: Il cinema prima di Hollywood* [Pordenone: Edizioni Studio Tesi, 1987]). The National Film Archive and the Museum of Modern Art both possess 35-mm prints of *Francesca di Rimini*. A 35-mm print of *Julius Caesar* is at the National Film Archive, and 35-mm prints of *The Life Drama of Napoleon Bonaparte and the Empress Josephine of France* and *Napoleon, The Man of Destiny* are at the National Film Archive and the Library of Congress. The National Film Archive has 35-mm prints of *Washington under the British Flag* and *Washington under the American Flag*; the George Eastman House also has a 35-mm print of the latter, although we have not seen it. A

16-mm print of all five reels of *The Life of Moses* is at the Museum of Modern Art. The Library of Congress has incomplete 35-mm prints of reels three and four as well as the complete five reels in 28 mm.

4. We use the terms *social formations*, *marginalized social formations*, and *dominant social formations* throughout the book in contrast to the more traditional *class*. The latter term, vexed as it admittedly is, has come to connote primarily an economic analysis of societal divisions, whereas *social formations* allows for the consideration of such factors as social, cultural, academic, and political capital that, while undoubtedly related to economics, are not necessarily economically expressed. The terms *dominant* and *marginalized*, then, relate to relative positions within any existing hierarchy.

5. Two provisos are necessary. While our approach potentially provides an almost infinite array of intertextual evidence, we seek to be exemplary rather than exhaustive, using cultural artifacts that suggest the broad expanse of reception and the probable response of hypothetical readers. And since all of these "intertexts" obviously existed in the world as "texts" in their own right, we use a relational sense of text and intertext. For example, when we discuss Vitagraph's *The Life of Moses*, we consider the Pentateuch itself an intertext, as we do the expressive forms related to it, such as commentaries and religious paintings. This distinction points to a particular object, the text—in this case the film—at the referential center of a wider range of intertextual expressions that help to delimit its meaning at any particular historical moment.

6. Antonio Gramsci, *Selections from the Prison Notebooks of Antonio Gramsci*, ed. and trans. Quintin Hoare and Geoffrey Nowell Smith (New York: International Publishers, 1971), p. 12.

7. Ibid.

8. For a useful discussion of the cultural aspects of hegemony, see T. J. Jackson Lears, "The Concept of Cultural Hegemony: Problems and Possibilities," *American Historical Review* 90:3 (1985): 567–593. For a broader consideration of the use of hegemony within Marxist thought and practice, see Perry Anderson, "The Antinomies of Antonio Gramsci," *New Left Review* 100 (1976–1977): 5–78.

9. Raymond Williams, *Marxism and Literature* (Oxford: Oxford University Press, 1977), pp. 112–113.

10. Lears, "Concept of Cultural Hegemony," p. 579. The sheer volume of historical monographs on the period's institutionalization of the hegemonic through the schools, professional societies, and the like, as well as its employment of the forces of political domination in terms of police forces, the militia, and armories, attests to the constant upheaval of these years.

11. Pierre Bourdieu, *Distinction: A Social Critique of the Judgement of Taste* (Cambridge, Mass.: Harvard University Press, 1984).

12. Ibid., p. 483.

13. These two paragraphs are a very quick gloss on Bourdieu's complex and multi-faceted theory of social reproduction, as presented in a myriad of books and articles. For a bibliography of Bourdieu's publications, see Loïc J. D. Wacquant, "Toward a Reflexive Sociology: A Workshop with Pierre Bourdieu," *Sociological Theory* 7:1 (1989): 26–63. For explications and critiques of Bourdieu, see Rogers Brubaker, "Rethinking Classical Theory: The Sociological Vision of Pierre Bourdieu," *Theory and Society* 14:7 (1985): 745–775, and David Gartman, "Culture as Class Symbolization or Mass Reification? A Critique of Bourdieu's *Distinction*," *American Journal of Sociology* 7:2 (1991): 421–447.

14. Pierre Bourdieu, "The Production of Belief: Contribution to an Economy of Symbolic Goods," in Richard Collins, James Curran, Nicholas Garnham, Paddy Schlesinger, and Colin Sparks, eds., *Media, Culture and Society: A Critical Reader* (London: Sage, 1986), p. 155.

15. The phrase "interpretive communities" will probably remind most readers of the work of Stanley Fish. In a recent formulation of the concept, Fish asserts that an interpretive community is "not so much a group of individuals who shared a point of view, but a point of view or way of organizing experience that shared individuals in the sense that its assumed distinctions, categories of understanding, and stipulations of relevance and irrelevance were the content of the consciousness of community members who were therefore no longer individuals, but, insofar as they were embedded in the community's enterprise, community property" ("Change," in *Doing What Comes Naturally: Change, Rhetoric, and the Practice of Theory in Literary and Legal Studies* [Durham, N.C.: Duke University Press, 1989], p. 141).

The period from 1880 to 1910 saw a rapid growth of authorized interpretive communities in the form of professional societies, empowered by tradition and self-appointment. The American Library Association was established in 1879, the Modern Language Association in 1883, the American Historical Association in 1884, the Academy of Political and Social Science and the American Economic Association in 1885, and the American Political Science Association in 1903. Others such as the National Education Association, founded in 1857, experienced a great growth in membership and influence during this period. For a discussion of the emergence of professional organizations, see Magali Sarfatti Larson, *The Rise of Professionalism: A Sociological Analysis* (Berkeley: University of California Press, 1977).

16. Some period observers noted this dynamic. Edward Alsworth Ross, for example, explored the mechanisms of social control, which he described as "that domination [by society over the individual] which is intended and which fulfills a function in the life of society." See his *Social Control* (New York: Macmillan, 1914; orig. pub. 1901). The substance of his book first appeared as a series of articles in the *American Journal of Sociology* between 1896 and 1898.

17. Our concept of institutions of cultural reproduction is more limited than Althusser's totalizing concept of ideological state apparatuses, which includes "institutions" such as the family. See Louis Althusser, *Lenin and Philosophy and Other Essays* (New York: Monthly Review Press, 1971), in particular "Ideology and Ideological State Apparatuses," pp. 127–186.

Of course, many institutions during the period served the function of cultural reproduction, not all of which dispensed valorized culture in the form of literature, history, or religion. A contemporary survey of leisure activities in Manhattan enumerated some of these, underscoring the motive behind their state support. "In devoting public funds to indoor and outdoor playgrounds, parks, lectures, libraries, museums, recreation centers, vacation schools, music, and popular festivals, civic leaders recognize that the municipality is not only offering its people something of positive value, but is also counteracting influences which are generally detrimental, and against which only the power of the municipality can effectively work" (Michael Davis, *The Exploitation of Pleasure* [New York: Russell Sage Foundation, 1911], p. 4). We shall later elaborate upon the counteracting of detrimental influences by institutions of cultural reproduction.

18. For a useful overview of current debates, see Martin Allor's "Relocating the Site of the Audience" and the responses to it in *Critical Studies in Mass Communication* 5:3 (1988): 217–254.

19. Janice Radway, *Reading the Romance: Women, Patriarchy, and Popular Literature* (Chapel Hill: University of North Carolina Press, 1984); David Morley, *The "Nationwide" Audience* (London: The British Film Institute, 1980); and Ien Ang, *Watching Dallas: Soap Opera and the Melodramatic Imagination* (London: Methuen, 1985).

20. Some of the key works here are Stuart Hall's "Encoding/decoding" and David Morley's "Texts, Readers, Subjects," both in Stuart Hall, Dorothy Hobson, Andrew Lowe, and Paul Willis, eds., *Culture, Media, Language: Working Papers in Cultural Studies, 1972–79* (London: Hutchinson, 1980), pp. 128–138 and 163–173; Tony Bennett, "Texts and History," in Peter Widdowson, ed., *Re-Reading English* (New York: Methuen, 1982); and Tony Bennett and Janet Woollacott, *Bond and Beyond: The Political Career of a Popular Hero* (London: Macmillan, 1987).

21. See particularly Christian Metz, *The Imaginary Signifier: Psychoanalysis and the Cinema* (Bloomington: Indiana University Press, 1982). Others have attempted to use cognitive psychology as a model for understanding cinematic spectatorship. See David Bordwell, *Making Meaning: Inference and Rhetoric in the Interpretation of Cinema* (Cambridge, Mass.: Harvard University Press, 1989). The reception/reader response tradition mapped out by Hans Robert Jauss, Wolfgang Iser, and Stanley Fish, among others, has contributed another perspective on textually extrapolated readers. For overviews, see Elizabeth Freund, *The Return of the Reader: Reader Response Criticism* (New York: Methuen, 1987), and Robert C. Holub, *Reception Theory: A Critical Introduction* (New York: Methuen, 1984).

22. For an overview of the theoretical approaches to female spectatorship, see Janet Bergstrom and Mary Ann Doane, "The Female Spectator: Contexts and Directions," *Camera Obscura* 20/21 (1989): 5–27.

23. Laura Mulvey, "Visual Pleasure and Narrative Cinema," *Screen* 16:3 (1975): 6–18; *Camera Obscura* 20/21. This particularly useful issue of *Camera Obscura* surveys the members of feminist film theory's interpretive community, seeking their latest formulations of spectatorship generally and female spectatorship in particular. The issue also contains a comprehensive general bibliography. See also E. Deidre Pribram, ed., *Female Spectators: Looking at Film and Television* (London: Verso, 1988).

24. See Patrice Petro, *Joyless Streets: Women and Melodramatic Representation in Weimar Germany* (Princeton: Princeton University Press, 1989), and Miriam Hansen, *Babel and Babylon: Spectatorship in American Silent Film* (Cambridge, Mass.: Harvard University Press, 1991). Hansen's work is particularly relevant to our own since several of her chapters deal with spectatorship in the early American silent cinema. The interested reader should also consult *Camera Obscura* 22 (1990), which focuses on feminism and film history.

25. See Janet Staiger, " 'The Handmaiden of Villainy': Methods and Problems in Studying the Historical Reception of a Film," *Wide Angle* 8:1 (1986): 19–27, and "Reception Studies: The Death of the Reader," in R. Barton Palmer, ed., *The Cinematic Text: Methods and Approaches* (New York: AMS Press, 1989), pp. 353–367. *Wide Angle* 8:1 is devoted to articles on the topic of reception. Unfortunately, Janet Staiger's important book, *Interpreting Films: Studies in the Historical Reception of American Cinema* (Princeton: Princeton University Press, 1992), appeared just as this manuscript was in the final stages of preparation.

26. See, for example, the spring 1990 issue of *The Velvet Light Trap* on the conditions of reception. See also Janet Staiger, "Announcing Wares, Winning Patrons, Voicing Ideals: Thinking about the History and Theory of Film Advertising," *Cinema Journal* 29:3 (1990): 3–31.

27. See, for example, Ben Singer, "Female Power in the Serial-Queen Melodrama: The Etiology of an Anomaly," *Camera Obscura* 22 (1990): 90–129; Susan Ohmer, "Female Spectatorship and Women's Magazines: Hollywood, *Good Housekeeping* and World War II," *The Velvet Light Trap* 25 (1990): 53–68; and Michael Renov, "Advertising/Photojournalism/Cinema: The Shifting Rhetoric of Forties Female Representation," *Quarterly Review of Film and Video* 11:1 (1989): 1–21.

28. Bennett, "Texts and History," p. 224.

29. Bennett and Woollacott, *Bond and Beyond*, p. 56.

30. We refer the reader to the work of Stanley Fish on readers and interpretive communities. See *Is There a Text in This Class? The Authority of Interpretive Communities* (Cambridge, Mass.: Harvard University Press, 1980), and *Doing What Comes Naturally*.

31. Much of our intertextual evidence is New York–centered, given the city's cultural primacy in turn-of-the-century America (as the headquarters of periodical publishing, of the theatre, and of the film industry) coupled with its importance in debates about the social/cultural crisis. We have not, then, addressed the problem of regional variations in intertextual exposures. We had initially intended to be more concrete, comparing New York City with a smaller community, but two factors prohibited this approach. More evidence survives for a major metropolitan center such as New York than for a smaller community. And, given that this was a period of an emerging mass culture, many of the surviving texts that circulated in smaller communities originated in New York City.

Chapter One
Responses to Cultural Crisis:
Political Domination and Hegemony

1. For details on the Haymarket incident, see Paul Avrich, *The Haymarket Tragedy* (Princeton: Princeton University Press, 1984).

2. *American Tribune*, July 1, 1890, cited in Wallace Evan Davies, *Patriotism on Parade: The Story of Veterans' and Hereditary Organizations In America, 1783–1900* (Cambridge, Mass.: Harvard University Press, 1955), p. 294.

3. Josiah Strong, *Our Country: Its Possible Future and Its Present Crisis* (New York: Baker and Taylor, 1885), p. 43. The fear of imminent social chaos is reflected in the building of armories during this period. By 1910, for example, New York City had nearly twenty armories. See Robert M. Fogelson, *America's Armories: Architecture, Society, and Public Order* (Cambridge, Mass.: Harvard University Press, 1989).

4. Daniel Coit Gilman, quoted in William Howe Tolman, *Municipal Reform Movements in the United States* (New York: Fleming H. Revell Company, 1895), p. 37.

5. Josiah Strong, *The Challenge of the City* (New York: Young People's Missionary Movement, 1907), p. 103.

6. "Foreign Born of the United States," *National Geographic*, September 1914, p. 271. For a detailed demographic breakdown of New York City, see *Federation*, June

1902, a special issue, devoted to the urban condition, of the publication of the Federation of Churches and Christian Organizations in New York City.

7. Of the United States' ten largest cities in 1910, only two had less than 25 percent foreign born; Chicago had 35.8 percent foreign born, Boston, 36.3 percent, Cleveland, 35 percent, Detroit, 33.8 percent, and San Francisco, 31.4 percent. See Robert A. F. McDonald, *Adjustment of School Organizations to Various Population Groups* (New York City: Teachers' College, Columbia University, 1915), p. 67.

8. Many of the social surveys conducted in New York City during this period detail the profound differences among ethnic communities. See, for example, Elsa G. Herzfeld, *Family Monographs* (New York: James Kempster Printing Company, 1905); Louise Bolard More, *Wage-earners' Budgets: A Study of Standards and Cost of Living in New York City* (New York: Henry Holt and Company, 1907); and Robert Coit Chapin, *The Standard of Living among Working Men's Families in New York City* (New York: Russell Sage Foundation, 1909).

9. Henry James, *The American Scene* (New York: Harper and Brothers Publishers, 1907), pp. 82–84.

10. Strong, *Challenge of the City*, p. 103.

11. For an analysis of the role of women in the emergence of mass culture, see Ann Douglas, *The Feminization of American Culture* (New York: Alfred A. Knopf, 1977).

12. *The Independent*, August. 2, 1877, p. 16, cited in Henry F. May, *Protestant Churches and Industrial America* (New York: Octagon Books, 1963), p. 93.

13. Richard Drinnon, " 'My Men Shoot Well': Theodore Roosevelt and the Urban Frontier," in Dave Roediger and Franklin Rosemont, eds., *Haymarket Scrapbook* (Chicago: Charles H. Kerr Publishing, 1986), p. 129.

14. "Moral Insurance," *New York Times*, November 30, 1900.

15. Matthew Arnold, *Culture and Anarchy: An Essay in Political and Social Criticism* (New York: Bobbs-Merrill, 1971), p. 6.

16. As Raymond Williams has said, "Culture is one of the two or three most complicated words in the English language" (Raymond Williams, *Keywords: A Vocabulary of Culture and Society* [New York: Oxford University Press, 1976], p. 76). Williams's discussion of the term can be found on pp. 76–82.

17. Arnold, *Culture and Anarchy*, p. 69.

18. Ibid., p. 56. But even Arnold himself was not above advocating violence when cultural incorporation failed to work. For a discussion of Arnold's repressive potential, see Raymond Williams, "A Hundred Years of Culture and Anarchy," in his *Problems in Materialism and Culture* (London: Verso, 1980), pp. 3–8.

19. The prevalence of Arnoldian discourse during the period has led other scholars to analyze cultural contestation in these terms. Thomas Bender, in his discussion of what he terms "the metropolitan gentry" (many of whom would have been numbered among our "progressives"), asserts that in the United States the notion of culture as a civilizing influence derives more from Ralph Waldo Emerson than from Matthew Arnold but that the prominence of the latter obscured the former's contribution (Thomas Bender, *New York Intellect: A History of Intellectual Life in New York City from 1750 to the Beginnings of Our Own Time* [Baltimore: Johns Hopkins University Press, 1987], p. 172). Daniel Czitrom provides a useful overview of the Arnoldian response to the motion picture industry in our period in a chapter of his *Media and the American Mind: From Morse to McLuhan* (Chapel Hill: University of North Carolina Press, 1992). But Czitrom

differs from us in not contrasting the Arnoldian extension of sweetness and light with the more repressive strategy of those who wished simply to eliminate popular culture, including the cinema, and in not discussing bottom-up negotiation and contestation.

20. Lawrence Levine has dubbed this process "sacralization." See his *Highbrow/Lowbrow: The Emergence of Cultural Hierarchy in America* (Cambridge, Mass.: Harvard University Press, 1988).

21. David Nasaw, *Schooled to Order: A Social History of Public Schooling in the United States* (New York: Oxford University Press, 1979). For more information on schools as institutions of cultural reproduction, see Diane Ravitch, *The Great School Wars, New York City, 1805–1973: A History of the Public Schools as Battlefield of Social Change* (New York: Basic Books, 1974); Stephan Brumberg, *Going to America, Going to School: The Jewish Immigrant Public School Encounter in Turn-of-the-Century New York City* (New York: Praeger, 1986); and Herbert M. Kliebard, *The Struggle for the American Curriculum, 1893–1958* (New York: Routledge and Kegan Paul, 1987). Although most members of this interpretive community agreed that the schools should serve as a primary instrument of Americanization, there was disagreement about how to achieve this goal. Debates over curricular tactics frequently divided educators, but general agreement existed regarding the particular subjects of literature, history, and religion that this book examines.

22. John Dewey, *The School and Society*, rev. ed. (Chicago: University of Chicago Press, 1915), p. 29, cited in Nasaw, *Schooled to Order*, p. 103.

23. Department of Education, New York City, *Course of Study and Syllabuses in Ethics, English, History and Civics for the Elementary Schools of the City of New York* (1909), p. 5.

24. *McGuffey's Fifth Reader* (n.p.: American Book Company, 1901), p. 3.

25. Frank V. Thompson, *Schooling of the Immigrant* (Montclair, N.J.: Patterson Smith, 1971; orig. pub. 1920), p. 16.

26. Andrew Carnegie, quoted in William S. Learned, *The American Public Library and the Diffusion of Knowledge* (New York: Harcourt, 1924), p. 70.

27. American Library Association, "Why Do We Need a Public Library?" *Library Tracts* (Boston: Houghton Mifflin, 1910), p. 18, cited in Rosemary Ruhig Du Mont, *Reform and Reaction: The Big City Public Library in American Life* (Westport, Conn.: Greenwood Press, 1977), p. 39.

28. "An Appeal to Friends of Libraries for Help," *Library Journal*, December 1891, p. 77, quoted in Esther Jane Carrier, *Fiction in Public Libraries, 1876–1900* (Metuchen, N.J.: Scarecrow Press, 1965), p. 91.

29. John Cotton Dana, *Libraries: Addresses and Essays* (New York: H. W. Wilson Company, 1916), p. 93. Dana's essay was originally written in 1902.

30. For more on these debates, as well as for more general information about libraries during this period, see Esther Jane Carrier, *Fiction in Public Libraries*, and Dee Garrison, *Apostles of Culture: The Public Librarian and American Society, 1876–1920* (New York: Free Press, 1979). See also Michael Denning's discussion in *Mechanic Accents: Dime Novels and Working-Class Culture in America* (New York and London: Verso, 1987), pp. 48–50, and John Cotton Dana's *Libraries: Addresses and Essays*, which sheds light on the factions within the library community.

31. Eugene V. Debs, "Crimes of Carnegie," letter printed in *The People*, April 7, 1901; September 10 and 17, 1892, issues of *Commoner and Glassworker*, cited in Sidney

Ditzion, *Arsenals of a Democratic Culture* (Chicago: American Library Association, 1947), pp. 163, 161. Contestation came from other quarters as well. Samuel Clemens, referring to Carnegie's library philanthropy, said, "He has bought fame and paid cash for it" (Samuel L. Clemens, *Mark Twain in Eruption: Hitherto Unpublished Pages about Men and Events*, ed. Bernard De Voto [New York: Harper, 1940], p. 309, cited in George S. Bobinsky, *Carnegie Libraries: Their History and Impact upon American Public Library Development* [Chicago: American Library Association, 1969], p. 105). Despite the protests, there is evidence that wage earners did use the public libraries in several cities. See Ditzion, *Arsenals of a Democratic Culture*, chap. 7.

32. The top-down control of schools and school curriculum resulted from a period of intense contestation. David Nasaw argues that, in urban centers across the nation, the issue of local versus citywide administration of the schools pitted immigrants and their representatives from the political machines against native-born Americans. The latter won, creating citywide school boards largely composed of white, male, Anglo-Saxon Protestants and their wives (Nasaw, *Schooled to Order*, pp. 105–113).

33. The Vice Commission of Chicago, *The Social Evil in Chicago: A Study of Existing Conditions* (Chicago: Gunthorp-Warren Printing Company, 1911), p. 230.

34. Space constraints force us to disregard much of the culture that the targeted social formations, the workers and the immigrants, actually engaged in. This disregard, although differently motivated, was shared in by the dominant social formations supporting the institutions of cultural reproduction, who either ignored or feared many of the existing cultural engagements of the targeted social formations. During this period, working-class and immigrant cultures (in the broadest sense of shared lived experience) included elements that were subsequently appropriated by dominant social formations into a newly constituted "high" culture. For example, as Lawrence Levine argues, in the first half of the nineteenth century, working-class engagement with Shakespeare was of such passionate intensity as to contribute to street riots. Immigrants also maintained some of the cultural values and traditions of their native lands, subsequently valorized by the dominant social formations as "folk" culture.

On the subject of cheap amusements, see Lewis Erenberg, *Steppin' Out: New York Night Life and the Transformation of American Culture, 1890–1930* (Westport, Conn.: Greenwood Press, 1981); John Kasson, *Amusing the Million: Coney Island at the Turn of the Century* (New York: Hill and Wang, 1978); Kathy Peiss, *Cheap Amusements: Working Women and Leisure in Turn-of-the-Century New York* (Philadelphia: Temple University Press, 1986); Roy Rosenzweig, *Eight Hours for What We Will: Workers and Leisure in an Industrial City, 1870–1920* (New York: Cambridge University Press, 1983); and Robert Sklar, *Movie-Made America: A Cultural History of American Movies* (New York: Vintage, 1975).

35. See Alan Havig, "The Commercial Amusement Audience in Early 20th-Century American Cities," *Journal of American Culture* 5:1 (1982): 1–19.

36. On the cultural associations of contemporary publications, see Christopher P. Wilson, "The Rhetoric of Consumption: Mass-Market Magazines and the Demise of the Gentle Reader, 1880–1920," in T. Jackson Lears, ed., *The Culture of Consumption: Critical Essays in American History, 1880–1980* (New York: Pantheon Books, 1983), pp. 39–64.

37. Julian Ralph, "Coney Island," *Scribner's Magazine*, July 1896, pp. 17–18. New York City had yet to build the subway line that prepared the way for the building of

Steeplechase Park, Luna Park, and Dreamland, transforming the resort into a haven for laborers and clerical workers.

38. Strong, *Challenge of the City*, p. 115.

39. For a discussion of cheap fiction during the period, see Denning, *Mechanic Accents*.

40. Francis Parkman, "The Failure of Universal Suffrage," *North American Review*, July–August 1878, p. 9.

41. Strong, *Challenge of the City*, p. 107. For a less damning view of the sensational press, see W. H. Bishop, "Story-Paper Literature," *Atlantic Monthly* 44 (1879): 383–393. For further discussion of the "moral panic in the late 1870s and early 1880s about sensational fiction," see Denning, *Mechanic Accents*, pp. 50–54.

42. Otto Peltzer, *The Moralist and the Theatre* (Chicago: Donald Fraser and Sons, 1887), p. 16.

43. By 1908 the fictional narrative or story film was the major product of the American film industry, but, as is typical of scholarship on the early cinema, a controversy exists, in this case concerning the exact point at which the story film became dominant. Robert Allen locates the shift between 1907 and 1908. "A dramatic change occurred in American motion picture production: in one year narrative forms of cinema (comedy and dramatic) all but eclipsed documentary forms in volume of production," by 1908 story films constituting 96 percent of the industry's output. (Robert C. Allen, *Vaudeville and Film, 1895–1915: A Study in Media Interaction* [New York: Arno, 1980], p. 212). Charles Musser argues, however, that Allen's methodology is fundamentally flawed by his reliance on "quantification of subject by title." Rather than count titles, Musser presents data about the quantity of actual film footage, both negative feet and print feet, a statistic he claims much better reflects what people were actually watching. Although actuality titles outnumber fiction titles, the latter seem to have been both longer and more popular. Musser concludes that "from the summer of 1904 onward, story films were made in substantial quantities and consistently outsold actualities that companies like Edison continued to produce, although with decreasing frequency" (Charles Musser, "Another Look at the Chaser Theory," *Studies in Visual Communication* 10:4 [1984]: 49, 40).

44. John Collier, "The Problem of Motion Pictures" (reprinted from the *Proceedings of the Child Welfare Conference*, Clark University, June 1910), p. 6, National Board of Review of Motion Pictures Clipping Files, New York Public Library for the Performing Arts at Lincoln Center.

45. Barton W. Currie, "The Nickel Madness," *Harper's Weekly*, August 24, 1907, p. 1246.

46. "The Moving Picture and the National Character," *American Review of Reviews*, September 1910, p. 316.

47. Some scholars have disputed the view that immigrants and the working classes formed the majority of the nickelodeons' audiences. On this point, see Russell Merritt, "Nickelodeon Theaters, 1905–1914: Building an Audience for the Movies," in Tino Balio, ed., *The American Film Industry*, rev. ed. (Madison: University of Wisconsin Press, 1985; essay orig. pub. 1976), pp. 83–102, and Robert C. Allen, "Motion Picture Exhibition in Manhattan, 1906–1912: Beyond the Nickelodeon," in John Fell, *Film before Griffith* (Berkeley: University of California Press, 1983), pp. 162–175 (essay originally published in *Cinema Journal* 17:2 [1979]). For a response, see Robert Sklar, "Oh!

Althusser! Historiography and the Rise of Cinema Studies," *Radical History Review* 41 (1988): 10–35.

48. Michael Davis, *The Exploitation of Pleasure* (New York: Russell Sage Foundation, 1911), p. 23.

49. Ibid., p. 34.

50. Currie, "The Nickel Madness," p. 1246.

51. "New York's Problem of the Nickelodeon," *New York Press*, February 23, 1908, box 38, PIR, RBMD/NYPL.

52. "Shutting Out the Children," *Motography*, March 1912, p. 100.

53. Davis, *Exploitation of Pleasure*, pp. 23–30. Social class was determined by observation: "Costume and demeanor enabled the observer, after a little experience, to place his people quite readily" (pp. 28–29).

54. Maude McDougall, "The Mission of the Movies: The Theatre with an Audience of Five Million," *The Designer*, January 1913, p. 160.

55. Davis, *Exploitation of Pleasure*, pp. 34–35.

56. Film scholars have sought, through the creative use of evidence, to determine the location of nickelodeons and, by implication, the composition of their audiences. Robert Allen, for example, extrapolating from such sources as *Trow's Business Directory of Greater New York* and fire insurance maps, argues that as early as 1908 nickelodeons ceased to be located primarily in working-class districts and that, by this time, middle-class viewers formed an important component of the audience (Allen, "Motion Picture Exhibition," p. 164). Russell Merritt, discussing Boston nickelodeons, uses sources ranging from the Boston *City Directory* to the *Annual Reports of the Navy Department* and reaches essentially the same conclusions as Allen ("Nickelodeon Theaters, 1905–1914," in Balio, ed., *The American Film Industry*, pp. 83–102). Calling both their methodology and their conclusions into question, Robert Sklar points out the limits of Allen's and Merritt's projects. He suggests that Merritt's focus on Boston proper predetermines his findings: "By defining his subject as Boston alone it may be that Merritt found the middle class because the working class audience was elsewhere" ("Oh! Althusser!" p. 23). He also suggests that Allen's reliance on *Trow's Business Directory* may exclude smaller, less stable theaters that may have catered to the working class.

57. For fascinating theoretical considerations of nickelodeon audiences, see Judith Mayne, "Immigrants and Spectators," *Wide Angle* 5:2 (1982): 32–41, and part one of Miriam Hansen's *Babel and Babylon: Spectatorship in American Silent Film* (Cambridge, Mass.: Harvard University Press, 1991).

58. Howard D. King, "The Moving Picture Show: A New Factor in Health Conditions," *Journal of the American Medical Association* 53:7 (1909), p. 519.

59. Vincent Pisarro, quoted in Frank C. Drake, "Real Danger of Moving Picture Shows," *New York World*, December 27, 1908.

60. "Cheap Amusement Shows in Manhattan: Preliminary Report of Investigation," January 31, 1908, p. 4. Subjects Papers, Papers Relating to the Formation and Subsequent History of the National Board of Review of Motion Pictures, box 170, RBMD/NYPL.

61. "Moving Pictures and Health," *The Independent*, March 17, 1910, p. 593.

62. King, "Moving Picture Show," p. 520.

63. "Commends the Mayor," *New York Times*, December 28, 1908.

64. "The Nation-Wide Wave of Moving Pictures," *New York Times*, January 3, 1909.

65. Kathleen D. McCarthy, "Nickel Vice and Virtue: Movie Censorship in Chicago, 1907–1915," *Journal of Popular Film* 5:1 (1976): 37–55.

66. "Admitting Children," *The Nickelodeon*, November 1909, pp. 135–136.

67. "Commends the Mayor," *New York Times*, December 28, 1908.

68. "Protected by Court, Shows Keep Open," *New York Daily Tribune*, December 28, 1908.

69. Letter from the Reverend A. B. Churchman, to Mayor George B. McClellan, Jr., March 3, 1909, McClellan Papers, container 4, Manuscripts Division, Library of Congress.

70. Ibid.

71. For a much fuller discussion of these closings, as well as a detailed analysis of New York City's attempts to control the nickelodeons, see Roberta E. Pearson and William Uricchio, *"The Nickel Madness": The Struggle over New York City's Nickelodeons* (Washington, D.C.: Smithsonian Institution Press, forthcoming).

72. "See in Cheap Shows Peril to Children," *New York Herald*, December 24, 1908.

73. "Mayor Hears Evidence," *New York Daily Tribune*, December 26, 1908.

74. "Say Picture Shows Corrupt Children," *New York Times*, December 24, 1908.

75. "Against Picture Shows," *New York Daily Tribune*, December 22, 1908.

76. "Licenses of Four Vaudeville Houses in Question," *New York Daily Tribune*, December 29, 1908.

77. "Showmen Enjoin Police," *New York Daily Tribune*, December 27, 1908.

78. Edwin R. A. Seligman, ed., *The Social Evil: With Special Reference to Conditions Existing in the City of New York* (New York: G. P. Putnam's Sons, 1912), p. 149. Extensive documentation on the committee's activities and those of its successor, the Committee of Fourteen, can be found in their papers in the Rare Books and Manuscripts Division of the New York Public Library.

79. Maurice Wertheim, "Suggestions for Legislation for the Improvement of the Condition of Moving Picture Shows in the City of New York," September 19, 1910, Subjects Papers, Papers Relating to the Formation and Subsequent History of the National Board of Review of Motion Pictures, box 170, RBMD/NYPL.

80. Charles Sprague Smith, quoted in "Seventh Anniversary of the People's Institute," *New York Times*, April 16, 1905, box 37, PIR, RBMD/NYPL.

81. Charles Sprague Smith, *Working with the People* (New York: A. Wessels Company, 1904), p. 109. Smith, descended from the same wealthy, aristocratic Smiths of Massachusetts who endowed Smith College, devoted his early years to intellectual pursuits, studying at the University of Berlin, the Sorbonne, and Oxford University. By age twenty-nine, he was professor of modern languages and German literature at Columbia University (Robert Bruce Fisher, "The People's Institute of New York City, 1897–1934: Culture, Progressive Democracy and the People" [Ph.D. diss., New York University, 1974], pp. 7–9). Having become disillusioned with the elitist, isolated position of the university, Smith determined to create an organization that would foster the peaceful social change necessary to correct the myriad ills of the country.

82. The explicitly political nature of many of the institute's activities did not escape notice. In fact, one of the organization's supporters, the Woman's Municipal League, which conducted a joint investigation of cheap amusements with the institute, felt constrained to temper its praise of Charles Sprague Smith by referring to his quasi-radical political stances. "One may totally disagree with Director Sprague Smith's ideal

of society—equality, liberty, democracy—but there can be no gainsaying that as between such educational means as he employs for the adult foreigner and the partisan newspapers, the local boss and heelers, the party political meeting . . . there can be no question as to which is preferable" ("February Meeting Subject—'The People's Institute,' " *Woman's Municipal League Bulletin*, March 1907, p. 1).

83. Charles Sprague Smith, "Saloon Substitutes in New York and Elsewhere," *Federation*, March 1903, p. 52.

84. Smith, *Working with the People*, p. 35.

85. Plays chosen for this program had to meet the standards of "an Executive Committee composed of twenty well known men and women of the community," who either rejected the production or recommended it for: (1) children under fifteen; (2) high schools; (3) teachers; (4) adult wage earners. The play committee insisted that the play "must be clean and wholesome . . . and if it deals with the problems of life must be right in their dramatic development. If anything is found objectionable in a play, morally, or if the play inculcates false ideas of life and character the committee . . . does not recommend it. . . . It also reports as to whether it interested the audience and whether it is instructive and inspiring" (Charles Sprague Smith, quoted in the *New York Herald*, January 26, 1908, box 38, PIR, RBMD/NYPL). For a more detailed description, including a reproduction of an evaluation form for plays, see "New York City's Censorship of Plays," *Theatre Magazine*, May 1908, pp. 134–136.

86. *Tenth Annual Report of the Managing Director to the Corporation of the People's Institute*, 1907, box 3, PIR, RBMD/NYPL.

87. *Addresses at the Eighteenth Annual Reunion and Dinner*, May 1908, Department of Education, Public Lectures, HLP, RBMD/NYPL.

88. Henry Leipziger, "A University for the People," *Addresses at the Seventeenth Annual Reunion and Dinner*, (New York: Department of Education, 1907), p. 10, HLP, RBMD/NYPL. Descended from German Jews who had emigrated to England, Leipziger came to New York City in 1864 when his family emigrated to the United States, where he attended City College and received a law degree and a Ph.D. from Columbia University.

89. Ibid.

90. Ruth Frankel, *Henry M. Leipziger, Educator and Idealist* (New York: Macmillan, 1933), pp. 155–156.

91. Henry Leipziger, *Annual Report of the Supervisor of Lectures to the Board of Education, 1911–1912* (New York: Department of Education, 1912), p. 172.

92. The Educational Alliance was formed from a merger of the Hebrew Free School Society, the Aguilar Free Library, and the downtown branch of the Young Men's Hebrew Association. At first called the Hebrew Institute, it changed its name and moved to its present location on East Broadway in 1892 (Stephen Brumberg, *Going to America, Going to School*, p. 65).

93. For information on the rising anti-Semitism in New York during this period, see David Hammack, *Power and Society: Greater New York at the Turn of the Century* (New York: Russell Sage Foundation, 1982), pp. 66–69.

94. "Report of the Special Committee on Reorganization," April 7, 1905, Records of the Educational Alliance, RG 312, #21, YIVO Institute for Jewish Research.

95. *Thirteenth Annual Report of the President and Board of Directors* (New York: Educational Alliance, 1905), p. 37.

96. For more on the alliance's efforts at Americanizing, see Cary Goodman, "(Re)creating Americans at the Educational Alliance," *Journal of Ethnic Studies* 6:4 (1979): 1–28.

97. *Thirteenth Annual Report of the President and the Board of Directors*, p. 52.

98. Yet the common desire of these uplift organizations to create cultural consensus should not mask the fundamental differences within and among their social agendas regarding the immigrant "problem." Although we have generally termed these uplift organizations, as well as other institutions of cultural reproduction, "assimilationist" to contrast them with more repressive forces, assimilation could itself have a repressive edge. Some assimilationists wished to efface ethnic differences and dissolve the newcomers into the famous "melting pot"; others strove to retain difference while preparing the newcomers to become fully empowered citizens of their new country. Of the three uplift organizations under discussion, the Educational Alliance most clearly epitomized the melting-pot strategy, since its raison d'être was to make the new arrivals indistinguishable from "real" Americans as quickly as possible and protect the wealthy, uptown German Jews from anti-Semitic attacks. In contrast, Charles Sprague Smith of the People's Institute articulated a fairly radical social program and labored for the political mobilization of workers and immigrants. Similar debates over the meaning and methods of assimilation took place both within and among other institutions of cultural reproduction. There was, for example, the debate between educators who advocated technical education and those who supported a more "academic" curriculum, the former wishing to create docile laborers, the latter wishing to give immigrants the cultural capital necessary to participate more fully in the society.

99. "Crucial Hour for the New York Shows," *Film Index*, January 2, 1909, p. 5.

100. "Say Picture Shows Corrupt Children," *New York Times*, December 24, 1908.

101. "Report of the Executive Committee of the Department of Drama and Music," January 27, 1908, CSS, CU.

102. [John Collier,] "Cheap Amusement Shows in Manhattan: Preliminary Report of Investigation," January 31, 1908, p. 4, Subjects Papers, Papers Relating to the Formation and Subsequent History of the National Board of Review of Motion Pictures, box 170, RBMD/NYPL.

103. John Collier, "Cheap Amusements," *Charities and the Commons* 20 (April 11, 1908), pp. 74–75.

104. Letter from Michael Davis to Howard Mansfield, March 23, 1908, CSS, CU.

105. Collier, "Cheap Amusements," p. 76.

106. Letter from Howard Mansfield to Michael Davis, March 30, 1908, CSS, CU.

107. See Nancy J. Rosenbloom, "Between Reform and Regulation: The Struggle over Film Censorship in Progressive America, 1909–1922," *Film History* 1 (1987):309–310. The *New York Times* claimed that the board reviewed 99 percent of all films ("Censors Destroyed Evil Picture Films," May 14, 1911).

The institute's involvement in censorship was a logical extension of the play review mechanisms that implemented the institute's reduced-price theatrical ticket program for wage earners, teachers, and school children. The standards of the National Board of Censorship clearly reflect the sensibilities of the People's Institute's Drama Department, which selected appropriate plays for the program. Circa 1911 the board published guidelines specifying how filmmakers should handle particular subjects. Regarding "barrooms, drinking and drunkenness," the board warned, "such scenes must be used with discretion and made significant in the drama." As for "infidelity and Sex Problem

Plays," "the Board has never denied that this is a legitimate subject for the motion pictures, but it has insisted that it be treated with seriousness and artistic reserve." Violence had to be approached with the same attitude. "The National Board requires that such violence be not degrading but rather have educational and social value" ("The Standards of the National Board of Censorship of Motion Pictures" [New York, n.d.], quoted in Tom Gunning, "D. W. Griffith and the Narrator System: Narrative Structure and Industry Organization in Biograph Films, 1908–1909 [Ph.D. diss., New York University, 1986], pp. 492–493).

Most scholars have focused on the connection of the People's Institute with the Board of Censorship rather than on their other cultural activities. See Daniel Czitrom, "The Redemption of Leisure: The National Board of Censorship and the Rise of Motion Pictures in New York City, 1900–1920," *Studies in Visual Communication* 10:4 (1984): 2. For further information on the Board of Censorship, see also Fisher, "The People's Institute of New York City," and Gunning, "D. W. Griffith and the Narrator System."

108. *Film Index*, April 16, 1910, p. 2.

Chapter Two
The Film Industry's Drive for Respectability

1. "Another Attack on Picture Shows," *Motography*, April 1912, p. 148.

2. Michael Davis, *The Exploitation of Pleasure* (New York: Russell Sage Foundation, 1911), p. 34.

3. John Collier, "The Problem of Motion Pictures" (reprinted from the *Proceedings of the Child Welfare Conference*, Clark University, June 1910), pp. 6–7, National Board of Review of Motion Pictures Papers, NYPLPA.

4. *Views and Film Index*, March 14, 1908, p. 3.

5. W. Stephen Bush, "Signs of a Harvest," *MPW*, August 5, 1911, p. 272.

6. "The Film Maker's Responsibilities," *MPW*, August 5, 1911, p. 271.

7. Lucy France Pierce, "The Nickelodeon," *The Nickelodeon*, January 1909, p. 8. Numerous articles in the trade press make the same point, one even using the term counterattraction. The *Salem News* editorialized that one reason for declining saloon profits was "the counter attraction of the moving picture. . . . It is figured that the people want a place to pass away the time and enjoy themselves a bit . . . the picture houses are a counter-attraction that serves to entertain quite a crowd" ("Hits the Saloon Trade," *Film Index*, June 5, 1909, p. 12).

8. K. S. Hover, "Motography as an Arm of the Church," *Motography*, May 1911, p. 86.

9. W. Stephen Bush, "The Film of the Future," *MPW*, September 5, 1908, p. 172.

10. Isaac Marcosson, "A Practical School of Democracy," *The World's Work*, July 1905, pp. 6414–6417; Henry Leipziger, "The People's University," *Addresses at the Eighteenth Annual Reunion and Dinner*, 1908, Department of Education, Public Lectures, HLP, RBMD/NYPL; Thomas Davidson, *The Education of the Wage Earners: A Contribution toward the Solution of the Educational Problem of Democracy* (New York: Ginn and Company, 1904), p. iii.

11. Pierce, "The Nickelodeon," p. 7; Joseph Medill Patterson, "The Nickelodeons," *Saturday Evening Post*, November 23, 1907, p. 10; "Buchwalter's Opinion," *Views and Film Index*, January 18, 1908, p. 3.

12. Bush, "Film of the Future," pp. 172–173.

13. "Moving Picture is an Uplifter; How It Reaches the Multitudes," *MPW*, May 28, 1910, p. 887.

14. General Film Company, *Education and Entertainment in Motion Pictures: Catalogue* (New York: n.d.); "Elbert Hubbard on the Moving Pictures" (reprinted from the *New York American*), *MPW*, January 10, 1910, p. 10.

Not everyone affiliated with the film industry, however, supported the headlong rush to respectability. The pseudononymous Lux Graphicus of the *Moving Picture World* feared that uplifting rhetoric might well have adverse consequences for the moving picture business, which, in his view, should not make the mistake of equating itself with the churches or the schools. "Positive morality and education are gotten in the churches and the schools, which are the proper places for them. They have nothing to do with a motion picture theatre. . . . When I go to a moving picture theatre it is for amusement. . . . If you want to make the moving picture theatre a losing proposition, why, then, turn it into a moral and educational shop; if you want to make it pay stick to clean amusements" (Lux Graphicus [Thomas Bedding], "On the Screen," *MPW*, April 10, 1909, p. 435).

Yet, while neither the trade press nor film producers and distributors unanimously pursued an alliance with cultural arbiters, prominent and increasingly powerful constituencies, such as the Motion Picture Patents Company, dominated discursive practices. For more on this debate, see Roberta E. Pearson, "Cultivated Folks and the Better Classes: Class Conflict and Representation in Early American Film," *Journal of Popular Film and Television* 15:3 (1987): 120–128.

15. The list includes Eileen Bowser, *The Transformation of Cinema, 1907–1915* (New York: Charles Scribner's Sons, 1990); Richard deCordova, *Picture Personalities: The Emergence of the Star System in America* (Urbana: University of Illinois Press, 1991); Thomas Elsaesser and Adam Barker, eds., *Early Cinema: Space, Frame, Narrative* (London: British Film Institute, 1990); Tom Gunning, *D. W. Griffith and the Origins of American Narrative Film* (Urbana: University of Illinois Press, 1991); Miriam Hansen, *Babel and Babylon: Spectatorship in American Silent Film* (Cambridge, Mass.: Harvard University Press, 1991); Charles Musser, *The Emergence of Cinema: The American Screen to 1907* (New York: Charles Scribner's Sons, 1990), *High-Class Moving Pictures: Lyman H. Howe and the Forgotten Era of Traveling Exhibition, 1880–1920* (Princeton: Princeton University Press, 1991), *Before the Nickelodeon: Edwin S. Porter and the Edison Manufacturing Company* (Berkeley: University of California Press, 1991), and, edited with Paolo Cherchi-Usai, *American Vitagraph* (Washington, D.C.: Smithsonian Institution Press, forthcoming); and Roberta E. Pearson, *Eloquent Gestures: The Transformation of Performance Style in the Griffith Biograph Films* (Berkeley: University of California Press, 1992).

The Brighton Project, more formally a symposium entitled "Fiction Film, 1900–1906" held in 1978, inspired the reinvestigation of the area. Some of the articles stemming from this conference appeared in the *Quarterly Review of Film Studies* 4:4 (1979). Since then, major retrospectives, such as the 1987 Vitagraph festival in Pordenone, Italy, as well as the founding of Domitor, an international organization to promote the study of early cinema, which sponsored its first conference in May 1990, attest to the vitality of ongoing scholarship.

16. In *The Transformation of Cinema, 1907–1915*, Eileen Bowser provides an excellent overview of the history of the entire transitional period that deals with all of these concerns. David Bordwell, Janet Staiger, and Kristin Thompson offer an exemplary detailing of the relationship between signifying practices and industrial history during

this period in *The Classical Hollywood Cinema: Film Style and Mode of Production to 1960* (New York: Columbia University Press, 1985).

17. For detailed accounts of the Motion Picture Patents Company see Tom Gunning, "D. W. Griffith and the Narrator System: Narrative Structure and Industry Organization in Biograph Films, 1908–1909 (Ph.D. diss., New York University, 1986), and Robert Anderson, "The Motion Picture Patents Company," (Ph.D. diss., University of Wisconsin, 1983).

18. The members of the Motion Picture Patents Company at its formation in December 1908 were: Armat, Biograph, Eastman Kodak, Edison, Essanay, Kalem, Kleine, Lubin, Pathé Frères, Selig, and Vitagraph. See Anderson, "Motion Picture Patents Company."

19. Letter from George F. Scull, assistant to vice president Frank L. Dyer of the Edison Manufacturing Company, to J. Stuart Blackton, September 10, 1909, Manufacturers Files, box 5, Motion Picture Patents Company Papers, Edison Archives, Edison National Historic Site, National Park Service, United States Department of the Interior (hereafter Edison Archives).

20. "See in Cheap Shows Peril to Children," *New York Herald*, December 24, 1908.

21. "Picture Theatre Inspection," *NYDM* April 10, 1909, p. 15.

22. Ibid.; "Insurance for Picture Houses," *NYDM*, April 10, 1909, p. 14.

23. "The Nation-Wide Wave of Moving Pictures," *New York Times*, January 3, 1909.

24. "Achievements of Nineteen-Eleven," *MPW*, January 13, 1912, p. 106.

25. "The Moving Picture Field," *NYDM*, May 30, 1908, p. 7.

26. John M. Bradlett, "The Open Market," *MPW*, February 18, 1911, p. 349.

27. "The Lost Gallery," *MPW*, July 29, 1911, p. 186.

28. Lux Graphicus, "On the Screen," *MPW*, April 10, 1909, p. 435.

29. "Room for Improvement," *NYDM*, August 22, 1908, p. 9.

30. Bordwell, Staiger, and Thompson, *Classical Hollywood Cinema*, pp. 163–166.

31. Richard deCordova, "The Emergence of the Star System in America: An Examination of the Institutional and Ideological Function of the Star (Ph.D. diss., University of California at Los Angeles, 1986), pp. 104–108.

32. Ibid., p. 176.

33. See Pearson, *Eloquent Gestures*.

34. C. H. Claudy, "The Educational Photo Play," *MPW*, June 10, 1911, p. 1300.

35. See Pearson, *Eloquent Gestures*, especially chapter 4. The use of narrative logic or characterization through internal means to produce realistically motivated characters was a relatively new strategy in 1908. As Charles Musser has shown, prior to 1907 most film narratives were not self-sufficient, film manufacturers and exhibitors employing a variety of devices to effect narrative coherence: intertextuality, redundancy (the chase), sound effects, and lectures (Charles Musser, "The Nickelodeon Era Begins: Establishing the Framework for Hollywood's Mode of Representation," *Framework* 22–23 [1983], pp. 4–11).

36. Gunning, "D. W. Griffith and the Narrator System," p. 59.

37. Ibid., pp. 73–74.

38. "Simpler Subjects Needed," *MPW*, March 13, 1909, p. 308.

39. Frank L. Dyer, "The Moral Development of the Silent Drama," *Edison Kinetogram*, April 15, 1910, p. 11.

40. Typescript, no title, author, or date (probably John Collier, circa 1909–10),

Subject Papers, Papers Relating to the Formation and the Subsequent History of the National Board of Review of Motion Pictures, box 170, RBMD/NYPL.

41. "Encourage Educational Pictures," *NYDM*, December 26, 1908, p. 8.

42. Catalogue, General Film Company (n.d.; probably circa 1912–13), National Board of Review Files, NYPLPA. As late as 1913 at least one of our quality films, *The Life of Moses*, was still being shown but not, it seems, by virtue of the General Film Company's educational division. A correspondent to *The Survey*, who had just seen *The Life of Moses* at Hull House, loved the film and thought that the church "ought to teach its lessons by the most effective means" but complained that "it is hard to get films that are suitable" ("Bible Story Films," *The Survey*, September 13, 1913, p. 724).

43. "On Filming a Classic," *The Nickelodeon*, January 7, 1911, p. 4.

44. This typology of literaries, historicals, and biblicals approximates the industry's own perception of film genres. A list found in the Motion Picture Patents Company Papers organizes the output of its member studios between January 1910 and April 1911 into the following categories: biblical, industrial, educational, legendary and historical, operas, classics and standard authors, and modern fiction. The list may have been a preliminary move toward establishing the educational section of MPPC's distribution arm, the General Film Company ("Some Pictures Produced," Administrative Files: Documents, 1908–1912, box 1, Motion Picture Patents Company Papers, Edison Archives).

45. We must add one proviso with regard to the film titles that follow. A late-twentieth-century notion of canonicity has influenced our selection of the literary films. In other words, the discourse of the period certainly valorized many authors no longer included in the canon, such as Charles Kingsley, Thomas Hood, and Ferenc Molnár, but we have chosen not to include cinematic adaptations of such authors' works in our lists. Since the issue of canon formation is a vexed one, we have attempted largely to avoid the problem by choosing Dante and Shakespeare to exemplify the literary films.

46. "The Success of the Moving Picture Business," *Views and Film Index*, May 12, 1906, p. 8.

47. "The Spectator's Comments," *NYDM*, May 1, 1909, p. 38.

48. See Gunning, *D. W. Griffith*, and Pearson, *Eloquent Gestures*.

49. "High Art in Picture Making," *NYDM*, May 1, 1909, p. 38.

50. "American History on Film," *Edison Kinetogram*, March 1, 1911, p. 2.

51. "American History Series," *Edison Kinetogram*, June 1, 1911, p. 13.

52. " 'Film d'art' Plays," *New York Daily Tribune*, December 13, 1908.

53. "First in Pantomime Art," *NYDM*, May 1, 1909, p. 38. Despite assertions of film d'art's influence and popularity, occasional dissenting voices were heard. The *Moving Picture World* reported that, despite their technical and artistic achievements, the films d'art not only were failing to achieve popular success but were being criticized by the Board of Censorship ("Films d'art for the Independents, *MPW*, May 14, 1910, p. 786).

54. Richard Abel's article "Before Fantomas: Louis Feuillade and the Development of Early French Cinema" (*Postscript* 7 [1987]: 4–26) discusses three quality films directed by Feuillade for Gaumont: *The Death of Mozart* (1909), *The Huguenot* (1909), and *Christopher Columbus* (1910). In *The French Cinema: The First Wave, 1915–1929* (Princeton: Princeton University Press, 1984), Abel briefly discusses French quality film during our period and elaborates on the development of the genre through the 1920s.

55. "The Qualities of Imported Films," *MPW*, November 6, 1909, pp. 635–636.

56. James B. Crippen, "Realism and the Photoplay," *Motography*, April 1911, p. 14.

57. See Pearson, *Eloquent Gestures*, especially chapter 6. The distinction was maintained well into the transitional period, as an examination of the performance styles in the four stories of *Intolerance* reveals (see Hansen, *Babel and Babylon*, part two). Indeed, we suspect—though this goes far beyond the purview of this book—that the distinction still exists to some degree even in late-twentieth-century film and television.

58. For a discussion of character motivation and narrative structure see Bordwell, Staiger, and Thompson, *Classical Hollywood Cinema*, pp. 12–23.

59. Richard Abel discusses the mix of "primitive" and "institutional" signifying practices in the Louis Feuillade qualities produced between 1909 and 1910. "They seem to occupy an unstable intermediate position between what Noël Burch defines as a 'Primitive' cinema versus an 'Institutional' cinema, and thus undermine the exclusivity of the distinction. That is, each film includes several 'Primitive' features, e.g., autonomous shot-scenes, non-centered compositions, and characters described exclusively in terms of behavior. But each also exhibits one or more of the opposite 'Institutional' features of a centered, linear, firmly closed narrative cinema, e.g., short sequences of shots based on spatial-temporal connections, centered compositions, and characters defined (even if crudely) through psychological interiority. This suggests that Feuillade's early films represent not so much a sharp break with a so-called primitive cinema but rather a particular form of what Tom Gunning has described as a synthesis of spectacle and narrative, beginning around 1906–1907, which in an earlier 'cinema of attractions' is integrated into a 'fully narrativized cinema' " ("Before Fantomas," p. 9).

60. As with performance codes, the distinctive and specifically extracinematic referencing of visual representation in the quality films continued well beyond the period under discussion, extending, in fact, to late-twentieth-century practice.

61. "The Old Lady in the Audience," *Motography*, May 1911, p. 78.

62. This is but a small sample of Vitagraph's quality film output between 1908 and 1913. For a complete filmography of the Vitagraph Company, see Paolo Cherchi-Usai, ed., *Vitagraph Company of America: Il cinema prima di Hollywood* (Pordenone: Edizioni Studio Tesi, 1987). This filmography will give the reader a better sense of the place of the quality films within Vitagraph's overall output.

63. A relative lack of available studio documentation has precluded the level of detailed historical investigation that characterizes the work done on Biograph or Edison. For more on the studio's history, see Cherchi-Usai, *Vitagraph Company of America*; Jon Gartenberg, "Vitagraph before Griffith: Forging Ahead in the Nickelodeon Era," *Studies in Visual Communication* 10:4 (1984): 7–23; Anthony Slide, *The Big V: A History of the Vitagraph Company, A New and Revised Edition* (Metuchen, N.J.: Scarecrow Press, 1987); and Charles Musser, "The American Vitagraph, 1897–1901: Survival and Success in a Competitive Industry," in John Fell, ed., *Film before Griffith* (Berkeley: University of California Press, 1983), pp. 22–66.

64. Gartenberg, "Vitagraph before Griffith."

65. Letter from Vitagraph Company of America to film exchanges, September 5, 1908, Manufacturers Files, M—V, box 5, Motion Picture Patents Company Papers, Edison Archives.

66. *NYDM*, November 14, 1908, p. 10.

67. See chapter 2 of Kristin Thompson, *Exporting Entertainment: America in the World Film Market, 1907–34* (London: British Film Institute, 1985).

68. Slide, *The Big V*, p. 16.

69. *VB*, November 16–30, 1909.

70. Gartenberg, "Vitagraph before Griffith," p. 8.

71. Charles Musser, "Early Cinema and Its Modes of Production," paper presented at the annual conference of the Society for Cinema Studies, Iowa City, 1989, pp. 8–9.

72. *VB* February 15–March 1, 1910.

73. *VB*, November 16–30, 1909.

74. Ibid.

75. *VB*, February 1–15, 1910.

76. "Vitagraph's Historical Department," *Film Index*, May 20, 1911, p. 5.

77. Slide, *The Big V*, p. 21. See also Slide's "J. Stuart Blackton," in Cherchi-Usai, *Vitagraph Company of America*, pp. 403–410.

78. Blackton, born in Sheffield, England, worked as a stringer sketch artist for the *New York Evening World*. Blackton, Smith, and another Englishman, Ronald Reader, formed a vaudeville act in which Blackton drew lightning sketches. Blackton and Smith formed the Vitagraph Company in 1897, with William T. Rock becoming a third partner in 1898. Up until 1905 Vitagraph was primarily an exhibition and distribution company, its production limited largely to actualities. The 1905 nickelodeon boom coincided with Vitagraph's shift to the production of story films. (Musser, "American Vitagraph"; see also Musser's "Forgotten Years: American Vitagraph: 1901–1905," in Cherchi-Usai, *Vitagraph Company of America*). In this year they produced *Monsieur Beaucaire* and *Sherlock Holmes, or Held for Ransom*.

79. Marion Blackton Trimble, *J. Stuart Blackton: A Personal Biography by His Daughter* (Metuchen, N.J.: Scarecrow Press, 1985), pp. 22–23.

80. Letter from Vitagraph Company of America to film exchanges, September 5, 1908, Manufacturers Files, M–V, box 5, Motion Pictures Patents Company Papers, Edison Archives.

81. *Vitagraph Life Portrayals: How and Where Moving Pictures Are Made* (New York: Vitagraph Company of America, n.d. [circa 1911]), box 3, Florence Lawrence Papers, Natural History Museum of Los Angeles County.

82. "The Great Development of the Vitagraph Company," *Film Index*, January 22, 1910, p. 1.

83. For a detailed look at distribution practices during this period, see "The Goat Man" and "On the Outside Looking In," *Motography*, November 1911, pp. 237–239. For further information of nickelodeon distribution and exhibition, see Bowser, *Transformation of Cinema*. On the subject of brand name recognition, see p. 105 of that volume.

84. *VB*, #203, January 1–15, 1910.

85. "Vanity Fair," *Vitagraph Life Portrayals*, December 17–January 1, 1912, p. 5.

86. Vitagraph advertisement, *NYDM*, February 19, 1910, p. 17.

87. *Vitagraph Life Portrayals*, December 17–January 1, 1912, p. 24.

88. *VB*, #209, 1910, pp. 26, 11.

89. "Richelieu," *MPW*, January 22, 1910, p. 92.

90. "The Great Development of the Vitagraph Company," *Film Index*, January 22, 1910, p. 1.

91. Frederick James Smith, "The Evolution of the Motion Picture," *NYDM*, April 23, 1913, p. 26.

92. *VB*, November 16–30, 1909.

93. *VB*, February 15–March 1, 1910.

Chapter Three
Literary Qualities:
Shakespeare and Dante

1. Transcript of Mayor McClellan's hearings on the moving picture shows, December 23, 1908, Mayor McClellan's Papers, MGB 51, folder 4, New York City Municipal Archives. Unfortunately, only half the transcript, that recording the statements of the industry's defenders, survives. Thus, we can only speculate as to the nature of the attacks on the Vitagraph *Julius Caesar*.

2. "Picture-Show Men Organize to Fight," *New York Times*, December 27, 1908.

3. "Show Men Will Fight," *New York Daily Tribune*, December 26, 1908. The exhibitors refer to several nineteenth-century actors who were well known for their enactments of various roles in the play: Edwin Booth, Lawrence Barrett, and Edward Loomis Davenport.

We should note that the Lubin Manufacturing Company copyrighted a version of *Julius Caesar* on March 20, 1908, shortly before Vitagraph released its film. The film appears to be lost, and Robert Hamilton Ball questions whether the film is even based on the Shakespeare (Robert Hamilton Ball, *Shakespeare on Silent Film: A Strange Eventful History* [London: George Allen and Unwin, 1968], p. 314).

4. "Picture-Show Men Organize to Fight."

5. *The Nickelodeon*, September, 1909, p. 71.

6. In November 1907 Chicago had passed an ordinance requiring the Police Department to inspect and grant a permit to every film shown in the city. See Kathleen D. McCarthy, "Nickel Vice and Virtue: Movie Censorship in Chicago, 1907–1915," *Journal of Popular Film* 5:1 (1976): 37–55. According to Will Irwin, Chicago censors also suppressed "the duel scene and suicide in 'Romeo and Juliet' [and] barred out 'Macbeth' altogether!" (Will Irwin, "How the Movies Were Saved," *The Metropolitan Magazine*, March 1913, p. 68).

7. *The Nickelodeon*, January 7, 1911, p. 12.

8. Among the many factors that account for the differing positions of Shakespeare and Dante in turn-of-the-century America are issues of national origin and linguistic access, which centrally inflect the cultural history of textual circulation.

9. The film, whose title employed a variant spelling of Dante's Francesca da Rimini, was produced in September 1907 and released in February 1908.

10. For an excellent overview of the Shakespeare films, see Ball, *Shakespeare on Silent Film*.

11. *Vitagraph Life Portrayals*, January 17–February 1, 1912, p. 21.

12. Stuart Hall, "Cultural Studies and the Centre: Some Problematics and Problems," in Stuart Hall, Dorothy Hobson, Andrew Lowe, and Paul Willis, eds., *Culture, Media, Language: Working Papers in Cultural Studies, 1972–79* (London: Hutchinson, 1980), p. 27.

13. Shakespeare's status as the greatest *English* poet has led to a more directly political appropriation in the United Kingdom than in the United States. The work of new historicist English and American Shakespearean scholars tends to reflect the differences in Shakespeare's cultural status in the two countries. As Louis Montrose puts it, in

Britain, with its clear class barriers and tradition of radical discourse, the study of Shakespeare "readily becomes the site of a struggle over the definition of national problems and priorities, a struggle to shape and reshape national identity and collective consciousness." In the United States, by contrast, "the presence and direction of such ideological processes are perhaps less easily discernible, and sometimes less comfortably acknowledged." Yet, as he points out, the study of Shakespeare "may be prescribed precisely to counter the perceived threat to Anglo-Saxon hegemony by forces of cultural and ethnic diversity" (Louis A. Montrose, "The Poetics and Politics of Culture," in H. Aram Veeser, ed., *The New Historicism* [New York: Routledge, Chapman, and Hall, 1989], p. 27).

For further discussions of the differences between British and American Shakespeare, see Jean E. Howard and Marion F. O'Connor, "Introduction," Walter Cohen, "Political Criticism of Shakespeare," and Don E. Wayne, "Power, Politics, and the Shakespearean Text: Recent Criticism in England and the United States," in Jean E. Howard and Marion F. O'Connor, *Shakespeare Reproduced: The Text in History and Ideology* (New York: Methuen, 1987), pp. 1–16, 18–46, and 47–67, respectively. For a discussion of Shakespeare's place in American culture, see Lawrence W. Levine, *Highbrow, Lowbrow: The Emegence of Cultural Hierarchy in America* (Cambridge, Mass.: Harvard University Press, 1988), and Michael D. Bristol, *Shakespeare's America, America's Shakespeare* (New York: Routledge Chapman, and Hall, 1990). On Shakespeare in English culture, see Terence Hawkes, *That Shakespeherian Rag: Essays on a Critical Process* (New York: Methuen, 1986). See also Gary Taylor, *Reinventing Shakespeare: Cultural History from the Restoration to the Present* (London: Hogarth Press, 1990), and Jonathan Dollimore and Alan Sinfield, eds., *Political Shakespeare, New Essays in Cultural Materialism* (Manchester: University of Manchester Press, 1985).

14. *Eleventh Annual Report of the President and Board of Directors* (New York: Educational Alliance, 1903), p. 82.

15. Theodore D. Weld, "Shakespeare in the Class-room," *Shakespeariana* 3 (1886): 437–438.

16. Letter from James Hamilton to Michael M. Davis, secretary, People's Institute, November 23, 1905, box 16, PIR, RBMD/NYPL.

17. Joseph Quincy Adams, quoted in Michael D. Bristol, *Shakespeare's America, America's Shakespeare*, p. 79.

18. Charles Sprague Smith, "A Theatre for the People and the Public Schools," *Charities*, February 4, 1905, p. 5.

19. Thomas Davidson, *The Education of the Wage-Earners: A Contribution toward the Solution of the Educational Problem of Democracy* (New York: Ginn and Company, 1904), p. 80.

20. Ruth L. Frankel, *Henry M. Leipziger: Educator and Idealist* (New York: Macmillan, 1933), p. 150.

21. Even those opposing the status quo valorized the Bard. The period's leading socialist, Eugene V. Debs, quoted Shakespeare extensively, perhaps trying to communicate with those in the reigning cultural orthodoxy by using "their" language. (This is not, of course, to deny that Debs himself may have experienced "pleasure" in his reading of Shakespeare.) Upon his release from Woodstock Prison in 1895 Debs delivered a widely reprinted speech in Chicago, in which he said:

The immortal bard also wrote that:

> This our life, exempt from public haunt,
> Finds tongues in traes (sic), books in running brooks,
> Sermons in stones, nd (sic) good in everything.

If to be behind prison bars is to be "exempt from public haunt," then for the past six months I may claim such exemption. . . . There is not a tree on the Woodstock Prison campus or nearby, to whose tongued melodies or maledictions I have not in fancy listened when liberty, despotism or justice was the theme.

(Eugene V. Debs, "Liberty," [Terre Haute, Ind.: E. V. Debs and Company, 1895], reprinted in Leon Stein, ed., *The Pullman Strike* [New York: Arno and the *New York Times*, 1969], pp. 22–23).

22. *MPW*, February 19, 1910, p. 257.

23. *VB*, December 1–15, 1909.

24. See, for example, Eileen Bowser, *The Transformation of Cinema, 1907–1915* (New York: Charles Scribner's Sons, 1990), pp. 53–55.

25. "Lecturing the Show," *The Nickelodeon*, December 1909, pp. 167–168.

26. W. Stephen Bush, "Shakespeare in Moving Pictures," *MPW*, December 5, 1908, pp. 446–447.

27. Bowser, *Transformation of Cinema*, p. 35.

28. *NYDM*, November 14, 1908, p. 10.

29. Palladium, "Moving Picture Is an Uplifter: How It Reaches the Multitudes," *MPW*, May 28, 1910, p. 887.

30. *VB*, November 16–30, 1909.

31. *MPW*, February 19, 1910, p. 255.

32. Montrose Moses, "Where They Perform Shakespeare for Five Cents," *Theatre Magazine*, October 1908, p. 264. A trade press report, however, indicates that the denizens of the lower East Side may not have been so eager for filmed Shakespeare. The *Film Index* spoke to the manager of a nickelodeon at 118 Rivington Street, who said of his audience that "the most elaborately produced Shakespeare plays don't appeal to them much; they don't understand them. . . . What our patrons like most is sentiment and emotionalism that appeals to their better nature" ("Seeing the Pictures: *New York Sun* Reporter Goes the Rounds of the 5¢ houses," *Film Index*, December 25, 1909, p. 4).

33. "People's Amusements," *New York Daily Tribune*, December 19, 1908.

34. Palladium, "Moving Picture Is an Uplifter," *MPW*, May 28, 1910, p. 887.

35. "Seeing the Pictures," *Film Index*, December 25, 1909, p. 4.

36. L. Ralston Irving, "Shakespeare's Plays and Public Opinion," *Overland Monthly*, March 1904, p. 188.

37. "Why Shakspere Is Not Understood," *The World's Work*, March 1903, p. 3249.

38. "Is Shakespeare Popular?" *North American Review*, February 1907, pp. 334–335.

39. Walter Field, *Fingerposts for Children's Reading* (Chicago: A. C. McClurg, 1907).

40. Maude Kingsley, "Outline Study of Shakespeare's *Julius Caesar*," *Education* 22:4 (1901), p. 229.

41. "Is Shakespeare Read?" *Harper's Weekly*, February 2, 1907, p. 152.

42. "A School Comment on Shakespeare's *Julius Caesar*," *Atlantic Monthly*, September 1905, p. 431.

43. *Cyclopedia of Useful Information and Complete Handbook of New York City* (New York: New York World, 1889), p. 48.

44. *New York American*, November 1, 1911.

45. Examples of the former are available in the stereograph collection in the Department of Prints and Photographs at the New York Public Library. For the latter, see album 93, Burdick Collection, Department of Prints and Photographs, Metropolitan Museum of Art.

46. Album 83, Burdick Collection.

47. Elsa G. Herzfeld, *Family Monographs: The History of Twenty-Four Families Living in the Middle West Side of New York City* (New York: James Kempster Printing Company, 1905), p. 15.

48. *New York Times*, April 20, 1902, p. 15.

49. "Food, Meat. Green Boxes." Bella C. Landauer Collection, New York Historical Society.

50. Broadside Collection, New York Historical Society.

51. *Annual Report of the Supervisor of Lectures to the Board of Education* (New York: Department of Education, City of New York, 1910), p. 185.

52. *Seventh Annual Report of the Educational Alliance* (New York: Hebrew Institute, 1899), p. 34.

53. *Eleventh Annual Report of the President and Board of Directors* (New York: Educational Alliance, 1903), p. 44.

54. "Peppery Literary Meeting," *New York Tribune*, April 1, 1900.

55. William Riordan, *Plunkitt of Tammany Hall: A Series of Very Plain Talks on Very Practical Politics* (New York: E. P. Hutton and Company, 1963), p. 52.

56. "Dramatic Soup Kitchens," *Boston American*, March 18, 1906, box 37, PIR, RBMD/NYPL.

57. "The Spectator," *The Outlook*, March 24, 1906, p. 639.

58. *Ninth Annual Report of the Managing Director to the Corporation of the People's Institute*, October 1906, box 1, PIR, RBMD/NYPL.

59. "Shakespeare on the East Side," *New York Evening Mail*, January 7, 1905, box 37, PIR, RBMD/NYPL.

60. Charles Sprague Smith, *Working with the People* (New York: A. Wessels Company, 1904), pp. 37–38.

61. *Seventh Annual Report of the Managing Director to the Corporation of the People's Institute*, 1904, p. 8, box 1, PIR, RBMD/NYPL.

62. Judging by the copious press books in the New York Public Library, the People's Institute was extremely astute about public relations, keeping the New York papers and the national press fully aware of its every activity. From January to July of 1906, for example, the institute placed 273 articles in both local and national outlets ("Memorandum in regard to Publicity Work," n.d. [July 1906?], CSS, CU). Perhaps they felt this exposure was inadequate, however, for in December 1906 they signed an agreement with a public relations firm, Michaelis and Ellsworth (letter from Michaelis and Ellsworth to Michael Davis, December 29, 1906, CSS, CU).

63. "Drama for Common Folk," *Journal/Gazette* (Fort Wayne, Ind.), February 17, 1907, box 37, PIR, RBMD/NYPL.

64. Ben Greet, "For the Greatest Theatre in the World," *The World's Work*, April 1911, pp. 14,222–14,229.

65. Untitled People's Institute proposal, April 23, 1912, People's Institute Correspondence, CU.

66. John Corbin, "How the Other Half Laughs," *Harper's Magazine*, December 1898,
p. 47.

67. Some encounters may have been with a Shakespeare slightly modified to accommodate Jewish folk tradition. See Cary Goodman, "(Re)creating Americans at the Educational Alliance," *Journal of Ethnic Studies* 6:4 (1979), pp. 5–6.

68. Bernard Gorin, "The Yiddish Theatre in New York," *Theatre Magazine*, January
1902, p. 17.

69. Clearly, those charged with designing the investigations and gathering the data
intended to counter the fears of the "respectable classes." Thus, one must exercise
caution in extrapolating from their findings.

70. Louise Bollard More, *Wage-earners' Budgets: A Study of Standards and Cost of
Living in New York City* (New York: Henry Holt and Company, 1907). The sample
consisted of 105 native born Americans, and 95 foreign born, including 35 Irish, 15
English, 17 Germans, and 15 Italians.

71. Robert Coit Chapin, *The Standard of Living among Workingmen's Families in New
York City* (New York: Russell Sage Foundation, 1909).

72. Chapin, *Standard of Living*, p. 211.

73. More, *Wage-earners' Budgets*, pp. 142–143.

74. Typescript (no author, no date; circa 1909), National Board of Review of Motion
Pictures, Subject Papers, Papers Relating to the Formation and Subsequent History of
the National Board of Review of Motion Pictures, box 170, RBMD/NYPL.

75. Michael Davis, *The Exploitation of Pleasure: A Study of Commercial Recreations in
New York City* (New York: Russell Sage Foundation, 1911), pp. 29–43.

76. Otto Peltzer, *The Moralist and the Theatre* (Chicago: Donald Fraser and Sons,
1887), p. 39.

77. James L. Ford, "Why Shakespere Languishes," *Munsey's Magazine*, January 1904,
pp. 629–630.

78. Sidney Lee, "Shakespeare and the Modern Stage," *Littel's Living Age*, February 10,
1900, p. 541.

79. Martin Meisel, *Realizations: Narrative, Pictorial, and Theatrical Arts in Nineteenth-
Century England* (Princeton: Princeton University Press, 1983), p. 30. Meisel discusses
the realization of Napoleonic paintings in the British theatre of the 1830s (pp. 201–
228). On this subject, see also Michael Booth, *Victorian Spectacular Theatre, 1850–1910*
(London: Routledge and Kegan Paul, 1981), especially chapter 1. We are indebted to
Booth for much of the present discussion.

80. Booth, *Victorian Spectacular Theatre*, pp. 58–59.

81. Ben Greet, "Shakespeare and the Modern Theatre," *Harper's Weekly*, November
4, 1905, p. 1604.

82. The popularity of Elizabethan staging at elite colleges such as Barnard and Harvard further complicates matters. In 1906 the *Tammany Times* reported that "society
and college folks are going wild about appearances in salon and al fresco plays. The Ben
Greet madness seems an epidemic North and South, and Barnard girls and Boston girls
talk about their make-ups and their characters more than they do about their studies
and their schools. If this keeps on the theatres will have to shut up shop. . . . Every
tinker to his trade . . . is a needed regulation at this age when all the men and women

are 'merely players' on and off the stage ("Shakespearean," *Tammany Times*, May 22, 1906, p. 8).

83. *Seventh Annual Report of the Managing Director to the Corporation of the People's Institute*, 1904, p. 8, box 1, PIR, RBMD/NYPL.

84. "Julius Caesar," *MPW*, December 15, 1908, p. 23. We viewed the National Film Archive's German print, which corresponds closely with the Vitagraph description.

85. "Reviews of New Films," *NYDM*, December 12, 1908, p. 6.

86. *MPW*, December 5, 1908, p. 447.

87. Montrose J. Moses, "Where They Perform Shakespeare for Five Cents," *Theatre Magazine*, October 1908, p. 265. Among its theatrical activities, the People's Institute sponsored a half-price ticket program for students, teachers, and wage earners, selecting beneficial plays, many Shakespearean productions among them, for their edification.

88. By 1916 issues of medium specificity constituted an important component of the conditions of reception for Shakespearean films. Even those critics who supported the Elizabethan style admitted that film's capacity for "realism" permitted a more spectacular presentation of Shakespeare than the theatre could hope to achieve, thus making filmed Shakespeare acceptable even without the verse. See William Uricchio and Roberta E. Pearson, "Shriekings from Below the Gratings: Sir Herbert Beerbohm-Tree's *Macbeth* and His Critics" (paper presented at the seminar on screening Shakespeare, annual meeting of the Shakespeare Association of America, Vancouver, 1991). While critics may have held these opinions about film and realism as early as 1908, we have found no evidence to document it.

89. Weld, "Shakespeare in the Class-room," p. 449.

90. "Moving Picture Shows," *New York Daily Tribune*, December 26, 1908.

91. *Film Index*, November 12, 1910, p. 1.

92. Advertisement, *Views and Films Index*, February 8, 1908, p. 16. Vitagraph seems not to have publicized this film very heavily, as we have been unable to locate reviews or, with the following exception, the kinds of stories that the publicity department later planted for the quality films. "The tragic story of 'Francesca da Rimini, or, The Two Brothers' has received frequent applause for the good acting, but nothing like the rounds of applause it is getting from crowded audiences this week in a theatre not a thousand miles from New York. The reason is that the dialogue between the leading actors in the plot is carried on in a realistic manner by people behind the screen. This idea could well be applied to many subjects which require more than pantomime to explain the situations" ("Films That Please," *MPW*, March 21, 1908, p. 233).

93. Most extant prints do have fifteen shots, though we have located two additional shots in the Paper Print Collection at the Library of Congress that may or may not have been included in the original release print. Given the unstable nature of film stock in this period, surviving prints often vary significantly from release prints, which further complicates textual analysis.

94. Henry Beers, *A History of English Romanticism in the Nineteenth Century* (New York: Henry Holt and Company, 1901), p. 104.

95. Angela LaPiana, *Dante's American Pilgrimage* (New Haven: Yale University Press, 1948), p. 148.

96. Album 452, Burdick Collection; More, *Wage-Earners' Budgets*, p. 135.

97. "Dante in America," *The Dial*, June 1, 1897, p. 327.

98. *Wilkes Spirit of the Times: The American Gentleman's Magazine*, September 28, 1867, Francesca da Rimini Clipping Files, NYPLPA.

99. "Francesca da Rimini, *New York Times*, August 28, 1883.

100. Katherine Merrill Graydon, "A Dante Society among Fishermen," *The Dial*, September 1, 1897, p. 110.

101. *Annual Report of the Supervisor of Lectures to the Board of Education* (New York: Department of Education, City of New York, 1907), p. 48.

102. *Annual Report of the Supervisor of Lectures to the Board of Education* (New York: Department of Education, City of New York, 1910), p. 185.

103. Edward Howard Griggs, *University Extension Lectures: Syllabus of Six Lectures on the Divine Comedy of Dante* (Philadelphia: American Society for the Extension of University Teaching, 1899), and *Fifth Annual Report of the Managing Director to the Corporation of the People's Institute*, 1902, p. 28, box 36 and box 1, respectively, PIR, RMBD/NYPL.

104. Some confusion exists over production credits for the last two films. Both the Museum of Modern Art and the National Film Archive have films titled *Dante e Beatrice* (Ambrosio, 1913), and both catalogues list the same credits. The films, however, are different. We believe that the National Film Archive's print is actually *Il Paradiso* (Psiche Films, 1911). Luke McKernan, of the NFA, agrees with us.

105. John W. Frick, *New York's First Theatrical Center: The Rialto at Union Square* (Ann Arbor, Mich.: UMI Research Press, 1985), p. 93.

106. *Second Annual Report of the Educational Alliance* (New York: Hebrew Institute, 1895), p. 36.

107. The wide divergences among the many Francesca's relate to a certain degree of indeterminancy in the original text. Dante reports in *The Inferno* that he was perplexed by his encounter with the lovers. "Why the poet was 'perplexed' we can only conjecture; but he undoubtedly has sorely perplexed posterity by placing the victims of the tragedy in his Second Circle of the Inferno, and then doing his utmost to engage the pity and sympathy of his readers for them" (Sir Theodore Martin, "Dante's Paolo and Francesca," *Blackwood's Magazine*, September 1907, p. 317).

108. *Dramatic Compositions Copyrighted in the United States* includes citations to these and other Francesca plays: Francesca da Rimini, by Gabriele d'Annunzio, trans. by Arthur Symons (New York, F. A. Stokes Company, 1902); Francesca da Rimini, a play in five acts, adapted from the Italian, by E. Elsner (1900); Francesca da Rimini, a play in four acts, by F. Marion Crawford (New York and London: Macmillan, 1902); Francesca da Rimini, tragedia [di] Gabriele d'Annunzio, (New York: V. Ciocia, printer, 1902); Francesca da Rimini, a tragedy, by G. H. Boker. (Philadelphia: George H. Boker, 1883); Francesca of Rimini, or The Hunchback's Bride, founded on the Italian story of the house of Maltesti, a tragedy in six acts by J. S. Macy (New York: J. Sydney Macy, 1902).

109. Letter from George Boker to Richard Henry Stoddard, March 3, 1853, cited in Oliver H. Evans, *George Henry Boker* (Boston: Twayne Publishers, 1984), p. 71.

110. John Ridpath, *The Ridpath Library of Universal Literature* (New York: Fifth Avenue Library Society, 1910), p. 290.

111. Program Files, *Francesca da Rimini*, NYPLPA. Though thirty-six years elapsed between this production and Vitagraph's, Barrett revived his version several times.

112. "Francesca da Rimini," *New York Times*, January 6, 1885.

113. George H. Boker, *Francesca da Rimini: A Tragedy in Five Acts*. (Chicago: The Dramatic Publishing Company, n.d.), act V, scene i, p. 130.

114. *New York Times*, January 6, 1885.

115. Claude R. Flory, "Boker, Barrett, and the Francesca Theme in Drama," *Players: The Magazine of American Theater*, February—March 1975, p. 80.

116. "Francesca da Rimini," *New York Times*, January 1, 1902.

117. *New York Times*, June 29, 1902, and November 12, 1902.

118. Jack Zipes, *Fairy Tales and the Art of Subversion: The Classical Genre for Children and the Process of Civilization* (London: Heinemann Educational Books, 1983), p. 34.

119. "Francesca da Rimini," *New York Times*, August 28, 1883.

120. LaPiana, *Dante's American Pilgrimage*, pp. 147–152.

121. Julie K. Wetherill, "Francesca to Paolo," *Atlantic Monthly*, November 1884, p. 594.

122. On the dime novels, see Michael Denning, *Mechanic Accents: Dime Novels and Working-Class Culture in America* (London: Verso, 1987), pp. 189–190.

123. Ouida, "Great Passions of History: Francesca da Rimini," *The Cosmopolitan*, January, 1895, p. 264.

124. Christian Gauss, "Syllabus of a Course of Six Lectures on Great Masters of Literature" (Philadelphia: American Society for Extension of University Teaching, 1908).

125. W. Barry, "Dante and the Spirit of Poetry," *New Catholic World*, May 1906, p. 153.

126. Ouida, "Great Passions of History," pp. 268, 264.

127. Edith Wharton, "The Three Francescas," *North American Review*, July 1902, p. 29.

128. Herzfeld, *Family Monographs*, p. 13.

129. Dante was occasionally employed for specifically political appropriations, as the following excerpt from a letter to *The Dial* illustrates. "The poem [*The Divine Comedy*] is a *practical* one,—it is the work of an ardent reformer. Many of his ideas on bartering and corrupt politics remind us irresistibly of Dr. Parkhurst and the Lexow Commission. His remarks on the evils of indiscriminate and unrestricted immigration might furnish our own congressmen with arguments on this live question of the day" (Oscar Kuhns, "Dante as a Tonic for To-day," *The Dial*, September 1, 1897, p. 110). The Reverend Charles Parkhurst's antivice agitation had led to the establishment of the Lexow Commission, a group of New York State legislators who in 1894 investigated corruption in New York City.

130. Pierre Bourdieu, "Social Space and Symbolic Power," *Sociological Theory* 7:1 (1989), p. 18.

Chapter Four
Historical Qualities:
Washington and Napoleon

1. James W. McGee, in the *New York American*, reprinted in *The Edison Kinetogram*, October 1, 1911, p. 18. McGee appears to have written a similar Chicago-oriented version of the poem for the *Chicago Examiner*, which *Motography* reprinted ("The Moving Picture Craze," *Motography*, April 1912, p. 150).

2. The Washington films include *Hands across the Sea in '76* (Eclair, 1911); *Battle of Bunker Hill* (Edison, 1911); *The Death of Nathan Hale* (Edison, 1911); *Before Yorktown* (Republic, 1911); *A Heroine of '76* (Rex, 1911); *A Daughter of the Revolution* (Rex, 1911);

Church and Country: An Episode of the Winter at Valley Forge (Edison, 1912); *Washington Relics* (Pathé, 1911); and *How Washington Crossed the Delaware* (Edison, 1911). Napoleon films that resemble the first reel of the Vitagraph production in recounting an incident in the emperor's life include *Napoleon and the English Sailor* (Gaumont, 1908); *Death of the Duke d'Enghien* (Pathé, 1909); *Napoleon's Game of Chess* (Le Lion, 1909); *An Episode of Napoleon's War with Spain* (Lux, 1909); *Napoleon and the Princess Katzfeld* (also known as Hatfeld, Halsfeld, and other variants) (Italia, 1909); *A Message to Napoleon, or an Episode in the Life of the Great Prisoner of Elba* (Great Northern, 1909); *Madame sans Gêne* (Great Northern, 1910, and Society Film d'Art, 1912); *Napoleon in 1814* (Gaumont, 1911); *The Price of Victory: A Story of Napoleon Bonaparte* (Edison, 1911); *The Little King of Rome, or Napoleon and His Son* (Gaumont, 1911); *Prisoner of War* (Edison, 1912); *At Napoleon's Command* (Cinès, 1912); *A Bogus Napoleon* (Vitagraph, 1912); *The Old Guard* (Vitagraph, 1913); and *His Life for His Emperor* (Vitagraph, 1913). Those that resemble the second reel in presenting a synoptic overview of the emperor's career include *L'Epopée Napoléonienne* (Pathé, 1903–1907); *Napoleon* (Pathé, 1909, two reels); and *Napoleon* (Pathé, 1910, one reel). In addition, through the use of stop motion and maps of troop movements, *The Battle of Austerlitz* (Gaumont, 1909) recreates Napoleon's famous victory. *Pimple's Battle of Waterloo* (Phoenix, 1913) and *Napoleon et Rigadin* (Pathé [?], 1912), two parodic films made by popular comedians, pose especially interesting questions about the (mis)use of authenticating strategies for comic purposes. (Dates given above are American review dates rather than country-of-origin release dates.)

3. The crucial differences between the historical positions of these two figures help to account for the differences in the forms of textual expressions, the patterns of textual circulation, readings, and appropriations characteristic of Washington and Napoleon. Those of Eurocentric inclination might have considered that Napoleon, "Emperor" of Europe, played a more significant role in world history than did Washington, the general of the ragtag Continental Army. Even during his own lifetime Napoleon was heavily romanticized, a trend that continues to the present day, whereas romantic treatments of Washington are fairly rare. After all, Napoleon's career, with its highs and lows and its great loves, seems almost inherently melodramatic whereas, by most accounts, Washington led a staid and quiet life.

4. As with Dante, we must assume that European immigrants may have had a more elaborated intertextual frame vis-à-vis Napoleon than native-born Americans possessed. Clearly, the complexities of national origin and ethnicity would have inflected reception of Napoleon texts, although full consideration of this issue falls outside the scope of this volume.

5. Michael Wallace, "Visiting the Past: History Museums in the United States," *Radical History Review* 25 (1981), p. 66.

6. The organizations chartered in this period include Sons of the American Revolution (1889), Daughters of the American Revolution (1890), the National Society of Colonial Dames of America (1891), and the American Scenic and Historic Preservation Society (1895). Although today one may think of the Daughters of the American Revolution—in some ways the most influential of these societies—simply as rabid genealogists, during this period the organization actively engaged in immigrant education, and some factions within the DAR supported immigration restrictions. For information on the DAR, see Martha Strayer, *The D.A.R., An Informal History* (Washington, D.C.: Public

Affairs Press, 1958); Margaret Gibbs, *The DAR* (New York: Holt, Rinehart, and Winston, 1969); and Peggy Anderson, *The Daughters: An Unconventional Look at America's Fan Club—the D.A.R.* (New York: St. Martin's Press, 1974).

7. "Topics of the Times," *The Century Magazine*, April 1894, p. 949.

8. The *New York Dramatic Mirror* review claims that the film included a final shot of a statue of Washington. "The film ends with a symbolical picture which should have been omitted, as it does not measure up to the rest. In it there is a scene-painted makeshift representing a statue of Washington that is a shock to the eye after the excellent scenes that have preceded it (July 17, 1909, p. 17). Even though the National Film Archive's print does not contain this shot, the fact that Vitagraph's *Napoleon* ends with a similar shot of a bust of Napoleon surrounded by French flags leads us to believe that Vitagraph's original release most probably did contain the shot the *Mirror* found objectionable. The company may have cut it from subsequent prints in response to the review, or perhaps it was missing from prints distributed to Europe.

9. In the Library of Congress print, this character introduction appears at the beginning of the first reel; the National Film Archive print has it at the beginning of the second reel. No trade press descriptions of the character introductions exist, but we believe that the Library of Congress print is correct. Much of the film is set in the throne room, where the characters are introduced. Moreover, all the characters appear in the first reel, with the exception of Marie-Louise, and the first reel is generally more character-centered than the second.

10. Advertisement, *NYDM*, April 3, 1909, p. 14.

11. Albert E. Smith, in collaboration with Phil Koury, *Two Reels and a Crank* (Garden City, N.Y.: Doubleday, 1952), pp. 113–114. Given that Smith wrote this book in his dotage, one should not give too much credence to this rather fantastic tale.

12. On historical representation, see Hayden White's *Tropics of Discourse: Essays in Cultural Criticism* (Baltimore: Johns Hopkins University Press, 1978), and *The Content of the Form: Narrative Discourse and Historical Representation* (Baltimore: Johns Hopkins University Press, 1987).

13. "An Impression: The Finest Films I've Ever Seen," *Kinematograph and Lantern Weekly*, May 20, 1909, p. 77.

14. Marion Blackton Trimble, *J. Stuart Blackton: A Personal Biography by His Daughter* (Metuchen, N.J.: Scarecrow Press, 1985), pp. 50–53.

15. "Vitagraph High-Art Production," *Film Index*, April 10, 1909, p. 14.

16. Ibid.

17. *MPW*, June 26, 1909, p. 871.

18. *NYDM*, July 10, 1909, p. 15.

19. *NYDM*, July 17, 1909, p. 17.

20. "Vitagraph High-Art Production," *Film Index*, April 10, 1909, p. 14.

21. Obviously, anecdotes often served to psychologize Napoleon by revealing various aspects of his character. Since the anecdotes circulated as historical "truths," we include them in the key-event category.

22. "The Drama," *New York Daily Tribune*, October 25, 1899, p. 9.

23. Program Files, NYPLPA.

24. *Film Index*, July 3, 1909, p. 9, and see also *MPW*, June 26, 1909, p. 884.

25. "Vitagraph High-Art Production," *Film Index*, April 10, 1909, p. 14.

26. "The Drama," *New York Daily Tribune*, October 25, 1899, p. 9.

27. Our primary sources for Napoleon imagery have been Ida Tarbell, *A Short Life of Napoleon Bonaparte* (New York: S. S. McClure, 1895), and John L. Stoddard, *Napoleon, from Corsica to St. Helena* (Chicago: Werner Company, 1894). We also consulted some of the memoirs that Vitagraph cites, many of which contain illustrations.

28. Department of Public Instruction, *A Course of Study for the Elementary Schools of Pennsylvania* (Harrisburg, Penn.: C. E. Aughinbaugh, 1910).

29. "For the Week of the Fourth," *Film Index*, July 3, 1909, p. 5.

30. "Vitagraph High Art Films: The Career of Washington in Film Form," *Kinematograph and Lantern Weekly*, August 19, 1909, p. 719. This strategy was not unique to Vitagraph. The Edison Company said about one of its Washington films, "The crossing of the Delaware River has become historic and the famous painting by E. Leutze, in the Metropolitan Museum of Art, New York City, is known to every school boy. This picture has been carefully reproduced in the film" (*Edison Kinetogram*, March 15, 1912, p. 11).

31. Clement Scott, "Mr. Scott Frowns on Josephine," *New York Herald*, October 25, 1899.

32. "Vitagraph High-Art Production," *Film Index*, April 10, 1909, p. 14. In 1908 Humphrey appeared in a road-company production, *The Imperial Divorce* ("At the Nesbitt," *Wilkes-Barre Times-Leader*, November 21, 1908, p. 10; we thank Charles Musser for this reference), and as late as 1929 again played Napoleon in the film *Devil-May-Care* (MGM). We have seen Humphrey's name spelled differently but take our lead from Anthony Slide, who spells it this way in *The Big V: A History of the Vitagraph Company, A New and Revised Edition* (Metuchen, N.J.: Scarecrow Press, 1987).

33. Trimble, *J. Stuart Blackton*, p. 50.

34. William Curtis Taylor, "What Did Washington Look Like? The Testimony of Contemporary Painters," *The Booklovers' Magazine*, February, 1905, pp. 155–169.

35. *NYDM*, July 17, 1909, p. 17.

36. "Charles Richman a Star," *New York Times*, November 24, 1903.

37. Roland Barthes, "The Realistic Effect," *Film Reader 3*.

38. *Film Index*, April 9, 1910, p. 5.

39. Henry Van Dyke, *The Americanism of Washington* (New York: Harper and Brothers, 1906), p. 2.

40. The fifth edition of Parson Weems' oft-reprinted book first introduced the cherry-tree anecdote. See Mason Locke Weems, *The Life of Washington the Great: Enriched with a Number of Very Curious Anecdotes, Perfectly in Character, and Equally Honorable to Himself, and Exemplary to His Young Countrymen* (Augusta, Ga.: Geo. F. Randolph, 1806).

41. Eugene Parsons, *George Washington: A Character Sketch* (Dansville, N.Y.: Instructor Publishing Company, 1898), p. 58.

42. "The Story of George Washington," in Parsons, *George Washington*, p. 110.

43. Frederick Trevor Hill, *On the Trail of Washington* (New York: D. Appleton and Company, 1910), pp. vii–viii.

44. Effie Louise Koogle, *The Heir of Mount Vernon: A Colonial Play* (Lebanon, Ohio: March Brothers, 1906), pp. 2, 5.

45. On the subject of the transformations of Washington's image, see Karal Ann Marling, *George Washington Slept Here: Colonial Revivals and American Culture, 1876—1986* (Cambridge, Mass.: Harvard University Press, 1988), and Barry Schwartz, *George Washington: The Making of An American Symbol* (New York: Free Press, 1987).

46. Melville W. Fuller, "Oration," *Congressional Record*, December 11, 1889, vol. 21, pt. 1, p. 148.

47. *The Study of History in the Schools: Report to the American Historical Association by the Committee of Seven* (New York: Macmillan, 1899), p. 160.

48. *MPW*, July 10, 1909, p. 51.

49. "Musings of the 'Photoplay Philosopher,' " *Motion Picture Story Magazine*, April 1912, p. 129. The style of the article makes it very likely that it was written by J. Stuart Blackton, publisher of the journal. Blackton had also testified at Mayor McClellan's hearings prior to the nickelodeon closings.

50. Fuller, "Oration," p. 151.

51. Henry C. Potter in the *Washington Centenary* (New York: n.p., 1889), quoted in Howard N. Rabinowitz, "George Washington as Icon: 1865–1900," in Ray B. Browne and Marshall Fishwick, eds., *Icons of America* (Bowling Green, Ohio: Popular Press, 1978), p. 78.

52. Van Dyke, *Americanism of Washington*, pp. 66, 67.

53. Barbara S. Groseclose, *Emmanuel Leutze, 1816–1868: Freedom Is the Only King* (Washington, D.C.: Smithsonian Institution Press, 1975), pp. 36–37.

54. W. W. Winters, "Filming a Historical Drama," reprinted in *The Nickelodeon*, May 15, 1910, p. 261. W. W. Winters is very possibly the same William Winters who was the premiere American drama critic until he was fired from the *New York Tribune* in 1909. The sarcastic tone of the article is consistent with Winters's dim view of moving pictures.

55. Lately Thomas, *The Mayor Who Mastered New York* (New York: William Morrow and Company, 1969), p. 114.

56. Trade card, Department of Prints and Photographs, New York Historical Society.

57. Caroline McQuinn, *The Wrong George Washington: A Dialogue and Drill* (Franklin, Ohio: Eldridge, 1912), p. 4.

58. Marling, *George Washington Slept Here*, pp. 186–189.

59. Rabinowtiz, "George Washington as Icon," pp. 70–71. Rabinowitz gives the following bibliographical information about these volumes: Henry F. Waters, *An Examination of the English Ancestry of George Washington* (Boston, 1889); Albert Welles, *The Pedigree and History of the Washington Family Derived from Odin* (New York, 1879); and Caroline Butler Powel Carothers, *Washington: The Most Distinctively American Character That Our Country Has Produced* (n.p., 1897).

60. Martin F. Tupper, *Washington: A Drama in Five Acts* (New York: James Miller, 1876), p. 3.

61. Elizabeth Stillinger, *The Antiquers* (New York: Alfred A. Knopf, 1980), p. 47.

62. Peter C. Marzio, *The Democratic Art* (Fort Worth, Tex.: Amon Carter Museum of Western Art, 1979), pp. 83–85.

63. These ephemera, especially commercial premiums such as trade cards, may have served as household decorations among immigrants and the working class. Elsa Herzfeld, who conducted a 1905 investigation of life in New York City's Hell's Kitchen, reported that some households had soap coupons of George Washington in "homemade frames of colored and gilt paper and ribbon" (Elsa Herzfeld, *Family Monographs: The History of Twenty-Four Families Living in the Middle West Side of New York City* [New York: James Kempster Printing Company, 1905], p. 15).

64. Arents Collection, RBMD/NYPL.

65. Department of Prints and Photographs, New York Historical Society.

66. *Report of the Sub-Committee on Army, Centennial Celebration of the Inauguration of George Washington as First President of the United States, Held at New York City, April 30 and May 1, 1889* (New York: Sub-Committee on Army, 1890). For more on parades and pageants, see Marling, *George Washington Slept Here*, pp. 201–207.

67. On the subject of pageants, see Ralph Davol, *A Handbook of American Pageantry* (Taunton, Mass.: Davol Publishing Company, 1914), and Kenneth Sawyer Goodman, *A Pageant for Independence Day* (Chicago: The Stage Guild, 1912). For a contemporary scholarly assessment of the phenomenon, see David Glassberg, *American Historical Pageantry: The Uses of Tradition in the Early Twentieth Century* (Chapel Hill: University of North Carolina Press, 1990).

68. William Orr, "An American Holiday," *Atlantic Monthly*, June 1909, pp. 782–783.

69. For an example of these activities, see Alice M. Kellogg, *How to Celebrate Washington's Birthday in the Schoolroom: Helps for the Primary, Grammar and High School* (New York: E. L. Kellogg, 1894).

70. See, for example, Department of Public Instruction, *A Course of Study for the Elementary Schools of Pennsylvania*, which includes a list of pictures suggested for classroom display. The New York City Board of Education recommended that students read Horace Scudder's *George Washington*, W. J. Abbott's *George Washington*, B. Seelye's *Story of Washington*, and E. S. Brooks's *True Story of George Washington* (*Catalogue of Books for Public School Libraries in the Boroughs of Manhattan, the Bronx, Brooklyn, Queens and Richmond* (New York: Board of Education, 1903).

71. Although state and city departments of education attempted to contain the potential polysemy of Washington through such standardizing mechanisms as teacher certification requirements, published lesson plans, endorsed textbooks, and wall decorations, one should not discount the possibility that individual teachers could have promulgated particular partisan appropriations of Washington texts.

72. "Pupils Exhibit Work," *New York Times*, May 28, 1900, p. 10.

73. *Fifth Annual Report of the President and Board of Directors* (New York: Educational Alliance, 1897), p. 21.

74. "Minutes of the Meetings of the Board of Directors," March 15, 1910, Records of the Educational Alliance, RG 312, #2, YIVO Institute for Jewish Research.

75. *Twelfth Annual Report of the Department of Education of the City of New York for the Year Ending July 31, 1909* (New York: Department of Education, 1909), p. 217.

76. *Announcement of Public Lectures* (New York: Department of Education, 1909), pp. 19 and 22.

77. "Simpler Subjects Needed," letter by JMB, *MPW*, March 13, 1909, p. 308.

78. "Reviews of New Films," *NYDM*, July 17, 1909, p. 17.

79. We viewed the National Film Archive print of the film and have translated the German intertitle.

80. "Vitagraph High Art Films: The Career of Washington in Film Form," *Kinematograph and Lantern Weekly*, August 19, 1909, p. 721. Although this review and others note that Washington is asleep, we disagree. For the first vision, Washington is in fact standing near the fireplace, leaning on the mantlepiece. He sits down for the second vision but still does not appear to sleep.

81. *MPW*, July 3, 1909, p. 12.

82. While we have no evidence proving that Blackton personally directed the Washington films, he did supervise all of Vitagraph's productions. Moreover, the Washington

NOTES TO CHAPTER FOUR

films were billed as a sequel to the Napoleon films, which Blackton did actually direct, leading us to believe that Blackton would, at the least, have taken a great deal of interest in these productions.

83. "Professor Sloane's 'Napoleon,' " *The Century Magazine*, October 1895, p. 950.

84. "The Vitagraph Napoleon," *MPW*, April 10, 1909, p. 439.

85. J. Holland Rose, "The Limitations of Napoleon's Genius," *Contemporary Review*, April 1906, pp. 549–550. This complaint typifies the contestation among interpretive communities as they tried to gain access to institutions of cultural reproduction.

86. Sarah Knowles Bolton, *Famous Leaders Among Men* (New York: Thomas Y. Crowell and Company, 1894), p. 86.

87. "The Vitagraph Napoleon," *MPW*, April 10, 1909, p. 439.

88. Richard Sheffield Dement, *Napoleon and Josephine, A Tragedy* (Chicago: Legal News Company, 1876).

89. See, for example, "Bonaparte and Josephine," *The Nation*, December 13, 1900, and M. M. Blake, *Courtship by Command: A Story of Napoleon at Play* (New York: D. Appleton and Company, 1895).

90. Marc Debrit, "Napoleon in the Light of Posthumous Testimony in Recent Historical Works," *International Quarterly* 6 (1902), pp. 44, 46.

91. Esse V. Hathaway, *"The Little Corsican": Napoleon Bonaparte* (Chicago: Rand, McNally and Company, 1909), p. x.

92. *The Independent*, August 2, 1877, p. 16, cited in Henry F. May, *Protestant Churches and Industrial America* (New York: Octagon Books, 1963), p. 93.

93. *Edison Kinetogram*, February 15, 1911, p. 7.

94. *New York Evening Call*, January 3, 1908, pp. 1 and 3, and June 12, 1908, p. 1.

95. John Higham, "The Reorientation of American Culture in the 1890s," in John Weiss, ed., *The Origins of Modern Consciousness* (Detroit: Wayne State University Press, 1965), p. 31. See also James C. Malin, *Confounded Rot about Napoleon: Reflections upon Science and Technology, Nationalism, World Depression of the 1890's and Afterwards* (Ann Arbor, Mich., and Topeka, Kans.: n.p., 1961), p. 205.

96. John Davis, "Napoleon Bonaparte: A Sketch Written for a Purpose," *The Arena*, April 1896, p. 783.

97. *New York Times*, November 4, 1894.

98. "The Vitagraph Napoleon," *MPW*, April 10, 1909, p. 439.

99. See James Westfall Thompson, "Napoleon as a Book-Lover," *Atlantic Monthly*, January 1908, pp. 110–118, and Edward Andrews, "Napoleon and America," *Magazine of History with Notes and Queries* 6 (1907), pp. 86–97.

100. Malin, *Confounded Rot About Napoleon*, p. 185.

101. For example, *The Critic* reported that in May 1902, Watson's *The Life of Napoleon* was the most widely circulated book in the Atlanta library while Roseberry's *Napoleon: The Last Phase* was sixth in circulation in Kansas City ("Library Reports on Popular Books," *The Critic*, May 1902, pp. 475–480). Earlier that year *The Critic* also reported that Watson's book was among the top ten in circulation at the Mechanics' Institute Free Library in New York City and that *With Napoleon at Saint Helena* was in the top ten at the Brooklyn Public Library ("Library Reports on Popular Books," *The Critic*, February 1902, pp. 188–192).

102. *Thirty Years of SLK: 1887–1917* (New York: Society for Literary Knowledge, 1917).

103. "Topics of the Times," *The Century Magazine*, October 1895, p. 950.

104. Malin, *Confounded Rot about Napoleon*, p. 188.

105. See Thomas Bender, *New York Intellect: A History of Intellectual Life in New York City from 1750 to the Beginnings of Our Own Time* (Baltimore: Johns Hopkins University Press, 1987), p. 213.

106. Christopher P. Wilson, "The Rhetoric of Consumption: Mass-Market Magazines and the Demise of the Gentle Reader, 1880–1920," in T. J. Jackson Lears, ed., *The Culture of Consumption: Critical Essays in American History, 1880–1980* (New York: Pantheon Books, 1983), p. 45. For fuller details on the *McClure's/Century Magazine* confrontation, see Malin, *Confounded Rot about Napoleon*.

107. "Topics of the Times," *The Century Magazine*, October 1895, p. 950.

108. Sloane, *The Century Magazine*, September 1895, p. 644.

109. "Topics of the Times," *The Century Magazine*, October 1895, p. 950.

110. Tarbell, *A Short Life of Napoleon Bonaparte*.

111. Ibid., p. 43.

112. Ibid., p. 166.

113. The Werner Company, a Chicago publisher, issued a book reproducing 331 engravings dealing with all phases of Napoleon's career. The company claimed that "it is a well known fact among book and print collectors that pictures illustrating the career of the 'Man of Destiny' are rapidly disappearing from the market, and are even now commanding fabulous prices" (Malin, *Confounded Rot about Napoleon*, p. 196).

114. Both are in the Arents Collection. The card series appeared somewhere between 1900 and 1917.

115. *Dramatic Compositions Copyrighted in the United States* includes the following: *Napoleon, A Drama*, by Richard Sheffeld (Chicago: Knight, Leonard and Company, 1893); *Napoleon, An Historical Drama*, by D. Welch (New York: Deshler Welsh, 1888); *Napoleon, A Play*, by E. W. Tullidge (Salt Lake City: Edward Tullidge, 1888); *Napoleon, A Play in 4 Acts*, by Henry Adams (New York: J. Selwin Tait and Sons, 1894); *Napoleon, A Spectacular Drama in 3 Epochs and 5 Acts*, by G. C. Miln (Brooklyn: George C. Miln, 1895); *Napoleon, A Study in 1 Act*, by J. V. Hood (Philadelphia: John V. Hood, 1895); *Napoleon, A Tragedy in a Prologue and 5 Acts*, by Avlys Richmond (pseud. of Richmond S. Dement) (Shelbyville, Ill.: R. S. Dement, 1875); *Napoleon, A Tragedy in 5 Acts*, by J. S. Norton (New York: J. S. Norton, 1873); *Napoleon I, or the Life and Death of Napoleon Bonaparte, An Historical Tragedy in 5 Acts*, by P. Wales (Minneapolis: Phillip Wales, 1884); *Napoleon at St. Helena, A Play in 5 Acts*, by F. L. Schmidt, Jr. (Richmond Hill, N.Y.: Fritz L. Schmidt, 1905); *Napoleon, A Drama*, by L. Stoddard (New York: Lorimer Stoddard, 1894); *Napoleon Bonaparte, Emperor of France, An Historical Drama in 5 Acts*, by E. E. Sherman (Buffalo: Ellen E. Sherman, 1884); *Napoleon Bonaparte, the Emperor of the French, His Life and Death in 6 Acts*, by J. J. Allen (Chicago: John J. Allen, 1891); *Napoleon the Great, in 5 Periods Dealing with the Main Incidents in the Life of Napoleon, From His Return from Egypt to Waterloo*, by Channing Pollock (Belfast, Me.: Thomas E. Shea, 1905); *Napoleon the Great, or Hero of a Hundred Battlefields, Historical Drama in 5 Acts*, by J. F. McDonell (Virginia, Nev.: John F. McDonell, 1895); and *Napoleon's Defeat, A Drama in 1 Act, 1 Scene*, by H. L. Holland (Oakland, Calif.: Harold L. Holland, 1908).

116. *Catalogue of Books for Public School Libraries in the Boroughs of Manhattan, the Bronx, Brooklyn, Queens and Richmond*, and Department of Public Instruction, *A Course of Study for the Elementary Schools of Pennsylvania*, p. 76.

117. "Cooper Union Forum Lectures, 1868–1939," typescript, People's Institute Papers, CU.

118. Trimble, *J. Stuart Blackton*, pp. 50–53.

119. "Broadway—More than a Queen," *NYDM*, November 4, 1899, p. 16. See also Emile Bergerat, "More than Queen," adapted in English by Frederic Nordlinger and Charles Meltzer (produced at the Broadway Theatre, October 24, 1899), NYPLPA.

Though the connection between play and film seems strong, we must, in all honesty, admit that reviewers complained about the play's lack of dramatic development. "The play becomes a series of detached pictures. It is fragmentary and disconnected in its narration of the story" ("More than Queen," *New York Times*, October 25, 1899). Even while foregrounding Napoleon and Josephine's emotional interactions, reviewers lamented the flatness of the characters, that is, the play's failure to provide access to the characters' interiority. Perhaps Blackton remembered these critiques when writing his film scenarios and sought cinematic means to externalize characters' thoughts and emotions.

120. "Vitagraph High-Art Production," *Film Index*, April 10, 1909, p. 14.

121. "Napoleon Bonaparte and Empress Josephine," *NYDM*, April 17, 1909, p. 13.

122. "An Impression: The Finest Films I've Ever Seen," *Kinematograph and Lantern Weekly*, May 20, 1909, p. 77.

123. *Film Index*, April 10, 1909, p. 8. The trade press reviews we have located insist that Napoleon falls asleep, as do Vitagraph's publicity releases. Napoleon's hyperactive gesticulation, however, does not appear to take place in a somnambulistic state, and neither the film nor the actor give any indication that the character falls asleep. Given that trade press copy on *Washington under the American Flag* also claims that Washington falls asleep prior to the vision effects, one might be tempted to speculate that period conventions required visions and memories to be motivated by sleep—except that counterexamples abound. Even Josephine is not said to be asleep for her visions.

124. Maureen Turim briefly discusses this film in her *Flashbacks in Film: Memory and History* (New York: Routledge, Chapman, and Hall, 1989), p. 28.

125. Strangely, a British review of the Vitagraph Washington films suggests that some viewers may have been familiar neither with Napoleon nor with Napoleonic paintings. Speaking of Vitagraph's "first two high art films," the review notes that "these subjects dealt with the history of a personage (Napoleon) of whom many English people knew very little" ("Vitagraph High Art Films: The Career of Washington in Film Form," *Kinematograph and Lantern Weekly*, August 19, 1909, p. 719). For such viewers, the intervening shots of the gesticulating Napoleon, with events and dates superimposed over the image, would at least have identified the event and indicated the character's affect.

126. Our only evidence regarding audience reception suggests that viewers liked the film. The *New York Dramatic Mirror* reported that "the picture was warmly applauded at the Union Square and other houses, proving that motion picture audiences appreciate the highest class production" (April 17, 1909, p. 13).

127. James Harvey Robinson's *The New History: Essays Illustrating the Modern Historical Outlook* (New York: Macmillan, 1912), for example, argued that great leaders and wars had been privileged over fuller accounts of the past, which should include economics, psychology, and so forth (Brook Thomas, "The New Historicism and Other Old-Fashioned Topics," in H. Aram Veeser, *The New Historicism* [New York: Routledge,

Chapman, and Hall, 1989], p. 194). Although the book was published in 1912, it undoubtedly reflected the period's reappraisal of historical paradigms.

128. "Incidents in the Life of Napoleon and Josephine," *MPW*, April 10, 1909, p. 443.

129. "The Vitagraph Napoleon," *MPW*, April 10, 1909, p. 439.

Chapter Five
Biblical Qualities:
Moses

1. "A Theater Showing Only Biblical Films," *Motography*, December 1911, p. 8.

2. "Vitagraph's 'Life of Moses,' " *Film Index*, November 27, 1909, p. 5.

3. "Moses," *Encyclopedia Judaica* (Jerusalem: Macmillan, 1971).

4. Lydia G. Robinson, "Moses: A Lecture Delivered at Breslau, October 19, 1908," *The Monist*, April 1910, p. 161.

5. Daniel Jeremy Silver, *Images of Moses* (New York: Basic Books, 1982), p. 18.

6. *VB* February 1–15, 1910.

7. " 'Life of Moses' A Hit," *NYDM*, January 1, 1910, p. 19.

8. "Vitagraph's 'Life of Moses,' " *Film Index*, November 27, 1909, p. 5.

9. Charlie Keil has attempted to account for the stylistically retrograde features of Kalem's *From the Manger to the Cross* in terms of the cultural prohibition against psychologizing Christ. See "*From the Manger to the Cross*: The New Testament Narrative and the Question of Stylistic Retardation," paper delivered at the Domitor Conference on Early Cinema and Religion, Quebec City, June 1990.

10. Laurence F. Cook, "Advertising the Picture Show," *The Nickelodeon*, August 15, 1910, p. 93.

11. K. S. Hover, "Motography as an Arm of the Church," *Motography*, May 1911, pp. 84–86.

12. Mark Ash and William Ash, *The Greater New York Charter as Enacted in 1897 and Amended in 1901* (New York: Baker, Voorhis and Company, 1901), p. 843.

13. "Theatres To Open for Shows To-day," *New York Times*, December 22, 1907.

14. "Few Arrests under New Sunday Law," *New York Times*, December 23, 1907.

15. *Film Index*, February 26, 1910, p. 5.

16. "Dodging Snakes," *Film Index*, February 5, 1910, p. 5.

17. "Moving Picture Sermons?" *Views and Film Index*, May 9, 1908, p. 8.

18. *Morning Telegraph*, October 4, 1908, box 37, PIR, RBMD/NYPL.

19. The Museum of Modern Art's catalogue card on the film credits Charles Kent as director.

20. *VB*, November 16–30, 1909.

21. Editorial, *Views and Films Index*, November 21, 1908, p. 3.

22. John Fraser, "Moses and Pharaoh: A New Departure in Stage Literature," in Otto Peltzer, *The Moralist and the Theatre* (Chicago: Donald Fraser and Sons, 1887), pp. 39, 42.

23. Hover, "Motography as an Arm of the Church," p. 85.

24. "Bible Teaching by Pictures," *Film Index*, December 4, 1909, p. 9.

25. Tom Gunning, "D. W. Griffith and the Narrator System: Narrative Structure and Industry Organization in Biograph Films, 1908–1909" (Ph.D. diss., New York University, 1986), p. 448.

26. *VB*, December 1–15, 1909.

27. *VB*, November 16–30, 1909.

28. *VB*, #203, January 1–15, 1910.

29. *VB*, #206, February 15–March 1, 1910.

30. *VB*, February 1–15, 1910.

31. *VB*, #207, March 1–15, 1910.

32. *The Life of Moses* provides an early example of the employment of publicity strategies discussed by Janet Staiger in her useful overview, "Announcing Wares, Winning Patrons, Voicing Ideals: Thinking about the History and Theory of Film Advertising," *Cinema Journal* 29:3 (1990): 3–31.

33. *VB*, February 1–15, 1910.

34. *VB*, #206, February 15–March 1, 1910.

35. *VB*, December 1–15, 1909.

36. *VB*, March 15–31, 1910.

37. *VB*, #206, February 15–March 1, 1910.

38. *VB*, #205, February 1–15, 1910.

39. "Vitagraph Notes," *Film Index*, January 8, 1910, p. 9.

40. *The Bioscope*, February 10, 1910, p. 15.

41. Luther A. Weigle, *The Pupil and the Teacher* (New York: Hodder and Stroughton, 1911), p. 165.

42. W. T. Harris, "Religious Instruction in Public Schools," *The Independent*, August 6, 1903, p. 1841.

43. Among elite interpretive communities these cracks in the facade of religious belief appeared much earlier. For example, the emergence of the new philology at the end of the eighteenth century challenged the primacy of Hebrew, effectively rejecting the divine origin of language (Edward Said, *Orientalism* [New York: Random House, 1978], p. 135). Questions regarding the assumed nature of biblical provenance and claims for the inerrancy of the Bible followed from such scientific challenges.

44. Grant Wacker, "The Demise of Biblical Civilization," in Nathan Hatch and Mark Noll, eds., *The Bible in America: Essays in Cultural History* (New York: Oxford University Press, 1982), p. 124.

45. See Virginia Brereton, "The Public Schools Are Not Enough: The Bible and Private Schools," in David Barr and Nicholas Piediscalzi, eds., *The Bible in American Education: From Source Book to Textbook* (Philadelphia: Fortress Press, 1982), pp. 40–75. These disputes concerned whether the Bible should be included in the public school curriculum and, if so, which version to adopt.

46. "The Pittsburgh Platform" (Central Conference of American Rabbis, 1885), in J. Gordon Melton, *The Encyclopedia of American Religions: Religious Creeds* (Detroit: Gale Research Company, 1988), p. 773.

47. Silver, *Images of Moses*, p. 290.

48. Ibid., p. 193.

49. R. J. Zwi Werblowsky, "Judaism, or the Religion of Israel," in R. C. Zaehner, ed., *The Concise Encyclopedia of Living Faiths* (New York: Hawthorn Books, 1959), p. 46.

50. Robert Emmett Curran, "American Catholic Thought," in Charles H. Lippy and Peter M. Williams, eds., *Encyclopedia of the American Religious Experience: Studies of Traditions and Movements* (New York: Charles Scribner's Sons, 1988), p. 1005.

51. Debra Campbell, "Catholicism from Independence to World War I," in Lippy and Williams, *Encyclopedia of the American Religious Experience*, p. 371.

52. Curran, "American Catholic Thought," p. 1006.

53. Ibid.

54. *Catholic Encyclopedia*, vol. 10 (New York: Encyclopedia Press, 1911), p. 596.

55. I. M. Haldeman, *How to Study the Bible* (New York: Fleming H. Revell Company, 1904), p. 538.

56. David L. Holmes, "The Anglican Tradition and the Episcopal Church," in Lippy and Williams, *Encyclopedia of the American Religious Experience*, p. 407.

57. *MPW*, December 18, 1909, p. 878.

58. "Activity at Vitagraph Studios," *Film Index*, August 28, 1909, p. 12.

59. *The Pictorial Bible* (New York: Robert Sears, 1857).

60. The *Select Notes on the International Sunday School Lessons* was published for thirty-four years and is estimated to have had a circulation of 1,450,000 volumes (*Who's Who in America* [Chicago: A. N. Marquis, 1908], p. 1468).

61. Rev. F. N. Peloubet, D.D., and M. A. Peloubet, *Select Notes: A Commentary on the International Lessons for 1902* (New York: Baker and Taylor Company, 1901), p. 186.

62. Ibid., p. 193.

63. Addie Grace Wardle, *History of the Sunday School Movement in the Methodist Episcopal Church* (New York: The Methodist Book Concern, 1918), p. 149.

64. J. L. Hurlbut, *Manual of Biblical Geography* (Chicago: Rand, McNally and Company, 1884).

65. Fred Lewis Pattee, *Elements of Religious Pedagogy: A Course in Sunday School Teacher-Training*, (New York: Eaton and Mains, 1909), p. 7.

66. *Moses; Or, The Bondage in Egypt, by the Order of Cincinnatus: A Biblical and Historical Spectacle, Designed and Painted by John Rettig* (Cincinnati: Sullivan Printing Works, 1890), pp. 4–5.

67. Ibid., p. 23.

68. "Vitagraph's 'Life of Moses,' " *Film Index*, November 27, 1909, p. 5.

69. "The Life of Moses, Part 2," *MPW*, January 15, 1910, p. 58.

70. "Vitagraph's 'Life of Moses,' " *Film Index*, November 27, 1909, p. 5.

71. Advertisement, *Film Index*, December 4, 1909, p. 13.

72. "Biblical Pictures," *The Nickelodeon*, December 1909, p. 167.

73. *VB*, #204, January 15–31, 1910.

74. "Vitagraph Notes," *Film Index*, September 4, 1909, p. 9.

75. *NYDM*, January 15, 1910, p. 14.

76. Harris, "Religious Instruction," p. 1842.

77. Lyman Abbott, "The Passage of the Red Sea," *The Outlook*, June 2, 1894, p. 974.

78. Ibid., p. 974.

79. D. R. Dungan, *Moses, The Man of God* (St. Louis: Christian Publishing Company, 1899), pp. 6, 285.

80. Pattee, *Elements of Religious Pedagogy*, p. 185.

81. See, for example, the Berean Lesson Cards, vol. 6, #11, June 1894, album 549, Burdick Collection, Metropolitan Museum of Art.

82. Harris G. Hale and Newton M. Hall, arrs., "Moses the Liberator in Biblical Drama" (Boston: Pilgrim Press, 1906).

83. The term was first used by Tom Gunning in "The Cinema of Attractions: Early Film, Its Spectators, and the Avant-Garde," *Wide Angle* 8:3/4 (1986).

84. "Biblical Pictures," *The Nickelodeon*, December 1909, p. 167.

85. Madison C. Peters, *Why I Became a Baptist* (New York: Baker and Taylor Company, 1901), p. 32.

86. Madison C. Peters, *What the Old Testament Has to Say about the Great Hereafter* (San Francisco: Jewish Times Press, 1911), p. 23.

87. "The Life of Moses," *MPW*, December 18, 1909, p. 878.

88. "The Life of Moses, Part IV," *VB*, February 1–15, 1910.

89. *Variety*, February 5, 1910.

90. "Dodging Snakes," *Film Index*, February 5, 1910, p. 5.

91. Their efforts were not greeted with universal approbation. In a letter to the *Moving Picture World*, one exhibitor complained about the shoddiness of the miracle scene. "I admit that the passage of the Red Sea would have required the skill of the most experienced stage managers and would have called for many tricks and illusions to give it the proper grandeur, and if I had been unable to produce a realistic scene I would have omitted the passage of the Red Sea, instead of contenting myself to show a little stream of which the waters are not parted but vanish away" (An Exhibitor, "Religious Productions," *MPW*, February 26, 1910, pp. 303–304).

92. *VB*, February 1–15, 1910. Compare this with the biblical version. "And Moses stretched out his hand over the sea; and the Lord caused the sea to go back by a strong east wind all that night, and made the sea dry land, and the waters were divided. And the Children of Israel went into the midst of the sea upon the dry ground; and the waters were a wall unto them on their right hand, and on their left"(Exodus 14:21–22).

93. See Ahad Ha-Am, *Selected Essays* (Philadelphia: n.p., 1912), excerpted in Israel H. Weisfeld, ed., *This Man Moses* (New York: Bloch Publishing Company, 1966), pp. 167–69.

94. "The Use of Stories," n.d, file 9, box 5, HLP, RBMD/NYPL.

95. Elbert Hubbard, *Little Journeys to the Homes of Great Teachers*, vol. 22 (New York: The Roycrofters, 1908), p. 25. Hubbard also wrote several other popular books, such as *Little Journeys to the Homes of the Great*, and edited three journals, as well as giving public lectures. See Freeman Champney, *Art and Glory: The Story of Elbert Hubbard* (Kent, Ohio: Kent State University Press, 1968).

96. "Dodging Snakes," and "Troubles of the M.P. Actor," *Film Index*, March 5, 1910, p. 8.

97. "Troubles of the M.P. Actor," *Film Index*, March 5, 1910, p. 8. Vitagraph's irreverence here was not unique. The *Albany Times* published a holiday greeting insert in 1889 speculating about how newspapers may have reported historical events. A line drawing shows Egyptians, wearing glasses and spats, carrying canes, and smoking cigars, but otherwise in correct period garb. One carries a tray full of foaming mugs of beer to the others, who are reading a newspaper with the following headline: "Holy Moses! Egypt Defenseless—Our Army Totally Destroyed. Death of Pharaoh. The Red Sea Closes Over the Army and Engulfs It In a Watery Grave. Full Account by an Eye-Witness" (Broadside Collection, New York Historical Society).

98. Rev. Dr. Isaac M. Wise, *Moses, The Man and Statesman, A Lecture Delivered in New York and Boston, January 23 and 25, 1883* (Cincinnati: Block and Company, 1883), p. 21.

99. Abraham J. Karp, "The Emergence of an American Judaism," in Lippy and Williams, *Encyclopedia of the American Religious Experience*, p. 275.

100. Henry Leipziger, "Moses,' unpublished lecture, January 26, 1902, file 2, box 7, HLP, RBMD/NYPL.

101. Wise, *Moses*, p. 27.

102. James Hamilton, *Moses, The Man of God, A Course of Lectures Delivered to the Congregation of Regent Square* (New York: Robert Carter and Brothers, 1871), p. 131.

103. Madison C. Peters, *The Jews Who Stood by Washington: An Unwritten Chapter in American History* (New York: Trow Press, 1915), p. 41.

104. Frances S. Kempster, "Report of the Flag Committee," *American Monthly Magazine*, August 1907, p. 458. Lest one think that the Daughters were being surprisingly tolerant, we should say that the same report also commented on a professor at one of our large universities who had said, "We have not as much to fear from the immigrants, as the immigrant has to fear from contact with American customs. It is a wonder this class does not hate the flag, considering the way we treat them." The report, which strenuously disapproves of the professor's sentiments, continues: "He who dishonors the flag in time of war, dies,—and he who does so in time of peace, — —." Ms. Kempster left it to the reader's imagination to supply the missing words.

105. Peloubet and Peloubet, *Select Notes*, p. 202.

106. Ibid., p. 223.

107. Marianna C. Brown, *Sunday School Movements in America* (New York: Fleming A. Revell, 1901), p. 87.

108. Charles H. Parkhurst, *Our Fight with Tammany* (New York: Charles Scribner's Sons, 1895), p. 272.

109. Ibid., pp. 139, 136.

110. Richard T. Ely, *Social Aspects of Christianity and Other Essays* (New York: Thomas Y. Crowell and Company, 1889), p. 11.

111. Henry George, *The Complete Works of Henry George*, vol. 7 (New York: Doubleday, Page and Company, 1911), pp. 19, 119, 12.

112. Campbell, "Catholicism," p. 371.

113. Ely, *Social Aspects of Christianity*, pp. 14–15.

114. Edward H. Rogers, *"Like Unto Me"; or, The Resemblance between Moses and Christ: A Workingman's Views of the Relation of the Church to the People*, (Chelsea, Mass.: n.p., 1876), p. 2.

115. Hubbard, *Little Journeys*, vol. 22, p. 21.

116. Herbert G. Gutman, *Work, Culture, and Society in Industrializing America: Essays in American Working-Class and Social History* (New York: Vintage Books, 1977), p. 103.

117. Quoted in Ibid., p. 94.

118. Minutes of the Meeting of the Board of Directors of the Educational Alliance, March 15, 1910, RG 312, #2, YIVO Institute for Jewish Research.

119. "Educational Movement among N.Y. Churches," *Film Index*, March 5, 1910, p. 1.

Conclusion

1. *Vitagraph Life Portrayals*, March 1–16, 1912, p. 6.

Index

Abbott, Lyman, 182, 185
acting styles: film industry parallels with theatre, 47
"actualities" (short nonfiction films), 27
Adams, Joseph Quincy, 70
advertising industry: use of Washington as image by, 128–29
Albany Times, 78
Americanism of Washington, The, 121–22, 124
American Library Association, 23
American Review of Reviews, 27
American Scenic and Historic Preservation Society, 232n.6
amusement surveys: attendance at Shakespearean productions, 84–87. *See also* reception studies
anarchists: cultural impact of, 18
Ang, Ien, 12
Ariel Shakespeare, The, 77
Arnold, Matthew, 21–23, 210n.19
art. *See* paintings
Assassination of the Duke du Guise, 52
assimilationism: Arnoldian response and, 33–40; cultural hegemony and, 22–24, 217n.98; historical films as vehicle for, 113–14; impact of, on film industry, 195–99; institutions of culture and, 133–34; repressive strategies for, 28–33; role of schools in, 211n.21, 212n.32
Atlantic Monthly, 77, 105

Barrett, Lawrence, 85, 99–100, 103
Barthes, Roland, 120
Battle Hymn of the Republic, 195
Beerbohm-Tree, 86
Ben Hur: copyright infringement case and, 49. 69
Bennett, Tony, 13–14
Bergerat, Emile, 116
biblical quality films: defined, 50; development of, 160–94; Holy Land depicted in, 179–80; *Life of Moses* as example of, 162–63;

natural and supernatural discourses in, 173–87; partisan appropriations of Moses in, 187–92; production practices for, 163–73; public response to, 192–94; special effects in, 184–85; theological disputes concerning, 161–62
biblical study: academization of, 174
Bingham, Theodore, 142
Biograph Bulletin, 72
Biograph Company: quality film production and, 44, 46–47, 51, 56–57
Birds of the Bible, The, 168
Blackton, James Stuart, 3; on content of films, 45; early life and career of, 223n.78; as film industry spokesman, 65–68; on necessity of period detail in historical films, 116; participation of, in Napoleon fad, 149–51; revisionist history and, 139; Vitagraph's quality film production and, 56–63, 90; Washington films and, 126, 236n.82
Boker, George H., 97–99
Bolton, Sarah Knowles, 141
Booklovers' Magazine, The, 120
Boston American, 80
Bourdieu, Pierre, 7–12; cultural hierarchy and, 22, 109–10
Boy's Life of Napoleon, 147
Briggs, Charles A., 176
Brighton Project, 219n.20
Bunnell, George B., 98
Bureau of Lectures, 43; founding of, 34, 36–40; lectures on Dante, 98–99; lectures on Napoleon, 147–48; Shakespearean productions and, 78–81; valorization of Shakespeare and, 71
Bush, Stephen, 42–43

Camera Obscura, 13
canonicity: concept of, 221n.45
Carnegie, Andrew: and attempts at cultural uplift, 70; funding of public libraries by, 23–24; nickelodeons and, 44